Sept 2005

Renovate Before You Innovate

RENOVATE BEFORE YOU Innovate

WHY DOING
THE NEW THING
MIGHT NOT
BE THE
RIGHT THING

SERGIO ZYMAN

with Armin A. Brott

PORTFOLIO

PORTFOLIO
Published by the Penguin Group,
Penguin Group (USA) Inc., 375 Hudson Street, New York, New York 10014, U.S.A.
Penguin Group (Canada), 10 Alcorn Avenue, Toronto, Ontario, Canada M4V 3B2
(a division of Pearson Penguin Canada Inc);
Penguin Books Ltd, 80 Strand, London WC2R 0RL, England;
Penguin Ireland, 25 St. Stephen's Green, Dublin 2, Ireland
(a division of Penguin Books Ltd);
Penguin Books Australia Ltd, 250 Camberwell Road, Camberwell,
Victoria 3124, Australia (a division of Pearson Australia Group Pty Ltd);
Penguin Books India (Pvt) Ltd, 11 Community Centre, Panchsheel Park,
New Delhi – 110 017, India;
Penguin Group (NZ), Cnr Airborne and Rosedale Roads, Albany,
Auckland 1310, New Zealand (a division of Pearson New Zealand Ltd);
Penguin Books (South Africa) (Pty) Ltd, 24 Sturdee Avenue,
Rosebank, Johannesburg 2196, South Africa

Penguin Books Ltd, Registered Offices:
80 Strand, London WC2R 0RL, England

First published in 2004 by Portfolio,
a member of Penguin Putnam (USA) Inc.

10 9 8 7 6 5 4 3 2 1

All the diagrams, charts and graphs in this book were
created by Judy Jacobs and Veda Sammy.

LIBRARY OF CONGRESS CATALOGING-IN-PUBLICATION DATA

Zyman, Sergio.
Renovate before you innovate : why doing the new thing might not be the right thing / Sergio Zyman with Armin Brott.
p. cm.
Includes index.
ISBN 1-59184-054-6
1. Market segmentation. I. Brott, Armin A. II. Title.

HF5415.127.Z96 2004
658.8'02—dc22 2004044569

This book is printed on acid-free paper. ♾

Printed in the United States of America
Set in Fairfield Light

To Jessy, Jenny, and Becky, who see me and help me renovate myself all the time.

I dedicate this book, as I did my first one, to the memory of Roberto Goizueta. After leaving The Coca-Cola Company the first time, I had never thought it made sense for me to come back. But Roberto changed my mind, and I'm grateful that he did. Over the next five years I began to realize that it might actually be possible to change the world of business by changing the way companies develop their market strategies and go to market.

And to Don Keough, who gave me my first big break when he hired me as his executive assistant in 1979. Thanks, Don, I wouldn't have grown up at all if you hadn't pushed me.

Acknowledgments

You wouldn't be reading this book right now if it weren't for the help I received from many, many people. At the Zyman Group, Ric Alvarez, Vinita Bali, Craig Binkley, Dave Singleton, and Jon Stewart all contributed greatly by keeping me honest and making sure I stayed true to the religion of renovation. A number of good friends outside my company took the time to read this book carefully and made extremely helpful comments. These include Alain Belda and Bill Christopher at Alcoa, Nick Shepherd at Blockbuster, Mike Spinozzi at Borders, and of course Bruce Rohde, the CEO of ConAgra and one of the greatest minds of all time. And throughout, Armin Brott was always there with a good sense of humor. He made me clarify my arguments, kept challenging me to go further and delve deeper, and then managed to say it all better. I've been incredibly lucky to have worked with Armin on my books. He's changed the way I think and write.

Contents

Introduction

Everywhere I go, it's the same story. Over lunch with a client, the VP of marketing talks my ear off about all the new products the company is planning to introduce. At the quarterly meeting of one of the firms whose board I sit on, the CEO spends twenty minutes describing the new markets the company is getting into and the acquisition deals they're working on. And these guys aren't alone. Overall, more than 60 percent of S&P 500 firms incorporate the concept of innovation into their mission statement, use the term "innovation" in marketing and branding communications, or cite innovation as part of their strategy in their annual reports.

What's the big deal with innovation? Well, most corporate execs know this basic formula for business success: Increased sales lead to increased cash flow, which in turn drives growth. And ultimately that's what it's all about: Firms that have a proven history of top-line and bottom-line growth get rewarded by Wall Street with higher valuations (price-earnings ratios) than other companies in the same category. Just think of Coca-Cola, L'Oréal, Procter & Gamble, and Sony.

However, since many attempts at marketing have failed to create both top-line *and* bottom-line growth, CEOs have decided that the only way to drive growth is to change the rules of the game, gut the old system, and build a new one from the ground up. In other words, innovate. Most dictionaries agree that innovation is "the act of introducing something new" or "a new idea, method, or device." Both of those definitions work for me, but I think it's also fair to say that innovation is "using your existing assets and core competencies to do something different from what you're already doing."

This fixation on innovation has spawned an entire industry of consultants and authors and businesses whose entire purpose in life is to support and promote innovation. If you do a quick search on Amazon.com for "business innovation" you'll find two thousand titles. And if you Google "innovation consultant" you'll get more than 450,000 hits.

Two of the biggest innovation gurus these days are Tom Peters and Gary Hamel. We're all Michelangelos, they say. We need to forget everything we know, "de-risk" unfamiliar opportunities. Distance is dead, destruction is cool. Innovation rules! Sounds fantastic and inspiring, doesn't it? And it is—except for one small thing: For the majority of companies out there, *it just doesn't work*. All it offers is a quick fix—kind of like a sugar high: You feel better for a while, but when the effect wears off you're in worse shape than when you started.

At its core, this approach to business growth is simply lazy. Actually, it's worse than that; it's dangerous. But both Peters and Hamel have struck a chord with a broad base of companies that are now trying to grow their business by turning their back on what they need to do first, which is fix their basic value proposition—what it is that they offer their existing and prospective customers.

So now we've got a bunch of companies that have forgotten all that boring stuff that made them successful in the first place and are getting into areas they don't know anything about and have no business being in at all. A lot of these companies are showing their commitment to this strategy by creating a new position: CIO. No, that's not Chief Information Officer. It's—yep, you guessed it—Chief Innovation Officer. And these CIOs are rattling on and on about how the company is "retooling" and "charting a new course" and "exploring new opportunities." And let's not forget about "driving double-digit top-line growth." The fact that all that top-line growth will probably come at the expense of the more important bottom line doesn't seem to bother anyone. Except me.

In my view, innovation is just another word for "giving up." It's saying that things are so bad that it's easier to get into an entirely different line of business than to deal with our problems. And this whole "innovation culture" is just the latest in a long line of business fads. Just think of all the ones that have come and gone over the years: We've had one-minute management, total quality management, management by walking around, matrix management, management by objectives, theories X, Y, and Z, reorganizing, restructuring, the experience curve, downsizing, right-sizing, sensitivity training, and quality circles. Every single one is dead and gone.

In defense of fads, most of them are actually based on a good idea. The problem, though, is that the fadmeisters too often try to condense complex ideas into a few sentences. All you have to do, they say, is attend our seminar (or hire us as your consultant) and we'll cure you of whatever ails you. Just a few years ago, for example, everyone was talking about CRM (customer relationship management), and companies ran out and plunked down tens of thousands of dollars for programs that promised them the moon—or at least well-managed customers. The smart ones figured out pretty quickly that good customer relationships don't come in a box. The rest kept trying to make the magic program work or moved on to the next trend.

In the 1990s, it was all about knowledge management and process reengineering. And technology, the Web, and the information economy. Managers stopped trying to drive growth the old-fashioned way and bought into the Wild West mentality instead: Get there first, pay exorbitant amounts of money for eyeballs, drive traffic at any cost. Business schools followed closely, starting MBA programs on entrepreneurship and information technology and forgetting about the basics—things like return on investment. Of course we all know how that turned out: Most of the high-flying dot-coms ended up sinking into the dot-swamp.

After a few decades of drinking bottle after bottle of corporate snake oil, an entire generation of managers and executives has now forgotten what it really takes to create organic growth. Even worse, there's a whole *new* generation of up-and-coming executives and managers who never even learned the skills necessary to drive organic growth in the first place. So we have a situation in business today where the old guard want to leave a legacy, and the new guard want to make a name for themselves on their way up. And both generations have come to the conclusion that there's no better way to make a big splash than by doing something totally new. In other words, innovating.

But too many of them—old and new—haven't really thought about what that means. Besides stroking their own egos, the implicit assumption behind most corporate philosophies of innovation is that Wall Street will continue to reward them with higher multiples based on the "higher optionality" that all that innovation is expected to yield. Unfortunately, as you've no doubt seen for yourself, and as we'll discuss in detail in the following chapters, it rarely works that way.

At this point, you may wonder where I get off making these pronouncements about what works and what doesn't. Well, here's your answer: I've spent more than thirty years managing and renovating some of the world's most successful brands. At one of those companies, The Coca-Cola Company, I put together a team that increased worldwide annual volume from nine to fifteen billion cases—the most explosive growth period in the company's history—and quadrupled the company's stock price. And since leaving Coke in 1998, I've consulted for leading companies in a variety of industries all over the world.

I'm not the kind of guy who spends a lot of time on theoreticals and hypotheticals. I deal in what works—not just on paper, but in real life. Throughout this book I'll tell you about dozens of companies that have either renovated successfully and gained tremendously, or that failed to renovate and have suffered the consequences.

In Chapter 1, I'll talk about the current obsession that companies have with innovation, and I'll show you how that obsession has caused companies to lose track of what made them successful. I'll also introduce an idea that I'll keep coming back to throughout this book: the critical difference between *core competencies* (what you know how to do) and *core essence* (who you really are as a brand) and why a solid understanding of core essence is at the heart of any business success. I'll finish this chapter with a discussion of some of the major pitfalls of innovation.

In Chapter 2 I'll discuss exactly why renovation is a far better alternative than innovation. On the most fundamental level, the difference between the two is one of competing philosophies. Innovators leverage their core competencies and say "Let's start with what we can build and let's see whether we can sell it." Renovators, however, leverage their core essence and say "Lets find out what we can sell and then we'll figure out whether we can make it." The former gets you into trouble. The latter helps you grow your business organically.

Chapter 3 is devoted to a thorough discussion of the first element of my renovation program: Renovate the way you think. Too many companies achieve a little success and then get fat and lazy. They see themselves as the undefeated champion and look down their noses at would-be competitors. I'll also talk about two other important ideas that get companies into trouble. First, too few companies track their spending, let alone measure the results. Second, they fall into the trap of constantly lowering their prices.

As simple as it sounds, if you don't know where you're starting from and where you're going, you can't get anywhere. In Chapter 4, I'll show you how to assess both of those questions and how to come up with a solid destination statement that clearly articulates how you want the consumer to think, feel, and act in relation to your company and your brand. I'll also discuss the importance of making any destination consistent with your core essence, because if you don't, you'll end up innovating instead of renovating and the results will be disastrous.

Knowing who your competitors are is a basic part of doing business. But most have it all wrong. For decades, the Big Three automakers, for example, thought they were competing only against each other. Meanwhile, the Japanese imports were gobbling up market share left and right. In Chapter 5, you'll learn how to define your competitive space and how to create preference for your brand.

In Chapter 6 we'll take a look at another side of the equation: your customers. I'll talk about a very different kind of segmentation than you're used to. Demographics and psychographics aren't enough anymore. Companies also need to know exactly why customers buy what they do, what they're doing when they buy, why they choose one brand over another, and specifically what would make customers buy more of their products.

In Chapter 7 it's all about taking and maintaining control of the dialogue between you and your customers. If you don't, your competition will, and they'll position you as irrelevant to the market. I'll show you how to create a positioning statement that will leverage your core essence to ensure that you position yourself—and everyone else—right where you want to be.

Although the quality of the product or service you're selling will contribute to customers' satisfaction or dissatisfaction, it's the quality of their *experience* that makes the biggest difference. In Chapter 8 I'll give you the recipe for creating a meaningful experience for your customers. I'll also highlight one of the most neglected aspects of most customers' experience: postpurchase, which is the time when consumers make usage and repurchase decisions.

Renovation isn't something that a company does just once. It's a process, one that needs to be ingrained in the company's overall philosophy and be a part of everything it does. But too often it's not. In Chapter 9, I'm going to talk about *forced* renovation, which is what happens when companies put off doing what they should have been doing all along. Either they renovate in a hurry or they die. I'll also talk about the brand life cycle—beginning, middle, and end—and show you how renovation can keep you away from the end stage.

In Chapter 10, I'll take you through a detailed look at several companies whose successes and failures perfectly illustrate all of the points I've made. Some of these companies are textbook examples (with this book as the text) of what to do right, and they've profited immensely. The others have blown every renovation rule I have, and they've suffered the consequence.

Then in Chapter 11—oh, wait a minute, there is no Chapter 11 in this book. But if you ignore what I say in the first ten chapters and you don't start making some changes pretty quickly, there could be one in *your* book.

I give dozens of interviews and keynote speeches every year. And in almost every one of them, questions come up about my experience at The Coca-Cola Company, even though I left more than five years ago. Because so many people want to know, I've told the story in the Appendix to this book. It's a great example of just how powerful renovation can be.

By the time you're done reading this book, you'll have the knowledge, insights, tools, and direction you need to renovate your company from top to bottom and to expand and grow your business as much as you want to.

1

So What's Wrong with Innovation?

Let me take a second to clear something up right here: I'm a big believer in innovation and risk taking, and I think both can be critically important elements of some companies' strategy. But for most companies it simply isn't the right way to drive organic growth. Believe me, I know about this firsthand. After all, I'm the guy who managed the introduction of New Coke—one of the more (in)famous product innovations of the twentieth century.

I must admit that the whole New Coke thing is a classic example of lazy business growth strategy. The fundamental issue was that our brand's value proposition was flawed. Pepsi had been repositioning us for years—the latest assault being the Pepsi Challenge, in which they were implying (very successfully) that Coke didn't taste good. Back in those days, marketers believed that if you grabbed people's hearts, their wallets would follow. So in an attempt to grab their hearts, we upped our ad spending. But we didn't change the value proposition. We acted basically like the tourist who goes to a foreign country where he doesn't speak the language and he keeps repeating himself over and over, louder and louder, thinking that eventually the locals will understand him.

We did exactly the same thing, telling consumers over and over, louder and louder, to just "have a Coke and a smile." What we really should have been doing was giving consumers a reason to drink Coke instead of mindlessly repeating that Coke was part of their life or that it was an advertising icon. Meanwhile, Pepsi was telling consumers that Coke was fat, lazy, and an outdated, stodgy way of drinking cola, and they offered the Pepsi Challenge to prove it. Unfortunately, Pepsi was right: We *were* fat and lazy. Rather than address the value proposition problem, we opted for the easy way out. We decided we needed to innovate, so we changed the formula to make Coke taste more like Pepsi.

It didn't take long to figure out that New Coke was a disaster. After only seventy-seven days we brought original Coke back (calling it Classic). Ultimately, we recovered from our little brush with lazy business growth strategy. We reconnected with our customers, deepened our relationship with them, and increased our sales. But most companies aren't that lucky—or honest enough to pull the plug on an expensive (and potentially embarrassing) project. But remember: Corporate graveyards all over the world are filled with companies that have innovated themselves right out of business.

So if innovation is such a rotten idea, what should you do instead? In a word, *renovate*. That means no longer doing *different* things with your existing assets and competencies, but doing *better* things with them instead. It means reengaging with your customers by using your relationship with them (your core essence) to provide the products and services that they truly want. Put slightly differently, renovation is starting with what you can sell and then seeing whether you can deliver it. But there's a big difference between what companies *should* do and what they actually end up doing.

The Value Equation

Dave Singleton, one of the senior people on my staff at the Zyman Group, always says that to grasp the difference between innovation and renovation, you have to understand how businesses create value. Essentially, your brand's value is a direct function of your ability to align three key things: your core competencies, your core essence, and your assets and infrastructure. If all three of these elements aren't working together, your business cannot succeed. "Assets and infrastructure" are

pretty self-explanatory, so I won't get into those, but let's talk a
other elements.

Your core competencies are *not* just a list of your products o
vices. They're based on four distinct factors:

- Knowledge: What you know and what you have learned
- Experience: What you've been through
- Resources: What you have
- People: What you do and how you do it

Overall, your core competencies are the things you're good at, the things you know how to do—or that you believe you know how to do—better than anyone else. And every company (and individual, for that matter) should have at least one.

Your accountant's core competency, for example, is probably knowledge of tax law and IRS regulations. Intel's is designing complex chips for computer applications. The Army's core competencies are deploying combat-ready soldiers, equipment, and systems. The Air Force defines theirs very differently: air and space superiority, global attack, precision equipment, rapid global mobility, information superiority, and agile combat support. Microsoft is a fast follower. Southwest Airlines is phenomenal at running short routes and turning planes around quickly. And McDonald's is better than just about everyone else at picking locations, sourcing products, and hiring people.

Core essence is somewhat more abstract. It's who you really are as a company or brand. It's the relationship customers and noncustomers alike have with your brand; it's what your brand stands for in their hearts and minds and the promises your brand makes to consumers. Coca-Cola's core essence, for example, is authenticity, continuity, and stability. Pepsi's is choice and change, British Airways' is British comfort, Apple's is community.

Your core essence is critical in determining where you can go as a business. If you try to extend your brand beyond your core essence, your customers won't cooperate. Would you go to an Amazon.com brick-and-mortar bookstore? Probably not. Amazon's core essence is allowing you to shop without ever having to leave your house. And what about a Disney cell phone? Yep, it's true. Part of Disney's core essence is family entertainment, but although sending text messages may be fun, it's not fun enough to be called family entertainment. I could see them renting walkie-talkies to families to use in the theme parks, but outside the park? And it's no wonder that New Coke failed—it violated the key elements of its core essence: authenticity, continuity, and stability.

On the other hand, IKEA has been remarkably consistent with its core essence of reasonable quality at a reasonable price. They're coming up with new products all the time; but if they can't get them designed and manufactured in a way that fits with the company's core essence, those products never show up in the stores.

If you succeed in leveraging all three of the elements of value I mentioned above (core competencies, core essence, and assets and infrastructure), you'll be able to grow your business successfully. Think about Starbucks. Their core competencies are building stores, motivating people, and sourcing the best coffee in the world. Their core essence is providing a great coffeehouse experience. Oreo's core competency and core essence are pretty much the same thing—"dependable, good cookie"—and their new Chocolate Creme Oreos has paid off handsomely. And think about Outback Steakhouses. Their core competency is grilling food, their essence is Australia, and their new chain of seafood restaurants, Fishbone (which is modeled on Outback), is a great success. The company has significant expertise in locating real estate, restaurant design, and staffing which they also leveraged in creating Fishbone. The basic Outback business model is the same, but the menu and the sign over the front door are different.

And let's take a look at a company that's constantly called innovative, when it's really practicing renovation: Apple. Sure the iPod is a great new design—but it's *not* a truly innovative product. Apple always starts the design process by asking itself, "What's the user's experience and what does he or she want?" as opposed to "Hey, look at this cool thing we can make." New products are a logical extension of Apple's core essence of fun through creative technology. They purchased some missing core competencies (such as how to store music files) and organized their assets to build the product as well as an online community where comsumers could legally download songs. Apple simply extended an existing idea—a lot of people are downloading music files—and found an easy way for consumers to store and retrieve those files. Thanks to a renovated idea, Apple has got itself a brand-new, multibillion-dollar iPod brand.

▪ ▪ ▪

So what does this whole value equation thing have to do with innovation and renovation? Plenty.

Businesses that pursue an innovation strategy generally identify new growth opportunities that allow them to leverage their core competencies and assets. The challenge for innovators is that no matter how well they deliver on the *opportunity* (in other words, how great the new product or service), they still have to persuade customers to buy. They're embracing a philosophy of "Let's start with what we can build and then see whether we can sell it."

Companies that rely on renovation, on the other hand, start with their core essence and identify new growth opportunities that are consistent with what consumers have shown they're willing to buy. What this means is that renovators know—way before they introduce anything new—that the product or service they're considering will be accepted. The challenge for renovators, then, is making sure that they have the right core competencies and assets to deliver what they're promising. The philosophy of renovation is "Let's find out what we can sell and see whether we can make it."

What this all comes down to is that the big difference between renovation and innovation lies not in the desired outcome, but in the approach you take to get there. Having tried both at Coca-Cola, and with the many clients I've worked for, I've figured out that most companies spend way too much time trying to innovate and not nearly enough time renovating. Because renovation is grounded on the company's core essences and established relationships with customers, it is almost always going to be more successful. It's far more difficult to persuade consumers to buy something that you can make than it is to make something you know they will buy. Unfortunately, far too many firms are so focused on innovation that they fail to grasp this fundamental truth. And that, folks, is a recipe for disaster.

▪ ▪ ▪

Over the past few pages I've been painting a pretty negative picture of innovation and I've taken some swipes at people and companies who pursue it. I haven't been too specific, though, just telling you that it's a dumb thing to do. Now let me tell you why that's true.

The Five Innovation Pitfalls

Most companies that consider innovation make at least one—usually more—of the following major mistakes:

1. They focus on leveraging their *core competencies* instead of their *core essence.*
2. They pursue creativity at any cost and treat all new ideas as potentially equal. (I call this the "big bang" approach.)
3. They limit their innovations to only new products and forget that innovation is about creating new value for customers, consumers, and the business.
4. They grow horizontally instead of vertically.
5. They try to innovate by acquiring other companies instead of growing organically.

Let's take a look at each of these blunders in some detail.

1. Core Competencies over Core Essence

A critical part of being able to leverage the three elements of the value equation is having a firm grasp of what they are. Sounds a little silly, but you'd be amazed at how many companies can't tell the difference between their core essence and their core competencies and end up confusing what they know how to do with what consumers will buy from them. I've seen this happen many times, up close and personal.

At one point in its history, Coke got into the shrimp farming business in Mexico and Hawaii. Why? No one's sure. But everyone agrees that it was a complete disaster.

It sounded—like so many things that turn out badly—like a good idea at the time: a way to build goodwill and to provide jobs in local communities. We knew we had world-class purchasing, distribution, and sales capabilities. Plus, we had distribution, and logistics assets that were being underutilized, and an overall competency of operating businesses all over the world. We were absolutely right about that—at least as it applied to selling sugar water. But where it fell apart was that we knew absolutely nothing about shrimp farming.

Yes, Coke knows how to run businesses in different countries, but the company's real strengths are in direct-store delivery and helping retailers sell those products to consumers. The venture was a complete failure for several reasons. To start with, it turns out that to be in the shrimp farming business you need to have the right kind of shrimp, otherwise they won't mate and you'll end up with no shrimp at all. But far more important that that, we never even thought about why consumers would buy shrimp from us in the first place. Shrimp farming couldn't have been further from the company's core essence. No one could make the connection between Coke and shrimp farming. Soft drinks, yes. But shrimp, no.

In the final analysis, we fell into the trap that so many other companies before and after us have: We confused our core competencies with our core essence, vastly overestimating the former and completely ignoring the latter.

The same basic thing happened with McDonald's not too long ago. For some reason they decided to go in the hotel business and built a few Golden Arches Hotels. Don't see the connection? Neither do I—and neither did anyone else.

Getting the right competencies is pretty easy; if you don't know how to do something, you can probably hire someone who does. But getting a new core essence is nearly impossible. Golden Arches Hotels may have taken advantage of McDonald's customer service and real estate competencies, and even if it didn't, they certainly had the resources to hire a top-level hotel management firm. But the company's core essence was nowhere to be seen. McDonald's core essence is that you always know you're going to get a reasonably good meal for a reasonable price. The meal won't be spectacular, but it won't be horrible either. You always know what you're going to get, and you'll be able to be in and out in a hurry.

It's easy to see how some of McDonald's core essence carries over into the hotel business. For example, a lot of people who stay in hotels want consistency at a reasonable price. That's how Holiday Inn, Motel 6, and some other chains have stayed in business. But where it falls apart is the "in and out in a hurry" part, which is completely incompatible with what people are looking for in a hotel.

2. Creativity at Any Cost

The innovation culture has developed a number of frameworks for business, most of which focus on getting people to be creative and "think outside the box." The more different the new product, the better, they say. Although the Chief Innovation Officers usually claim that their innovations will drive sales and increase the bottom line, there's often a hidden agenda that comes from higher up in the organization: Do something—anything—with idle capacity or underutilized assets. But the push for creativity at any cost has a number of very negative side effects.

To start with, a huge amount of time and money goes into exploring and developing every new idea that comes down the pike. Everyone knows that all ideas are not created equal in their potential to create new value. Unfortunately, a lot of companies don't have the knowledge and ability to differentiate between the good ones and the bad ones, and it doesn't seem to occur to them to ask consumers to tell them which products they might actually buy. And if they do ask, they tend to ask either the wrong people or the wrong questions, or they put together focus groups that are stacked with people who enjoy doing focus groups and are happy to pat the company on the back. As a result, a lot of really dopey ideas don't get weeded out when they should. Consider the following:

- Porsche. These guys have come out with some very creative—yet incredibly dumb—product innovations in the past few years. First there was the rear spoiler that popped up at 65 or 70 miles per hour. Great idea. That way even the cops who didn't have radar could tell when you were speeding. Then they came out with an automatic transmission. Excuse me, but most of the fun of having a Porsche in the first place is driving it, and shifting gears is an integral part of the Porsche experience. If you're going to have an automatic transmission, you might as well drive a Ford Escort. What's next, a Porsche minivan? And speaking of minivans, why doesn't Volvo, the ultimate safe family car, have one? And why did it take them forever to introduce an SUV?
- Pepsi Blue. This "berry fusion" cola was on the market only a few months before reporting dismal results. I understand that Pepsi was trying to duplicate the success of Mountain Dew's successful Code Red, one of the most successful soda launches in years—teens couldn't seem to get enough. Pepsi, which owns Mountain Dew, apparently thought that teens would like Blue as much as Red. But did you ever try it? In the interest of checking out new products, I went down to my local store just after Blue was introduced to give it a try. On my way through the checkout line, the checker tried to talk me out of buying it. I should have listened to him. Pepsi claims they had teenagers help develop the taste, but teens rejected it as much as adults did. It's no wonder that Blue was soon nowhere to be found on Pepsi's Web site or in grocery stores.
- Nestea's bubbly yellow tea drink called "Tea Whiz." Really. What I want to know is, with the dozens of people who must have been involved in the R&D process, why didn't anyone notice that there was something very, very wrong?
- Kimberly-Clark's and Procter & Gamble's wet toilet paper on a roll. Could have been the punch line of a grade school joke, but it wasn't. Somehow both of these giant consumer products companies came up with the same idea at about the same time. Consumers had absolutely no interest and sales were nonexistent.

P&G had the good sense to flush the idea after only a few weeks, but K-C dug in their heels for a while longer.

Creativity at any cost also results in products or offerings that confuse customers or don't offer them any real benefits. For example:

- Taco Bell Lites, a low-fat, more health-conscious version of the taco. Sounds like a great idea, right? But the new tacos had lettuce, cheese, sour cream, salsa, and a shell—just like the old ones—so customers were confused about what was so great about Lites. And even after they figured it out, they interpreted Lites as an admission that Taco Bell had been serving unhealthful food until then.
- Family-friendly Las Vegas. A few years ago, Las Vegas tried to shake its Sin City image and remake itself into a haven for families. They spent millions on advertising, roller coasters, family shows, and restaurants. It was wonderful, except that parents couldn't figure out why they would want to spend their family vacation in a place where prostitution is legal. Eventually Las Vegas realized that the whole thing had been a mistake and they went back to doing what they do best: adult entertainment.
- Friskies cat food in the cat-shaped foil pouch. Cute idea, I suppose, but what was the point? They must have spent a huge amount of money designing the packaging, which may explain why, at about 63 cents per ounce, it cost consumers *seven times more* than the exact same product in a regular can. It's entirely possible that some cats preferred the cat-shaped packaging, but people—who are usually the ones with the wallets in the family—generally need a better reason than "It's new!" to spend money.

There's something else, too. With the tremendous number of new products hitting the market every day, warehouse and shelf space is extremely limited. More and more retailers are going to just-in-time inventory management systems, which push responsibility for warehousing back upstream, and they don't have patience—or space—for products that don't sell. That was clearly something that Friskies didn't consider when they came up with their cat-shaped packages: Unlike the cans, the new product couldn't be stacked, which meant stores couldn't keep as much of it on the shelves. It also meant that they couldn't fit as much volume into shipping crates, which translated into higher shipping costs and more warehouse space. Bottom line is that if retailers can't move your products, you're out of luck.

In their rush to carpet bomb the market with creative new offerings, a lot of companies try to sell their products to people who just aren't interested. RJR Nabisco, for example, spent more than $500 million developing and marketing smokeless cigarettes, which seemed like a wonderful concept. The cigarette industry, which was still denying that cigarettes cause cancer, tried to define the problem as smoke—"People don't like the way I smell after I've had a few." The only problem was that smokers themselves aren't bothered all that much by the smoke—only the nonsmokers who happen to be in the same general area are. Since smokers don't care and nonsmokers don't buy cigarettes, the whole thing was a tremendous flop.

In 1994, General Mills came out with a Wheaties cereal called Dunk-A-Balls. The idea was that kids would love to play with the basketball-shaped puffs. I'm sure they were right. But the problem is that very few parents are looking for a way to get their kids to spend more time playing with their food. Heinz made a similar mistake with their new Ore-Ida Cocoa Crispers—yep, chocolate French fries, designed for "kids with a sweet tooth." Heinz actually did some market research, asking kids what would make them want to eat more French fries. But they didn't ask parents, very few of whom are looking for creative ways to get their kids to eat more chocolate and French fries.

▪ ▪ ▪

Now, I don't want you to get the wrong idea. As with innovation, I have nothing against creativity. *Au contraire*. Businesses absolutely need creativity—it just has to be properly channeled to develop organic growth opportunities that have a high probability of success. By success I mean coming up with something you can actually sell! Quit worrying about new businesses, new brands, and new customers. Instead, worry about how to make better use of the ones you already have. The bottom line is this: You don't have to abandon everything you know in order to achieve breakthroughs that lead to top-line growth.

3. New Products Only

When it comes to identifying organic growth opportunities, an amazingly large percentage of companies are one-trick ponies, focusing only on coming up with new products to the exclusion of everything else. Even worse, the emphasis is clearly on quantity over quality. Some firms set ridiculous goals for themselves, which they then go out and publish in their annual report—comments like "over the next twelve months, 40 percent of our sales will come from new products." Recent data I've seen indicate that only one of every fifty-eight new product introductions succeeds. But that doesn't stop corporate R&D departments from taking the shotgun approach and churning out as many new products as they can come up with. According to a February 2003 article in *Stagnito's New Products Magazine,* 55 percent of drinks, 35 percent of prepared meals, 32 percent of mixes and sauces, 32 percent of snacks and bakery products, and 29 percent of dairy products had been introduced within the previous twelve months. This narrow-minded approach can easily do more harm than good, in a number of ways:

a. Conflicting with core essence. As I've said, renovation attempts to leverage core essence, core competencies, and existing assets and infrastructure. Innovation is also often about leveraging core competencies and assets; but too often, innovation misses the mark because companies neglect core essence and spend too much time pursuing ideas that aren't consistent with where they want to be. This past summer I was at Ace Hardware looking for a barbecue grill. There were a dozen of them in all shapes and sizes, but the one that I found most puzzling was the one manufactured by Thermos. Thermos's essence is containing beverages and keeping them hot or cold. It has nothing to do with steak. I bought a Weber.

   When Starbucks installed wireless networks in their stores, they were extending the Starbucks experience—giving you yet another reason to hang out, eat biscotti, and drink coffee after mocha after cappuccino. But when McDonald's did the same thing, the result was exactly the opposite. Part of the McDonald's essence is "in and out quickly," but Internet surfers don't want to be rushed. And it's hard to imagine even the most loyal McDonald's customers spending the afternoon sitting at one of those incredibly uncomfortable molded plastic tables munching on Chicken McNuggets and fries while they surf the Net.

If you think of Gerber, chances are you think of baby food and babies. So can anyone explain to me what Gerber was thinking when they decided to come out with a line of foods aimed at adults? None of us is looking forward to getting old, and no one wants to eat stewed prunes out of a jar any sooner than we have to.

On the other hand, take a look at Evian. Back when they were one of the first bottled waters, their core essence had nothing to do with taste, clarity, or purity. In fact, it didn't have anything at all to do with the water itself. The Evian core essence was all about status, about being able to say "I'm such a big shot that I can pay a dollar for something that would cost a penny if it came out of my tap." And, as snotty as that sounds, people loved it. Unfortunately for Evian, their customers had a firmer grasp of the Evian essence than the company did. In the perfectly reasonable search for added distribution channels, Evian got into bars and dance clubs. But to save money, they shipped the product in large bottles. So when Mr. Cool sidled up to the bar and ordered an Evian, the bartender poured some into a glass and charged a premium price. But with an unmarked glass of water, Mr. Cool couldn't impress Ms. Cool or anyone else with his sophisticated taste, and Evian's club sales dried up. Eventually Evian got wise: They got rid of the large tanks and started selling small labeled bottles.

b. Small ideas. Incremental thinking is different from innovative thinking. Too many companies believe in the "If you build it they will come" philosophy. In other words, introduce a new product and customers will beat a path to your door. As a result, many firms keep extending their lines, trying to create consumer needs rather than being driven by them. But sticking "New" or "Improved" on a package doesn't do much to make consumers drop it into their shopping carts. In fact, more often than not it makes them wonder what was wrong with the original version.

If you want to see what I mean, just take a walk down to your neighborhood grocery store. Frito-Lay sells at least nine types of barbecue potato chips. Do they really need that many? And does Crest *really* need to have fifty different kinds of toothpaste on the shelf? Procter & Gamble (which owns Crest) spent millions formulating their new products and millions more designing new tubes and packages and retooling production lines, distribution, advertising, and marketing. (Remember the Pump? What ever happened to it?) Sure, Frito-Lay will sell a lot of each kind of chips, and P&G will sell a lot of each kind of toothpaste, but their respective shares of the overall chip and toothpaste markets won't change. Even if there is a small increase in sales, it rarely justifies the additional operational and advertising expenses it took to launch the product. (They may be introducing all these new products in an attempt to squeeze the competitors off store shelves, but even if that's true, it will never work. If Crest comes out with two new products, Colgate will be right behind. It's a zero-sum game.) Instead, they'll cannibalize their own brands. "Dual Action Whitening" customers will be people who used to buy "MultiCare Whitening" or "Extra Whitening" or "Baking Soda with Peroxide Whitening."

c. Increased spending without increased revenues. New products usually require new financial outlays for R&D, manufacturing, distribution, and marketing. Is all that really necessary? Well, nearly half of all the money that U.S. firms spend on product development is spent on products that end up getting pulled or that never pay off. Nowhere is this more true than in areas where new products can be easily imitated. Coke spent a ton of money coming up with Diet Coke with Lemon. Pepsi wasn't far behind with Pepsi Twist. A massive waste of money and resources for both companies. If your new product isn't going to increase your market share or help you command a premium price, you have no business introducing it. Or, as my old boss Don Keough used to say, "New products that have a low velocity don't belong in a high-velocity environment."

All too often, line extensions end up fragmenting the brand and increasing the cost of doing business. But that didn't stop Delta from launching a new airline, Song. Reeling from the terrorist attacks on 9/11 and increased competition from low-cost airlines such as JetBlue and Southwest, Delta responded by coming up with a discount airline of their own. But they decided to use current Delta pilots because they didn't want to upset their unions. That meant that Song would be saddled with the same high costs that brought Delta to its knees. (In 2002 Delta's labor costs were about 40 percent of sales; compare that with 25 percent of sales at JetBlue.) So who would choose to fly on Song? Probably people who were already flying Delta. But now their margins would be even lower than before.

Other companies, under the guise of driving top-line growth, do even more damage to their bottom line by subsidizing their cannibalizing new products, often to the point of giving them away. To make things worse, they actually convince themselves that all the people who have gotten used to getting the free product love it and will suddenly start paying full price for it when the freebies and promotions are over. Consumers don't always act like it, but they're often more sophisticated than marketers give them credit for being. And while some of them may buy the new product, profits are built on repeat purchases, not one-offs.

d. It's too easy to jump on the bandwagon. Back in the early 1990s consumers suddenly started getting concerned about healthful eating. Evian and Perrier came into the market positioning themselves as healthier—and safer—alternatives to your local tap water. Manufacturers saw how successfully water was doing and decided to jump on the bandwagon. But instead of pursuing the health angle, they latched on to the color of the water. Amoco, Miller, and Pepsi jumped headfirst into the "clear craze" at about the same time, introducing clear motor oil, clear beer, and Crystal Pepsi. All may have been interesting ideas, but when consumers found out that the only difference between the old stuff and the new stuff was color—actually, the lack of color—they laughed and closed their wallets, clearly fed up with the whole thing. One of the few successes was Ban, whose clear deodorant communicated the added benefit of "doesn't stain your clothes."

The next bandwagon we'll see will be disposable products. Everyone seems to be coming up with an "on the go" version or a "use-it-once-and-toss-it" version of their existing brand—and they'll charge you a premium for the "convenience." The cleaning aisle of your grocery store, for example, is well stocked with single-use wipes and cloths. While you're in the store, check out some of the food products for children. Yoplait's Go-gurt, which comes in a lunchbox-friendly tube, has been extremely successful. In the same vein, Stonyfield Farm's Yo-Baby organic yogurt comes in a four-ounce package instead of the usual six-ounce ones.

e. Possible damage to existing brand equity. The Gap decided to take a bold, innovative step and created a completely new brand: Old Navy. That was a great move, except that consumers perceived Old Navy as essentially the same as the Gap but cheaper. So they abandoned the Gap in droves. The same thing can happen any time consumers and customers get mixed messages that confuse them.

f. Corporate schizophrenia. In some cases, being truly innovative means betting the farm in the hope of realizing an uncertain return. Despite all their bravado, most executives aren't ready to do that. Innovations are usually long-term investments with very few short-term prospects. Even for less risky ventures, most corporate executives aren't ready to put their money where their mouth is. Ted, United's new "discount" airline, is a good example. Using current United employees has prevented Ted from breaking away completely from the bankrupt main brand. And since an airline ticket costs the same on United and Ted, there's nothing discount about it. So don't expect United's A-320 planes to fly with a Ted logo for long.

Of course, being willing to get 100 percent behind an innovative new project is still no guarantee that it will succeed. Just think of all those dot-coms that leased huge lofts, paid outrageous salaries and bonuses to lure top-notch people, poured money into R&D, and lost it all. Of course the fact that the money came from some venture capital firm instead of out of their pockets probably made it a little easier to spend.

g. Customer frustration. Before you start making new-product promises, you'd better be sure you can deliver. Hewlett-Packard ran some television ads in which they asked us to imagine the future, with ant-sized cell phones and lightbulbs that never burn out. Sounded fantastic. But neither of those products will be available in anything less than ten years. In the meantime, HP's customers may get tired of waiting and take their business elsewhere. And Sprint PCS, which not so long ago was ranked among the top five of "trusted brands," is treading a very thin line. Recent television ads about their nationwide network have led consumers to believe that they'll have service no matter where they go. But Sprint PCS has as many, if not more, dropouts as anyone else. And when you get frustrated enough with your shattered expectations and try to get out of your plan, they charge you $150. The message is "We're not going to give you decent service and we aren't going to apologize for it either."

4. Horizontal vs. Organic Growth

Trying to grow a business through innovation means spreading resources horizontally—developing new businesses, new markets, new customers, new brands, and new directions. As we've discussed above, that's all tremendously expensive—and tremendously risky. Winning over a new customer costs six times more than retaining an old one. Organic growth, on the other hand, maintains relationships with existing customers and deepens the connection between them and the brand. We'll talk a lot more about this in the next chapter.

This isn't to say that it's not possible to grow a business horizontally. When the Berlin Wall fell, all of a sudden there were more than two billion new consumers clamoring for American products and services. American companies started doing what I call *brand arbitrage*—taking brands that were well developed in one area and extending them into completely new areas in which they were underdeveloped. In cases like that—which are few and far between—you don't have to worry about retaining old customers, (at least for a while) because you don't have any. And you don't have to worry about one of your products cannibalizing any of the others, because all of your products are new.

But after a while, when the market starts to mature and the battles for mind share and wallet share have settled down, you're right back to dealing with the very same issues you faced in the more established markets. And the choice is the same: Grow horizontally by chasing new customers and getting into new markets and new businesses, or grow organically by focusing on existing customers, existing businesses, and existing markets. You know where I stand on this one.

5. Innovation by Acquisition

In the year 2000 alone, there were almost 9,500 mergers and acquisitions in the United States—with a total value of about $2 trillion. Acquiring another company or brand is the Hail Mary pass of innovation: a desperate last-ditch attempt to get out of trouble. And, as with the Hail Mary pass, there's a pretty good chance that things will go exactly the opposite from the way they were supposed to.

To start with, being acquired more often than not destroys or at least reduces a company's or brand's value. Prior to being acquired, 24 percent of companies were performing better than their industry average and another 53 percent performed better than 75 percent of the industry average, according to management consultants McKinsey & Company. After the acquisition, though, those percentages dropped to 10 and 16 respectively. The outlook for the bigger fish—the companies that do the acquiring—is just as gloomy. Here's a play-by-play description of a typical acquisition:

a. Acquisition candidates are screened on the basis of industry and predicted company growth and returns, not on the current and future potential strength of their brands. (Plus, it's extremely difficult to put a firm dollar value on what a brand is worth at any given moment. A building, yes, but a name?) Frequently, no destination planning is involved. Instead, it's all about ghost economics, economies of scale, "fit," and synergies. One of the best examples of this was United's acquisition, in the early 1980s, of Hertz and Westin Hotels. The idea was that the airline's customers could be funneled into the hotels and rental cars. In a wide-eyed fantasy that revenues from the whole company would be greater than combined revenues from each individual company, they changed the name from United to Allegis. Unfortunately, consumers didn't see the connection between the airlines, rental cars, and hotels. And even if they had, the new corporate entity—which was run by airline execs—had absolutely no idea how to rent cars or book hotel rooms. The whole thing was a complete flop.

b. Occasionally, one or two perfectly good candidates are screened out based on projected cash flows that are too low. But eventually frustration sets in and the pressure mounts to get the deal done. Cash flow analysis is tainted by unrealistic expectations of synergies between the brands and the organization's processes, most of which either never materialize or require massive additional investment. A huge amount of time and energy is spent trying to justify the purchase price and very little time is spent worrying about the most important question: Will consumers continue to buy? One major consumer products conglomerate sent me a package they put together because they want to sell a number of their well-known (but languishing) national brands. They've included all sorts of suggestions on how the brands could be revitalized, new markets to get into, new brand extensions, and, of course, rosy cash flow predictions based on all that. I've been through the proposal at least twice and I don't think the words "customer" or "consumer" show up at all.

If you were buying a house you'd go inside and take a look around to make sure it was solid and that it would stand up to the elements. And if you didn't know what you were looking for you'd probably hire a contractor to check it out for you. You'd think companies would do the same basic thing when shopping for new businesses: send in a team of accountants and sharp marketing people to figure out whether the target company can generate enough cash flow to justify the purchase price. But they don't, instead falling into the same synergy (or "fit") trap that United did. @Home, for example, thought that its high-speed Internet service and Excite's web content would be a natural combination. It wasn't. Sony must have thought that being able to make good quality VCRs made it a natural fit with Universal Pictures' filmmaking. And AOL and Time Warner convinced themselves that their operations meshed well together. Now Time Warner has lost 75 percent of its value and the company just dropped "AOL" from its name for what they called "marketing purposes."

At last, the deal is consummated at an outrageous premium (the average is approximately 40 percent), which makes it difficult if not impossible to achieve a satisfactory return on the investment. If someone wants to acquire a company or a brand badly enough, they can value it any way they want to. Selling companies contributes to the problem by coming up with overoptimistic estimates of future cash flow and value. In 1994, Quaker bought Snapple for $1.7 billion, thinking (or dreaming) that Snapple could piggyback on Quaker's incredible supermarket distribution networks. What they didn't take into account, though, was Snapple's existing distribution. It turned out that half of Snapple's sales came from gas stations, liquor stores, convenience stores, and other places where Quaker had no expertise at all. When all was said and done, they sold Snapple for $300 million—a $1.4 billion loss.

c. Postacquisition experience reveals that all those wildly optimistic synergies never materialize. Of mergers with strategic motivations (a move upstream or downstream in the value chain, or an attempt to add capabilities or develop a new business model), only 32 percent achieve their vision and objectives, according to a study by Booz Allen Hamilton.

d. The acquiring company's returns are reduced and stock price falls. Overall, about two thirds of all mergers fail to reach their objectives, whether that's measured by stock price, sales, revenues, or something else. Both companies' brands often suffer as confused customers bail on them; disenchanted employees run, which further impacts service, causing even more customers to leave. Costs go up, management starts to panic, and stockholders start looking for someone to blame. That helps explain why Booz Allen found that 42 percent of the CEOs whose companies didn't achieve their merger/acquisition objectives were gone within two years.

There are, of course, plenty of merger success stories. But those successes are almost always the result of solid research, good planning, and realistic thinking as opposed to wide-eyed optimism. Although Quaker's acquisition of Snapple was an unqualified disaster, its purchase of Gatorade has been a big success, largely because Quaker used a completely different approach. Quaker tried to change Snapple's brand image from quirky, fun, and alternative to little more than juice in a bottle. They fired Wendy, the spokeswoman who read fans' letters, and replaced her with traditional advertising, and people immediately stopped buying. Perhaps having learned their lesson, Quaker left Gatorade's core essence of "scientifically proven energy boost" alone and didn't try to make it just another drink. As a result, most consumers probably didn't even know that Gatorade had changed hands.

Taking this up a level, ever since Pepsi purchased Quaker in 2001, consumers have been able to eat Pepsi-owned products for breakfast. And the company has made good use of Frito-Lay's tremendous convenience store distribution to get Quaker's granola snacks into more outlets. As the country becomes more concerned with healthful eating, consumers will have a choice between granola and chips—both of which will help Pepsi. This strategy is working: Quaker has grown every year under Pepsi's leadership and contributed $470 million in operating profit to PepsiCo in 2003.

Although I take a lot of swipes at McDonald's for things they do wrong, I also think they do plenty of things right. One of those is their acquisition of Boston Market, which fits McDonald's core essence of reasonable food at a reasonable price. Now McDonald's can use their core competencies of real estate planning, operations, and employee hiring to capture more of the convenient family dinners sector. Boston Market was on the brink of bankruptcy when McDonald's bought them, but they're recovering. And licensing the Boston Market brand name to H. J. Heinz Company was a great way to expand the business destination to include grocery store shoppers who like to buy their meals ahead of time.

As we've discussed in this chapter, innovation is an attempt to leverage existing infrastructure and core competencies in order to launch completely new business initiatives. And as we've seen here, that approach is remarkably unsuccessful for most companies: It's expensive and time-consuming and can even hurt your brand.

There are, of course, plenty of situations where innovation is absolutely essential, but for most companies, the downside risk far outweighs any upside reward potential. The solution? Forget about innovating and start renovating!

Next, we'll talk about what renovation is and how it differs from innovation, and we'll give you the tools you need to quit doing *different* things with your existing competencies and assets and start doing *better* things instead.

2

Renovate Instead

I've been a consultant for a long time and I know how people react to new ideas. Clients pay me money and I do a lot of research, come up with an action plan, and present it to the company. I'd say that about 90 percent of the time the first reaction I get is "We can't possibly do that." And when I ask why, the answer is almost always the same: "Because we've always done it" some other way. When I keep pushing, I know I'm going to get one of three responses: "Yeah, but . . . ," "Wait, you don't understand . . . ," and "Let me explain. . . ." What a waste of time.

So I know that even though I've made a very strong case for why innovation isn't all it's cracked up to be, you may be thinking that since everyone else is doing it, you'd better, too. Unfortunately, I can't hold your hand and personally convince you that the first thing you need to do is get rid of those old ways of thinking or you could end up innovating yourself to death. What I can do, though, is take some time here to tell you a little more about what I mean by "renovation" and explain why it's so important. After that, you'll have to make up your own mind.

Innovation/Horizontal Growth	Renovation/Organic Growth
New business Who's going to own it? Environment of ambiguity/where is the expertise What defines success	**Existing businesses** You know who's responsible Operating in an area of expertise Parameters of success are known
New brands Expensive to build new equity	**Existing brands** Leverage existing equities
New customers Develop relationships with new set of people	**Existing customers** Sell to customers you already have a relationship with
New competencies Must develop new knowledge, systems, people, and processes	**Existing competencies** Leverage the knowledge, resources, people, and processes you already have

Defining the Terms

To start with, renovation is *not* a back-to-the-future kind of thing. It's not about burying your head in the sand and forgetting about the competition. It's not about going back to the horse-and-buggy days and door-to-door salesmen. Not at all. It's also not making minor changes to something that already exists. (That's incremental improvement, which is things like "new and improved" formulas, condoms with reservoir tips, or chocolate chip cookies with nuts. If you think of it in terms of your house, it's refacing the kitchen cabinets or painting the living room.)

True renovation is making changes to something that already exists, leaving the essence intact but giving it new vigor and perhaps a new life. It's also a lot more than that. Renovation is also rethinking your value proposition—figuring out what brought you here and where consumers will allow you to go. It's reconsidering trends in the marketplace and giving your consumers and customers more reasons to buy your brand. It's analyzing your resources and skills and leveraging them to make a bigger impact. It's like remodeling your kitchen: The basics—counters, dishwasher, refrigerator, wet bar—will still be there, but they'll be upgraded. You're doing better things with existing assets. (Contrast this with innovation, which, as we saw in the previous chapter, is doing *different* things with existing assets. It's like buying an empty lot, designing a house, and building it from the ground up.)

Conditions are changing all the time: weather, economics, the aging population, technological advances, gas prices, politics, and so on. If you think that your business is immune from any of those factors, you're wrong. They may not affect you directly, but ultimately they do. And unless you keep up, you'll become irrelevant.

In the previous chapter I touched on the difference between horizontal growth (which is what innovation tends to be) and organic growth (which is renovation). Because this is such an important distinction, I want to go into the idea in a little more detail. This table will give you a better idea of what I'm talking about.

The Big Question

Okay, now that we know what renovation is, we can move on to the next big question: Why bother to do it? After all, innovation is a lot more flashy. The simple answer is that you have to renovate, at least if you want to drive your company's value, grow your market share, increase your standings in the polls, or achieve any kind of long-term success. Ultimately, it all comes down to one thing: money.

As I pointed out in the table, when you're innovating you're basically starting over—new markets, resources, new people, new customers, new advertising—and that's not cheap. Plus, what are you going to do with all your existing resources and people and machinery and customers? If those assets aren't already underutilized or completely idle, they soon will be. Let me give you a few specifics:

- Attrition. Some industry experts maintain that the average company in the United States loses half its customers every five years—that's an average of 13 percent every year. Trying to grow a business is tough enough these days without having to increase sales 13 percent just to stay even. There are two approaches to solving this problem: You can either go out and try to get new customers, or you can keep your existing customers from going elsewhere in the first place.
- The 80/20 rule. In nearly all industries, 80 percent of sales come from what the fast food and commercial products people call "heavy users"—the same 20 to 30 percent of current customers.
- Profits. That same group of heavy users contributes essentially 100 percent of a firm's profits. In the airline business it's even worse, with nearly all the profits generated by the same 5 to 6 percent of customers. No wonder the airlines are all going broke.
- Retention. Depending on the industry, it can cost between five and twenty times more to land a new customer than to retain an old one. Studying our consulting clients, we've found that increasing the customer retention rate by only 5 percent can boost profits 50 percent or more. In addition, loyal existing customers are cheaper to maintain (they don't require as much hand-holding as new customers); they're also a great source of free advertising and can help bring in new customers for free. Finally (and don't tell your customers this), you can charge more for your product or service because your loyal customers are less likely to wait for special promotions or sales.

Leveraging Your Core Essence

In Chapter 1 we introduced the idea that the value of your brand and your company and their ability to grow organically are a function of how well you leverage these three things in order to develop and deliver products and services that more people will buy, more often, and for more profit to your company:

- your core competencies
- your core essence
- your assets and infrastructure

By far the most important of these three elements, particularly when it comes to renovation, is *core essence.* Without a firm grasp of your core essence you'll have no idea what your consumers will allow you to do; and if you don't know that, you won't be in business long.

JCPenney has been stumbling for the past few years as they've lost track of their core essence. Expanding into insurance, drugstores, Internet retailing, and fancier designers stretched the brand too thin, and frequent reorganizations muddied the JCPenney message even more. Consumers don't know what the brand stands for anymore or why they should shop there instead of Sears, Target, Kmart, or Wal-Mart. Penney's has recently started unloading some of their unrelated "innovations" such as direct-marketed insurance and financial products. That's going to help, but they've still got a way to go. In my view, the next step should be to ensure that everything they do or say (including their slogan "It's all inside") reinforces the company's original essence of clothing, home furnishings, and accessories—all at a good value.

Similarly, my New Coke innovation failed because I didn't pay enough attention to the company's core essence. In fact, the ads we ran conflicted with Coke's so much that they were very successful in convincing consumers that New Coke was a product they wouldn't want to buy. As a result, customers subconsciously scratched their heads and wondered how New Coke could possibly stand for authenticity, continuity, and stability when it had a new formula. Good question. And the answer was simple: It didn't. Sales tanked so fast that we had no choice but to change the formula back.

Figuring out Your Core Essence

Although the term *core essence* sounds fairly self-explanatory, there's more to it than you might think. A lot of people confuse core essence with jingles or logos or advertising slogans. While there can be some overlap there, true core essence is—in no more than three or four words—the most powerful, compelling attributes of your brand. The core essence of Windows, for example, is "user-friendly"; for Pepsi, it's "revolution, choice, and change"; for Doublemint it's "distinctiveness"; and for Crest it's "fights cavities."

Your core essence is probably your most important asset. It's expressed and supported by every single thing your company does—from the way your receptionist answers the phone and the uniforms your drivers wear to your thirty-second television ads and the way your CEO responds to corporate emergencies. In a sense, your core essence is the seed from which your corporation evolves. Without one, you simply can't grow—you'll be stuck flitting around from idea to idea, never building an organization that will be able to endure over the long haul.

Think of Cummins Engine. Their core essence is "powerful," according to Pyramid, a brand consulting firm. And everything they do reinforces that idea. They make the most powerful engines, as measured in horsepower and torque; they focus their R&D on creating more powerful, more efficient engines; and they forge partnerships with suppliers who can help them stay on top of new developments in engine technology.

The most important thing to remember about core essence is that what *you* say it is is completely irrelevant. It's what consumers and customers think that counts. Chances are that they aren't even consciously aware of the words you use to describe your core essence. You can tell people all day long what you want them to believe about your core essence, but none of that matters. What matters are the feelings and emotions and images that are evoked by their interactions with your company and your brand.

The essence of the Four Seasons Hotels, for example, is "I care," and usually that's precisely the impression that guests get. The hotel staff keeps track of every special request you make and they incorporate those requests into the basic service you receive. A few years ago I asked for an extra blanket, and since then every time I've stayed at a Four Seasons hotel anywhere there's always an extra blanket neatly folded at the foot of the bed.

Awhile back, though, I stayed at a different hotel in New York that also wants to convey the "I care" core essence. A few minutes after I checked in I got a call from someone saying "Hi, this is Guest Services. Welcome to the hotel, we're very happy to have you here. Let us know if you need anything." Very nice, I thought. Only a few hours later, though, I wasn't nearly so impressed. I went to the lobby to ask the concierge whether there was a gym nearby. He was on the phone when I got there, talking about the score of the Yankees game. As I stood there, he mouthed "one moment" to me and went on with his personal phone conversation. So much for "I care."

As you can see, there's often a big disconnect between what you think your core essence is and what it actually is in the minds of consumers. So, as counterintuitive as it sounds, you're going to have to do some research to find out exactly what your own core essence really is. And the only way to do that is to hit the street and start asking people—customers and noncustomers alike—questions about three things that they perceive about your company or your brand:

- Emotional benefits. This is what customers buy—it's the sizzle, not the steak. It's how your brand makes them *feel*. Offering the right emotional benefits makes customers feel that you understand and respect what's in it for them.
- Functional benefits. These are the elements that, in the customer's mind, make your brand superior to any of the competitors'. If you don't deliver the functional goods, the emotional benefits you offer won't help for very long.
- Attributes. These are things that affect the functional and/or emotional benefits even though they aren't benefits themselves.

Let me show you in greater detail the kinds of answers you're likely to get by giving you a specific example using a brand you know well: the National Basketball Association (NBA).

The NBA has two different kinds of attributes: those that have to do with individual athletes and those that have to do with specific teams or the league itself. When it comes to player attributes, two factors are strongly related to fans' interest: the athletes' passion for the game and the fact that they're among the world's best. Fans tend to divide players into three distinct groups:

- Good players and solid citizens
- Superstars and past heroes
- Bad boys

In the past, there was a good mix of all three player attributes. But in the late 1990s and early 2000s, the bad-boy image dominated. Add free agency, labor disputes, and the media's emphasis on players' legal problems and soaring salaries and it's no wonder that the NBA lost some of its appeal—and a lot of viewers.

Recently, though, the league has begun to renovate itself, starting with strengthening its relationship with fans. For example, the NBA and individual teams are making significant contributions to local communities. Charity basketball games, fund-raisers, and free clinics are being offered all over the United States. Teams give millions of dollars to charities and players volunteer thousands of hours of their time. And the NBA has donated more than 350,000 books and more than a million magazines to needy children, schools, and local organizations.

The league is even building stronger connections with fans overseas. Its new Basketball Without Borders program is designed to "promote friendship, goodwill, and education among young people through sport." Through this program, the NBA has also helped develop grassroots basketball programs, donated equipment, and encouraged

HIV/AIDS awareness throughout the world. Basketball fans in 212 nations can now watch NBA games, most of which are presented in their native languages. And today, more than sixty-five players from at least 30 countries and territories play in the NBA.

By listening to its fans, identifying the crucial attributes and benefits that matter most, and by not being afraid to tackle issues head on, the league has made major progress in polishing its tarnished image. Their renovation strategy seems to be working. Television ratings for ABC, TNT and ESPN's 2003–2004 NBA coverage are up and the NBA expects to top the NFL in licensed merchandise sales with revenue of more than $3 billion.

Ordinarily, it's very hard to change your core essence. And in most cases you wouldn't want to even if you could. But there are times when you may have to tweak or expand your core essence in response to people's changing priorities. Remember the whole fiasco with the Ford Explorer and Firestone tires? All of a sudden all the things the Explorer stood for and that had made it America's best-selling SUV—adventure, freedom, and power—weren't as important as safety. They tried to recover by falling back on the laziest marketing tactic in the world: price reductions, and they offered zero percent financing and rebates. But none of that helped them do what they needed to do: reconnect with consumers on the basis of differentiating the brand.

Polaroid had a similar problem. The company sold its first product in 1937 and for many years was synonymous with instant photography in the same way that Kleenex became synonymous with tissue. Over the past few decades, the photography industry has changed dramatically, but Polaroid didn't seem to notice and kept right on defining itself as the leader in instant photography. Amazingly, they still haven't learned from this mistake. In March 2003 their new CEO announced a drive to "realize the tremendous potential of our instant digital printing technology"—the same emphasis that landed the company in bankruptcy court awhile back. Gee, where have we heard that before? So while consumers are out there shopping for the latest and greatest digital cameras and photographic printers, I doubt that many will be coming home with a Polaroid.

The Democratic Party is an even better example of needing to allow for some flexibility in its core essence. For generations, the party's core essence has been education, race relations, social security and social services, and rights (reproductive and civil). But for the past few years those things haven't been part of the national dialogue—now it's all about the economy, health care, and national security. Sure, people still care about education and social security and choice, but not as much as they used to—or at least not as much as they care about these other things.

The results of the 2000 election are a great example of what happens when a brand refuses to adjust. Bill Clinton added the economy (remember "It's the economy, stupid"?) to the Democrats' core essence, but Al Gore felt he had to distance himself from Clinton, so he went back to the traditional Democratic platform. At the same time, George Bush and the Republicans co-opted education and social security. Left with nothing that anyone cared very much about, the Democrats lost the election. Could this change? Look at the way Clinton summed up the core essence of Wesley Clark, one of the many candidates vying for the 2004 Democratic nomination. "He is brilliant, he is brave, he is good." Who (or what political party) wouldn't love to be associated with those characteristics?

This reminds me of the fable about the scorpion who wanted to cross a river. He asked a duck to carry him to the other side, but the duck refused, saying, "If I carry you on my back, you'll sting me." The scorpion scoffed. "That would be pretty stupid; if I did that we'd both die." After some arguing back and forth, the duck finally gave in and the scorpion climbed aboard. In the middle of the river the scorpion stung the duck. "Why did you do that?" the duck asked as she and the scorpion started sinking. "Because I'm a scorpion," he replied, "and that's what scorpions do." The bottom line is that not being flexible enough to make minor adjustments to your core essence to keep your offerings relevant to consumers will kill you.

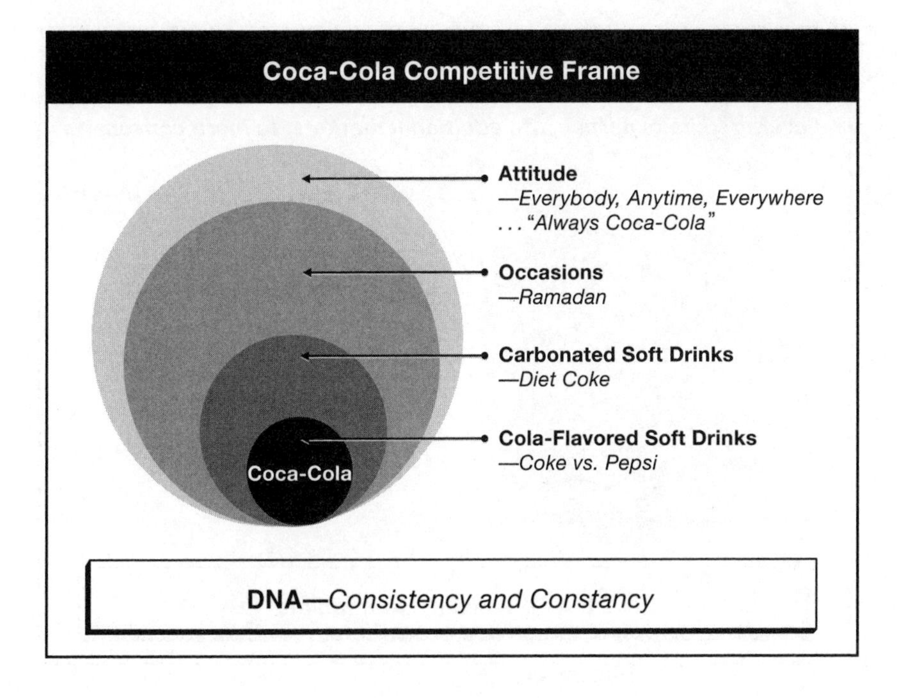

Doing the kind of research I'm suggesting here will enable you to see your company the way consumers do. Once you've determined your core essence, you'll be able to use that knowledge to renovate every aspect of your business and start generating, evaluating, and developing organic growth opportunities. In the next chapter, I'll tell you the six principles that will help you do just that.

Is Your Company a Business or a Franchise?

Don't worry, I'm not asking whether you're running a particular McDonald's outlet or whether you're planning to franchise your own busi-

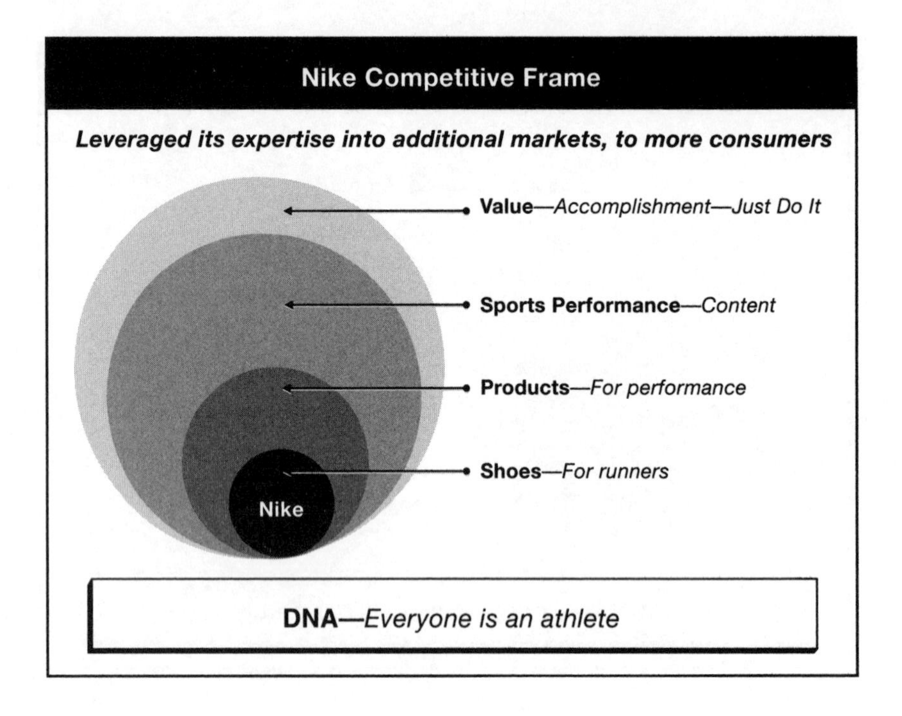

ness. What I mean by the word *franchise* is whether your business is truly in a position to grow beyond what you're doing now.

A *business* can grow, but only in its defined area. A *franchise,* on the other hand, can expand far beyond its perceived area of expertise. Being a franchise enables a company to:

- redefine its competitive frame
- broaden its market
- redefine its basis of competition
- leverage its unique expertise

Sounds great, doesn't it? Obviously, being a franchise gives you some very powerful advantages that your competition doesn't have. But be-

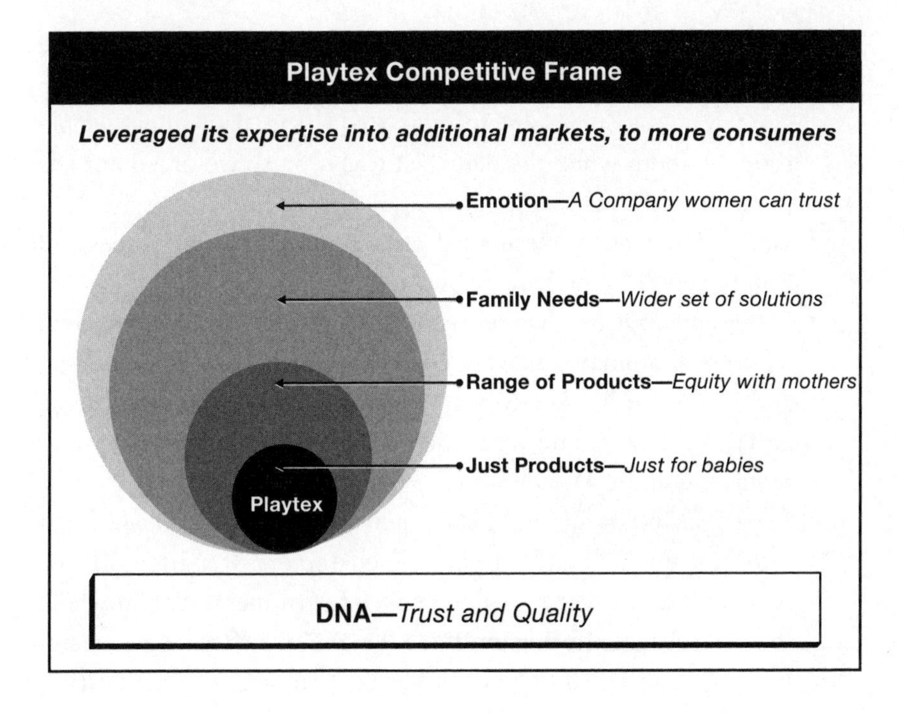

coming a franchise isn't a question of just deciding to do it and flipping a switch. In order to be a true franchise, a company has to have at least one of the following:

- Attitude. Coke, for example, has been able to expand into many other areas besides soft drinks by establishing that Coke is for everybody, anytime, everywhere—"Always Coca-Cola." The company started off in a relatively small market—selling cola-flavored soft drinks—competing mostly with Pepsi. They expanded into the overall carbonated soft drink market by introducing Diet Coke and Sprite. They expanded further by making Coca-Cola a drink for more occasions, even Ramadan! (A lot of companies don't advertise any kind of food or beverage product during this month-long Muslim holiday when it's forbidden to eat during the day. Food and drink ads weren't considered a good idea—no sense trying to sell something to someone who can't buy it. But Coke wanted to be the first thing people thought about when the daily fast was over, so we timed our ads to run at sundown.)

- Value. Wal-Mart has leveraged its commitment to low prices and value to get into the grocery business.
- Experience. Disney has taken the Disney experience far beyond its original animated movies. Snow White, Alice in Wonderland, and of course Mickey Mouse expanded into destination theme parks and resorts and from there to cruise ships, theme restaurants, and entire Disney stores.
- Expertise. Nike has used its expertise in athletic shoes to get into new markets and attract new customers. It started off in a relatively small sector, making shoes for runners. After a while, they expanded, offering products for sports performance—water bottles, running shorts, and other athletic gear. After that they expanded into an even bigger sector: overall performance products. Finally, they took it up another notch by getting into *any* area (at least any *athletic* area) that values accomplishment—Just Do It.

Another good example of leveraging expertise is Playtex. The company started off in 1932 as International Latex. Business really took off when they leveraged their expertise in latex to create a line of foundation garments—bras and girdles. In 1960, they came out with infant feeding products. Less than a decade later, they used the equity they'd built up with women to offer feminine hygiene products. Today, Playtex has a full line of baby products—from bottles and diaper wipes to shampoo and kid-friendly dishes—and feminine products. The company has been so successful at extending the brand that it's even got a line of intimate apparel. But as they've expanded, they've always remained a brand that women can trust for their children and themselves.

Going from Business to Franchise

I'm not suggesting here that only franchises can renovate—far from it. What I *am* saying, though, is that businesses *become* franchises by continually renovating, following the steps I'm going to take you through in the rest of this book. It's only by renovating that you'll learn the kind of information about your customers, your company, your market, and your competitors that you'll need to grow and expand your business.

To start with, if you're going to turn your business into a franchise, you're going to have to hit the street to talk to customers and noncustomers alike to find out whether they'll even let you extend your brand. Let me give you an idea of how this might work by taking a look at studies we did on two different companies.

AutoZone is a major player in the do-it-yourself (DIY) auto parts and accessories market. They have more than a thousand franchised stores, but are they a true franchise? Can they leverage their expertise and expand their competitive frame?

Theoretically, yes. They could expand beyond the DIY market and get into the DIFM (do it for me) market, providing auto service and repair in addition to parts and accessories. Beyond that, they might be able to provide education and training—call it the "teach me" sector. And finally they might be able to go into the car experience area, offering things like travel gear and road trip planning for family vacations.

But making these theoretical possibilities a reality isn't up to AutoZone. It's up to the people who currently buy from AutoZone, those who buy from the competition, and those who've never even heard of AutoZone. So we sent a team of researchers out to find out how AutoZone compared to the following in a number of different areas:

- New car dealerships
- Large specialty auto centers like Sears and Wal-Mart

- Specialty auto repair chains like Midas and Jiffy Lube
- Independent garages and service stations

Here's what we learned:

1. AutoZone pretty well owns the DIY space. When we asked customers to name their first choice (selecting from the list above) for where they'd go to purchase a part or accessory for their car, they said:

AutoZone	75%
Independent garages and service stations	6%
Large retailers	10%

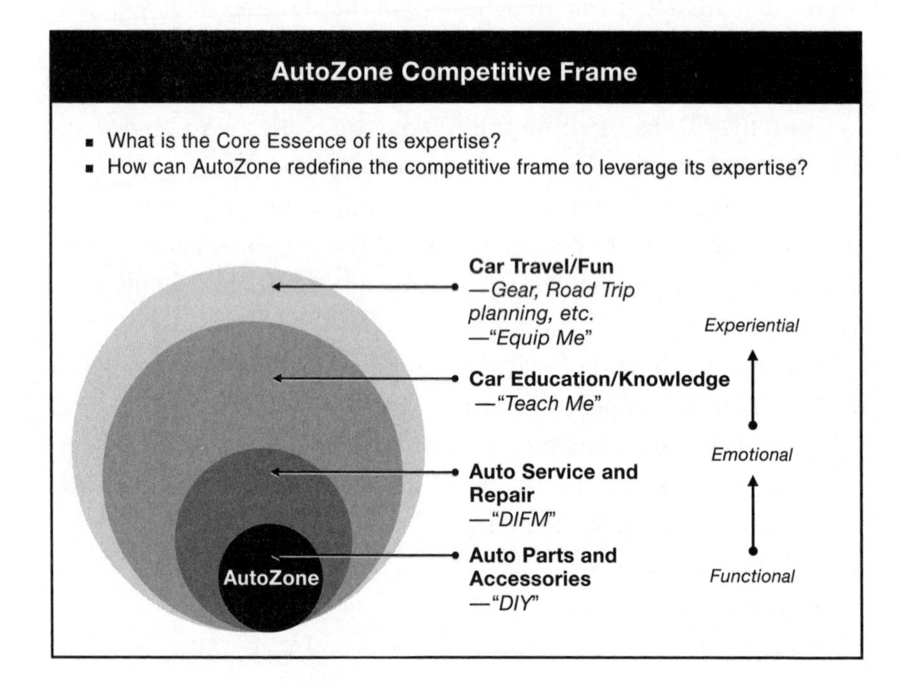

New car dealerships	8%
Specialty auto repair chains	1%

2. But they aren't even close to owning the DIFM space. When we asked customers to name their first choice for where they'd take their car to get it repaired or serviced, they said:

AutoZone	8%
Independent garages and service stations	45%
Large retailers	6%
New car dealerships	32%
Specialty auto repair chains	9%

3. Currently, no one owns the "teach me" space. When asked who knows how to teach people about cars, consumers said:

AutoZone	34%
Independent garages and service stations	35%
Large retailers	15%
New car dealerships	36%
Specialty auto repair chains	13%

4. The "equip me" space is wide open too. When asked who could offer the right advice and accessories to make car travel and family road trips more enjoyable, consumers said:

AutoZone	36%
Independent garages and service stations	24%
Large retailers	36%
New car dealerships	44%
Specialty auto repair chains	15%

AutoZone has some great opportunities to leverage their existing expertise with consumers, based on two important factors:

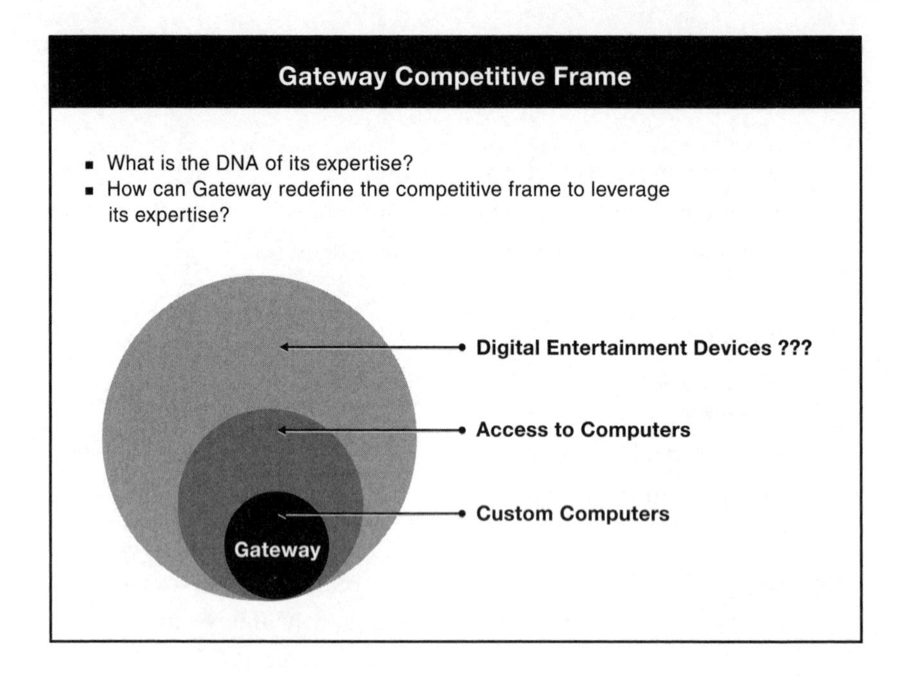

- Only about 40 percent of consumers are in the DIY market anyway, meaning that the other 60 percent need someone either to do it for them or to teach them how to do it.
- There's an increasing trend in the United States toward car travel (80 percent of all vacations and trips are taken by car, within six hours of home).

AutoZone also has an excellent opportunity to position other automotive retailers as impersonal or as offering purely functional benefits. As a result, they'll be able to own the more compelling emotional and experiential dimensions of the car experience. To do this, the company will have to very clearly define its:

- Technical expertise
- Knowledge expertise

- Experience expertise
- Status expertise

After that, they'll have to figure out:

- How to translate their various kinds of expertise into specific categories and products
- How their customers can have the best possible AutoZone experience
- How they can leverage that experience against the competitive alternatives

▪ ▪ ▪

Gateway Computers faced the same basic questions as AutoZone (and, perhaps, as your company): What is the essence of Gateway's expertise, and how can they leverage that expertise to redefine the competitive frame?

We found that in the minds of consumers, Gateway has significant expertise in the technology area—not quite as much as Dell or IBM or even Sony, but still enough to be able to redefine its competitive frame.

We also found that while most consumers say they know something about technology, they still need and want access to technology expertise. Almost everyone expresses interest in the latest technology and wants to know more. When it comes to home entertainment and home computing, only 6 percent of consumers don't know where to get the expertise they lack. But when it comes to truly cutting-edge innovations and applications that go beyond home electronics, they feel lost. For example:

- 34 percent don't know where to find out about voice recognition technology for computers or televisions.

- 34 percent don't know where to find out about digital cable.
- 41 percent don't know where to find out about video intercom systems for their home.
- 43 percent don't know where to find out about using their television for video conference calling.
- 47 percent don't know where to find out about using wireless technology to manage home security systems.

Given Gateway's perceived expertise in technology, there are great opportunities to redefine their competitive space, to position other electronics retailers as "impersonal big box warehouses," and to position other competitive computer manufacturers as "nothing more than computer manufacturers."

Although most of the examples I've given you in this chapter have focused on big companies, the basic ideas—understanding your core essence and connecting with consumers—apply to small businesses as well. If you own a neighborhood dry cleaning shop, for example, you could conduct research to find out how consumers value your service and your brand—especially in relation to your competitors'—and what their additional needs could be. If your customers get to know you and see you as a company that meets their needs, they'll keep coming back, and you'll be able to expand your brand's core essence beyond "friendly, convenient, good-quality dry cleaner." For example, you might expand into personalized valet services to help handle more chores for your busy customers.

Making a Franchise out of TACOS

No, I'm not selling shares of a new Mexican food startup. In fact, the kind of tacos I'm talking about aren't food at all. TACOS is a formula that you can use to evaluate your prospects of turning your business into a franchise. As I mentioned above, it's perfectly possible to do a fantastic job of renovating your company *without* being a franchise. Plenty of companies either can't or don't want to make the transition. But since being a franchise offers so many advantages, isn't it worth at least checking out the possibility? Here's the formula:

Trademark + Area + Customer Offer = Success

Trademark is a manifestation of your core essence. It's your unique selling proposition, what you offer that no one else does. And everyone has one. My unique selling proposition is a strong point of view, controversy, a willingness to attack the status quo, and a proven ability to provide solutions. Besides working with me, my coauthor is a well-known author of books on fatherhood. He's also branded himself as Mr. Dad, hosting a radio show, maintaining a Web site, and writing a syndicated column that offers advice to parents.

▪ ▪ ▪

Area is where you place your trademark. And one of the major factors in determining that is the trademark's relevance. Sometimes your area is more limited than others. The Sergio Zyman trademark, for example, is pretty well established in business and marketing. But if I were suddenly to try to do consulting in supply chain economics or manufacturing, my trademark—even though I've got some name awareness in those areas—wouldn't get me too far. In the same way, if Armin were to try to leverage his Mr. Dad brand to establish himself in the world of technical books, he wouldn't have much chance of success because the Mr. Dad trademark isn't worth much to people who buy technical books. Similarly, eBay has gone from being an electronic garage sale to a place where people can sell anything and everything, even new products. But it's still a marketplace of a kind.

The size and power of the trademark play an important role in determining its relevance. When Coca-Cola first introduced Diet Coke, the diet drink market was very small. And when we positioned Diet

Coke in that market, the Coke trademark was so huge that it overwhelmed the market and basically lost its relevance. (How could the Coke brand ever be irrelevant—especially in a cola market? Simple. There's a difference between a big brand and a relevant one. With the exception of four months in 1980, the Coca-Cola brand had been losing share for twenty years. Yes, twenty years. Since Coke was no longer giving people a reason to buy, fewer and fewer people did.) As a result, all we could get was a three share of that small market. When we repositioned Diet Coke in the overall carbonated beverage market, as "Coke without the calories," we got an eleven share of a far bigger market, where the Coke trademark was big, but not so big that it overshadowed everyone else. People don't drink Diet Coke to diet. They like the taste and don't feel that they're sacrificing anything. And the fact that it doesn't have any calories is an unexpected bonus.

▪ ▪ ▪

Customer Offer is your product or service. And what you're able to offer your customers is going to be a function of your trademark and where you place it. If for some reason Armin decided to get into technical books, he'd have to provide a consumer offering that would be absolutely huge in order to overcome the weakness of the Mr. Dad trademark in that area. On the other hand, Mr. Dad could successfully extend his brand by offering advice on general parenting topics, relationships, helping women understand men, and other related areas.

Because Richard Branson's Virgin trademark and attitude have become almost synonymous with choice and change, Virgin has become the ultimate franchise, able to enter areas where the emotional benefits of the brand are more important than the functional ones. In other words, what a particular Virgin product does—whether it's an airline, a television station, or a phone company—isn't as important as how consumers feel when they sit in a Virgin seat, watch Virgin TV, buy a Virgin CD, or make a call on their Virgin cell phone.

▪ ▪ ▪

Success. In order to transform your business into a s
chise, all the TACO ingredients have to fit together
trademark has to be properly placed in an area where
whelm or get lost, and you have to offer your customers
evant that capitalizes on your expertise in other areas.

If any one of the ingredients is missing, the whole thing will collapse. McDonald's, for example, has a huge trademark in fast food. But, as we discussed earlier, that trademark is all but worthless in the hotel area. As a result, the Golden Arches customer offering was completely irrelevant and rejected by consumers.

American Airlines has been trying to get into the very lucrative executive jet leasing market. As one of the biggest commercial airlines in the world, they have a huge amount of expertise in leasing jets—arguably more than just about anyone else around. But the American Airlines trademark is way too big for the relatively tiny private plane leasing market—so big that it's not relevant. This doesn't mean, of course, that American can't get into that market. It just means that they'd have to come in on a more equal footing with the rest of the players. That would require starting a completely different company, one with a new name that no one would associate with American Airlines. That way they could bring their leasing expertise to the market without shooting themselves in the foot by being the eight-hundred-pound gorilla.

▪ ▪ ▪

Okay, so you think you're ready to renovate? Well, hold on. A truly effective renovation involves overhauling six key components of your business:

1. The way you think
2. Your destination
3. Your competitive frame
4. Your segmentation (how you think about customers)
5. Your brand positioning
6. Your customers' brand experience

Depending on your situation, you may feel that one or more of these components is perfectly fine and doesn't need to be changed. You may be right. But before you make the final decision to leave things alone, I strongly suggest that you carefully read each of the chapters that follow. Things may not be quite as rosy as you think. Okay, let's take a look at each step in detail.

3

Renovate Your Thinking

The fact that you're reading this is an indication that you're at least willing to consider the idea that renovation could be a worthwhile approach. That's great. But while being open-minded is a great way to start, the process of renovating begins with renovating your mindset and the way you think about a number of basic business and marketing ideas. Actually, you'll need to change the way you act, too, but I'll get to that in a minute.

Developing a renovation mentality involves several steps:

1. Train yourself to think like the challenger rather than the champion.
2. Commit *before you even start* to measuring the results of every single dollar you spend on marketing.
3. Get the idea of giving price concessions out of your head right now.

Aggressors vs. Leaders

The leader is the big player in the market. He's cautious and cumbersome, content to kick back and rest on his laurels, not bothering to change anything because "we've always done things like this."

The aggressor is the new kid on the block. Or sometimes he's a kid who's been successful somewhere else and is trying to make inroads into a new market. He's fast, smart, and hungry, and has nothing to lose. And by the time you realize he's there, he's already taken some of your market share.

If you go and check your e-mail right now you'll probably have twenty messages telling you that size matters. And they're right. Except that when it comes to doing business, being big can be a problem. If you're the market leader in your sector, you can't afford to get complacent—some punk upstart with little to lose and everything to gain might catch you completely by surprise. The only solution is to keep renovating, remain true to your core essence, and keep doing better and more relevant things with your existing assets.

Of course, if *you're* the upstart, you'll need to make some bold innovations every once in a while, just to get your foot in (or further in) the door. But once you're there, the key to your long-term survival—and the only way to avoid being surpassed by the next upstart—is to make renovation a central part of your corporate structure and mindset.

If you think about your market as a football game, the leader is the team that's ahead with one minute to play and all they want to do is hold on to the ball. So the quarterback (read CEO) takes the snap, falls down on one knee, and lets the clock run out. But the aggressor is hungry. He knows that the only way he'll be able to come from behind is to shake things up and really make something happen. So while the leader is clinging to what he's got, the aggressor finds an opportunity, snatches away the ball, and takes off running.

This kind of thing happens all the time. Don't believe me? Well, maybe you can explain to me why:

- Diet and caffeine-free soft drinks weren't introduced by Coke.
- Overnight package delivery wasn't introduced by the United States Postal Service.
- Online mapping wasn't introduced by Rand McNally.
- E-commerce wasn't popularized by offline retailers.
- Cell phones weren't introduced by AT&T.

- Spreadsheets weren't introduced by Microsoft (and neither was e-mail).

It's all true. Not a single one of the above innovations was developed by industry leaders—the folks who developed the previous breakthrough in the field. But each one forever changed its industry. Had they been introduced by the leader (which they should have been), each of these products would actually have been a renovation—a natural extension or enhancement of an existing brand, a perfect way of doing something better with existing corporate assets. As long as it was consistent with the company's core essence, it would have generated organic growth. But none of that ever happened, because these companies were asleep at the wheel.

I learned firsthand how important it is to act like the challenger and come out swinging. In 1999, I launched my own consulting firm and entered a marketplace that was dominated by only a few firms (even fewer today) worth billions of dollars and employing thousands of people (fewer of those today, too). Clearly, I had to differentiate Zyman Group from the pack. So I developed a new value proposition and an aggressive new way of doing consulting. Instead of hiring people right out of business school like the other guys were doing, I hired only experienced people who had done similar strategic work at leading consumer and consulting companies. The average consultant at my firm has over fourteen years of experience. And instead of selling our clients the hot new idea-of-the-day like the other guys do, we use proprietary methodologies that have driven organic growth at many of the biggest Global 1000 firms. We teach our clients how to do the work and measure the results, and we're now one of the fastest growing consulting firms in the United States.

A few more examples for you to consider: Joe Owades, brewmaster for Edison, a small independent regional beer brewer, came up with the idea for a light beer. It wasn't until a few years later that Miller got into the act, misspelling "light" in the process. And it took even longer before the industry leader, Anheuser-Busch, finally caught on and introduced Bud Light.

Back in the early 1970s, a guy named Bernie Sadow was working for United States Luggage when the lightbulb went on. Coming back from a vacation, he noticed how easily porters were able to maneuver their suitcase-laden wheeled carts, so he put some wheels on a regular suitcase and showed the idea to his boss, who told him he was nuts. So did buyers at all the major department stores in New York. Sadow persisted and was so successful that he eventually bought out the dinosaurs he'd worked for. Where was Samsonite while all this was going on?

The same kind of thing happened back in the 1960s to the two Swiss watchmakers who came up with the idea for a digital watch. But their employer didn't care. In fact, they were so uninterested that they didn't even bother to patent the idea. So the two watchmakers sold their concept to some investors who took it to Japan, where it was embraced wholeheartedly and immediately put into production. Over the course of a few short months the Swiss went from being the biggest name in watchmaking, with about a 75 percent market share, to an also-ticked with about 15 percent.

Interestingly, the Swiss learned their lesson and were able to start thinking like aggressors again. Rather than spend a bunch of time figuring out how to play catch-up, they basically started from scratch, as if they were just getting into the watch market. They took a long, hard look at their current environment and asked what products consumers wanted and needed. What they came up with was the Swatch, which was a big departure from the durable, prestigious, and expensive watches they used to make. Plus, Swatch was targeted at a completely different audience, one that values color and funky design over traditional luxury and accuracy. Regardless, the Swatch was still very consistent with the industry's destination: to be the biggest maker of watches in the world. Even more important, it leveraged the three components of value that I talked about in Chapter 1: core competencies (making reliable watches), assets and infrastructure (they manufactured Swatch in existing facilities), and core essence (trusted, quality watches). The result has been billions in sales.

Let's get back to the size thing for a second. Big companies are by no means the only ones that act like leaders, and small companies are absolutely not the only ones that act like aggressors. And, unfortunately, today's aggressors have a nasty habit of turning into tomorrow's leaders, admiring the view from on high.

Virgin is the classic example of a large company that acts like an aggressor. It's continually renovating its existing businesses to protect market share and expanding into completely new categories. Today Virgin operates two hundred individual companies worldwide, generates $5 billion in annual sales, and employs more than twenty-five thousand people under the Virgin brand alone. Each of these companies has its own mission statement, but they all work together to leverage Virgin's core essence: revolution and change.

Amazon is another example of a massive company that's always one step ahead of the competition. In 1994, Amazon was the ultimate aggressor, launching an Internet bookstore to go head-to-head with industry giants Borders and Barnes & Noble. They quickly positioned those two as stodgy and outdated, still putting books on shelves in alphabetical order. And they innovated the customer experience by offering home delivery, product reviews and recommendations, and lower prices on a selection that was infinitely larger than what any brick-and-mortar store could stock.

Amazon quickly became the dominant player in the book business and could have stopped right there to smell the library paste. But they didn't. Instead, they applied their business model to other industries: music, videos, cameras, toys, tools, kitchen utensils—you name it, and they probably sell it. If you're in retail, chances are you've lost share to Amazon. Some of those former customers may still come into your stores to browse, but they do their buying online. In less than a decade the aggressor who seemed to come from out of left field has a market capitalization of $23 billion and annual sales of $4 billion.

If Virgin and Amazon are at one end of the insurgency scale, Domino's Pizza is at the other. Now don't get me wrong: Domino's $4 billion in annual sales is nothing to sneeze at; but Pizza Hut knocked them out of the number one spot in the industry and hasn't looked back. Domino's practically invented the concept of delivering a hot pizza directly to your door. But then they got fat—maybe it was all those trans fats in the cheese. They let their food quality slip and stood idly by as everyone from neighborhood pizza places to other national chains established their own delivery services. All of a sudden they were repositioned as "quick pizza whose low price is matched by its low quality."

If Domino's had been on the ball and continually renovating, they would have known that pizza customers value taste and they would have paid more attention to quality; they might have leveraged their competencies, core essence, and assets and infrastructure to expand into frozen pizzas, instead of letting Kraft's Tombstone and DiGiorno brands chew through Domino's market share; and they would have added buffalo wings and chicken tenders to the menu sooner. But they didn't do any of these things, because they were the leader. (In all fairness, I should mention that Domino's international business has done a far better job: They customize their pizzas to accommodate local tastes, and they allow local franchisees to aggressively find ways to gain market share in new locations.)

Duracell offers a very interesting example. It was a leader in a specialized market but became an aggressor in a far larger one. In 1970, Duracell was a $25 million brand, selling batteries primarily through camera shops. But Duracell had developed a new technology, alkaline, that made their batteries last significantly longer than the commercial zinc-carbon batteries that Eveready was selling everywhere for $1.09 for a pack of four. Duracell managed to persuade a couple of mass marketers to take a chance on them, partly because they promised to invest a big chunk of the profits in marketing.

So Duracell revised its packaging, ran commercials that demonstrated the long life of its batteries in everyday use, and introduced a four-pack for $2.09. Portable electronics like boom boxes were getting more popular and consumers loved the longer-lasting batteries. At the same time, retailers enjoyed the increased sales.

Eveready, the leader in the consumer battery market, had avoided getting into alkaline because zinc-carbon batteries were immensely profitable and they didn't want to cannibalize their own sales by launching a new product; so they let a nobody beat them to the punch. As a result, they lost a huge chunk of market share, jeopardized their current and future profit streams, and ended up having to share the title of "leading battery company."

In 1985, Quaker had a roughly 50 percent share of the highly profitable moist dog food market. A few years later, after paying $200 million to acquire Anderson Clayton, which owned Gaines, Quaker upped that share to 90 percent. Meanwhile, on the other side of the kennel, Ralston Purina was worried that Quaker might use its soft food profits to get into the dry food market, where Purina had a 40 percent share.

Purina's then-chairman, Bill Stirtz, wanted to put a dent in Quaker's cash flow and keep them out of his market. So he bought a small private-label moist food franchise, which he tasked with developing a new national brand that would undercut Quaker's near-monopoly pricing and achieve a 50 percent share within three years. Amazingly, it took soft-food aggressor Purina only two years. The dramatic drop in leader Quaker's cash flow kept them from seriously challenging Purina in dry food.

There's a story brewing right now that I find absolutely fascinating: In 2002, Eveready (now chaired by former Duracell chair Bill Stirtz—yep, the same one who chaired Purina) acquired Schick and became the aggressor, trying to break into the razor business. In an interesting rematch, the leader is Gillette, which owns, you guessed it, Duracell. You've got to wonder what Stirtz is up to. Could he be repeating his pet food gambit, trying to shave away some of Gillette's profits in order to keep it from investing more in batteries? With aggressors, you never know what they're going to do. Duracell knows Stirtz's record, and I'm sure they're running scared.

The automotive industry is a great source of aggressor vs. leader stories. Back in the early 1980s, Chrysler recognized that the baby boomers were looking for a "family hauler" that was more versatile and more fun than the station wagons they grew up with. So they took a big gamble and came out with the industry's first minivan. It was an immediate success and was partly responsible for getting the company out of bankruptcy.

Interestingly, General Motors had come up with the same concept five years before. But they were afraid that it would cannibalize their highly profitable station wagon sales, so the GM minivan never made it off the drawing board. As it turns out, they were absolutely right: The minivan *did* take sales away from GM's station wagons. But since

Chrysler hadn't been producing station wagons at the time, its minivans were pure profit for them. So GM enjoyed five years of strong station wagon sales, but that whole market almost disappeared entirely after Chrysler's minivan hit the streets.

▪ ▪ ▪

Despite all these examples, the truth is that there aren't that many large companies that act like aggressors—I just wanted to demonstrate that if a multi-billion-dollar behemoth can do it, so can you.

What's a lot more common, unfortunately, is smaller companies that act like leaders, resting on their laurels and refusing (or not even recognizing the need) to renovate. When was the last time anyone in the dry cleaning business renovated? Must be fifty years. But they're due for some changes, partly in response to those new dry cleaning products for the home washer that could make them less relevant.

And look at what's happening to hospitals. Most of them seem to be in some kind of financial trouble, and I believe that their problems are self-inflicted. For decades, hospitals have thought of themselves as public works, never worrying about things like relevance, differentiation, positioning, destination, or even their customers. If you're sick or injured, you come; if not, you don't. Fortunately, there are a few agile aggressors out there acting like regular service businesses, offering special services to different groups (such as pregnant women and cancer patients) and advertising themselves as *the* place for elective surgery.

Marketing Like the Aggressor—Making It More Effective

Customer loyalty is one of the most perishable commodities in the world. Sure, customers will tell pollsters all day long how much they love your brand and how they buy it all the time. But at that critical moment—when the choice comes down to your brand or the other guys'—those same loyal customers will turn their back on you in a second if you haven't given them a compelling reason to buy.

Obviously, reminding people about why you're so great is always important. But there are two situations that stand out because nearly every company finds itself in one of them at some point:

- You're under assault by aggressors and it's getting harder and harder to stay afloat. Delta Air Lines is a good example.
- You're an also-ran in a stagnant category—exactly what's happening with Budget Rent A Car.

Let's start with Delta, which is getting blown out of the water by the discount carriers who are stealing market share and building customer loyalty—in particular, Southwest, which reports profitable quarters as reliably as the sun comes up in the morning, and JetBlue, which is doubling operations out of its base at JFK.

Clearly, what Delta has been doing for the past few years hasn't been working. The company's been hemorrhaging money and teetering on the brink of bankruptcy. They know they need to combat the discounters head-on, but introducing their own discount carrier, Song, hasn't done much but cannibalize Delta's own business. Part of the problem is that Song has no core essence. Delta has one, but I'm not convinced that much of the senior management staff knows what it is.

If they're going to survive, Delta has to redefine its positioning against the discount carriers in a way that not only differentiates, but that also creates preference. More important, they need to figure out what their core essence is, as well as who their customers are, why they fly Delta when they do, and what makes them pick other carriers when they don't. Then, they need to focus on keeping their regular customers and increasing usage among light users.

In my mind, the perfect place to start doing that is with SkyMiles, Delta's vastly underutilized frequent flyer program. As it stands, 3 percent of Delta's customers account for 45 percent of their seats and 60 percent of their revenue. But loyalty is slipping. Their various Medallion members choose and fly Delta for only about a third of their flights. Why? Partly because Platinum Medallion members—the ones who fly Delta the most—don't like being treated the same as Gold or Silver members, who also fly Delta, just not as often. So there's no real reason for Platinum members to do what it takes to maintain their elite status (which is to fly a hundred thousand miles per year). Similarly, when Gold members see that Silver and Platinum levels offer the same benefits, they lose their motivation to fly Delta any more frequently, since it won't get them anything more than they already have.

Clearly, Delta has a lot of work to do. Basically, they're going to have to gut the entire SkyMiles program and redesign it from the ground up, based on a clear understanding of what motivates customers to do what they're currently doing and what would motivate them to spend more time waiting at Delta's gates than at anyone else's. In most cases, it's risky to make big changes to something loyal customers like and are used to. But in Delta's case it's riskier to leave it alone.

The benefits the company offers to Gold and Platinum members will have to make them feel special and unique and appreciated enough at least to maintain their current level of flying. The benefits will also have to be attractive enough to motivate Silver and Gold members to go the extra mile, so to speak, without feeling rejected. And then of course Delta will have to deliver (actually overdeliver) the goods in as individualized a way as possible.

SkyMiles—especially Medallion—members are so important to Delta's business that Delta needs to find ways to make SkyMiles relevant—they're useless if you can't use them. SkyMiles members would enjoy their flights a lot more if they could use miles instead of cash to pay for things like drinks or movie headsets. And they'd feel even more positive about their Delta experience if they could use their miles elsewhere in the airport, say to pay for their Starbucks and *Wall Street Journal*. The flight staff and airport merchants already use scanners for other purposes; why not use them to scan SkyMiles cards and deduct the miles from the member's account?

And while they're at it, Delta really needs to make more award travel seats available for their best customers—again, Medallion level flyers, in particular Gold and Platinum. If these people can use their miles to take their family to Europe at the height of the tourist season, you know they'll call Delta first for their next business trip.

If Delta can successfully make the transition from the all-things-to-all-people approach to individualized-things-for-individual-people, they'll build value with their most profitable customers and turn their financial situation around.

▪ ▪ ▪

Okay, let's talk about Budget. Like the airline industry, the rental car business has become stagnant in terms of marketing and brand positioning. But there are a lot of differences too. In the airline business, the big guys are going broke but the little guys are making a good living picking up the pieces. With rental cars, the big boys are getting bigger and a few bottom-feeding smaller firms have been doing okay, but there's not much in between. (Enterprise is the only company that's done anything remotely new lately, picking up market share by targeting a different segment of the market: people getting their cars repaired.)

The top-tier players have essentially turned car renting into a commodity business, leaving customers without any real way to tell them apart. The business category is focused on corporate deals. Price is the top motivator, and customers control the dialogue. In the leisure category, price is also the big differentiating factor. Most of the big companies have positioned themselves in the same way, presenting essentially the same brand image and offering the same benefits. They all say they want to beat Hertz, but their strategy is closer to "Be Hertz."

This is an unhealthy situation for the overall industry, and particularly for Budget. Whenever this kind of stagnation happens, the market leader (in this case, Hertz) has the most to gain, mostly because when everything else is equal, people go for the bigger brand—it makes them feel they're getting a deal. In politics, it's a very similar situation: Sameness doesn't change votes, which is why leaders win about 90 percent of the time. Faced with no significant difference, voters pick the devil they know over the devil they don't know.

If it's going to survive, Budget is going to have to give current customers a reason to rent from them more often, and the only way to do that is by offering them more than just a cheap car. With that name, though, they won't be able to get too far away from having customers use price as a benchmark. This is a great example of how a company's core essence can limit its ability to move. I can't imagine that anyone would rent a Jag from Budget. On the other hand, Budget can still leverage its core essence (easy, affordable travel) to bring some aggressor mentality to their competition with Hertz. That attitude will have to permeate everything the company does. And rather than "Be Hertz," it's going to have to be "Anything they can do we can do better."

Actually, as I discussed in the case of Chrysler and the minivan, being an aggressor isn't limited simply to doing things better. It can also be about doing something completely new that the lazy leader hasn't done.

And Now for Something Completely Different

In some rare cases, the best way to increase marketing effectiveness may be not to do any marketing at all. Sounds crazy, but sometimes it works.

Pabst Blue Ribbon Beer was once a big name with blue-collar workers, but as their customer base got older, Pabst wasn't able to retain them and didn't have enough money to spend on an aggressive campaign to attract a new generation of drinkers. Pabst's last television ad aired more than ten years ago, and they hadn't done much print or radio advertising either. But in a truly bizarre twist of fate, being half dead and not doing any advertising helped resurrect the brand.

Turned off by the huge corporations that produced most beers and the slick ads that hawked them, skateboarders, bike messengers, and other twentysomethings were attracted to Pabst precisely because it seemed small, casual, completely uncorporate, and free from the scandals and corruption that plague big business these days. When Pabst ended up in *The Hipster Handbook,* sales took off.

A lot of companies would have taken advantage of the increased revenue and sunk some of their profits into a big ad campaign and celebrity endorsers. But the Pabst folks were smart enough to have connected with their customers, and they knew that big ads would undermine their success. Instead, they do the kind of advertising that most of their competitors would never touch: sponsoring small concerts by indie bands, as well as skateboard and snowboard competitions and similar events.

Red Bull was in a similar situation but did exactly the wrong thing. For a long time, their caffeinated drink was an underground hit sold mostly in bars. But then they launched a series of pointless commercials which did nothing but alienate their customer base and turn a small, popular brand into a commercial brand that trendsetters wouldn't go near.

Krispy Kreme has also had a lot of success with no-marketing marketing. But while Pabst's success was completely accidental, Krispy Kreme's has been very carefully planned. Knowing it didn't have a lot of money to spend on ads, the company played up the Krispy Kreme *experience*. Customers can watch the entire doughnut making process through a glass wall, and the funky "Hot Doughnuts Now" sign lets people know that they can come in, have a sample or two, and walk out with a doughnut that's still warm.

Besides freshness, a big part of the KK experience is based on scarcity. The company is very careful to open up only one store per community, which gives the impression that KK doughnuts are a hot commodity in short supply. When McDonald's or 7-Eleven opens up a new store, no one cares anymore. But a Krispy Kreme Grand Opening is an event, as evidenced by the hundreds of people who drive for miles and stand in line whenever a new one opens up. That's exactly the kind of thing that generates a lot of free publicity.

Commit to Measuring Your Results *Before* You Start Anything

In my book *The End of Marketing As We Know It,* I introduced the notion that marketing is a science, not an art. In *The End of Advertising As We Know It,* I went deeper and showed how continuing to treat advertising as an art does tremendous damage to companies of all sizes. Besides those books, I give speeches all over the world and dozens of media interviews every year. But no matter how hard I try, people keep slipping back into their old habits, practically worshipping marketing (and advertising) as something mysterious and intangible when there's nothing mysterious or intangible about it at all.

…aven't read any of my books or heard me speak, it's critical …ay attention to the following discussion. Even if you *have* read …s or heard me speak, listen up anyway: Sometimes hearing th… …nore than once can help drive the point home more forcefully.

On the most basic level, artistic marketing is used to drive awareness, and the emphasis is often on coming up with clever, award-winning ads. It's also fairly touchy-feely, focusing on questions such as:

- What do I *feel* like doing today?
- What does my *gut* tell me to do?
- Do I *like* this advertising campaign?
- Does it entertain me and appeal to me?

To paraphrase Rhett Butler in *Gone with the Wind,* frankly, my dear, I don't give a damn about how you *feel* about your advertising, or what your *gut* tells you, or whether you *like* the campaign or not, or whether you even find it entertaining or appealing. You shouldn't care about any of those things either, because none of those *feelings* is worth anything.

If you take away from this book only one idea, it should be this: The purpose of marketing is to drive sales, and every dollar you spend on marketing should generate measurable results. Period. If you need a quick break to get that "Yeah, but . . ." or "You don't understand . . ." or "Our situation is different . . ." out of your system, go ahead. Done? The truth is that I *do* understand, and your situation *isn't* different from what I've seen with hundreds of other companies.

The other thing to remember here is that you absolutely need to have a plan to measure the results of your marketing activities *before* you put them in place. Disciplined marketers don't wait until the advertising/promotion/sponsorship is in the field to think about how they are going to measure its impact or results; they create control markets and build in measurement criteria up front.

Let me take you through a process that I use with most of my business consulting clients. I always start by asking the same three questions that I'll put to you right now:

- How much are you spending on marketing?
- What exactly are you spending it on?
- What are you getting for it?

How'd you do? If you're like most managers, you had a pretty good idea of the answer to the first one, were a little less sure of the second, and couldn't even come close on the third. Don't feel bad—most companies are in the same spot. And that's a real tragedy, because the answers to these deceptively simple questions are vital to your company's success.

I absolutely guarantee that if you know how much you're spending, what you're spending it on, and what you're getting for it, you will ultimately sell more stuff to more people, more often, and more efficiently.

Your overall goal must be to maximize the returns generated by your marketing investments (and I use that word deliberately—they really are investments, not just expenditures). You'll never be able to achieve that goal, though, unless you know exactly how much you're spending on each specific marketing activity (advertising, promotions, sponsorships, price discounts, etc.). When you've got a handle on spending, you'll be able to figure out the return each activity generates. Once you've done that, you'll be able to focus your efforts on the activities—or combination of activities—that produce the best returns, instead of wasting money on things that make you feel all warm and fuzzy.

I know what you're going to say: How can you possibly track one specific sale to one specific marketing initiative? Admittedly, it can be complicated, but it can be done. In fact, you've probably participated in some other company's tracking program. Whenever you call a company to order a product from a catalog and a telephone sales rep asks you to read aloud those seemingly nonsensical letters and numbers from the mailing label on your catalog, you're telling them which specific catalog or ad you're responding to, along with a lot of other stuff about who you are and what your buying habits are. Same goes for when you enter a coupon or discount code in your online order form. Of course, Internet marketing offers all sorts of other ways to match up sales with ads, tracking which popup or banner ad you responded to and from which site. It's a very effective way of getting a lot of critical data.

But most companies rarely do this, complaining that this type of data mining is too complicated or too expensive. Instead, they tend to fall into one of the following traps:

- They don't track what they do and they don't measure the amounts they invest.
- If they do use any kind of metrics to link activities, investments, and sales, they're rarely consistent from one element to the next.
- They rarely measure systematically the volume of response generated from any specific activity.
- There's no structured approach that links marketing investment with brand objectives.

So what's the cure?

1. To start with, you need to change the way you think, beginning with the following:
2. Next, go back to the second and third questions I asked a few paragraphs ago and make a serious attempt to answer them. Assuming you know your overall marketing budget, break it down

Get rid of this thought:	. . . and replace it with:
What do I *feel* like today?	**What is the next step in my marketing *process?*** (not just any process, but one that is based on real numbers)
What does my *gut* tell me to do?	**What do my *data* tell me?**
Do I *like* this advertising campaign?	**Does this advertising campaign appeal to my *target market?***
Does it entertain me and appeal to me?	**Does it drive increased *sales and profits?***

and determine exactly how much you spend on each element (advertising, sponsorships, coupons, etc.).

Macy's, for example, should know how many pairs of socks and underwear they sell on a typical weekend when they aren't running a sale. They should also know how much they sell on the weekend immediately after they run full-page ads in the local newspapers. The difference between their non-ad results and the post-ad results are most likely the result of that specific element of Macy's marketing mix.

The same applies to every other element. If your company sponsors a breast cancer walk, or hires some famous person as a spokesman, or changes packaging, or opens a new store, or distributes coupons, you should see a before-and-after change in sales. Of course, you're not always going to see results overnight. But whether it's a day, a week, a month, or a quarter later, results *must* be quantifiable.

3. The next step is to calculate how much of your sales are being driven by each individual marketing element. At the same time, you need to determine the net profitability of those elements. How much gross profit does each one generate? How much does it cost? Is there anything left over?
4. As you do all of this number crunching, a clear picture should emerge of the efficiency of each piece of your mix. From there, it's simply a matter of focusing your efforts on the things that generate the highest return and dumping the ones that either lose money or don't bring in much profit.
5. Until now I've been talking about the impact of individual marketing elements on a total brand level. If you do that alone, you'll be able to change your spending patterns and you'll end up a lot better off than where you are right now. But looking at results for the total brand doesn't deal with more subtle and specific business objectives. For example:
   - How should spending be allocated to convert competitive users?
   - What is the optimal level of spending to increase usage among current brand users?

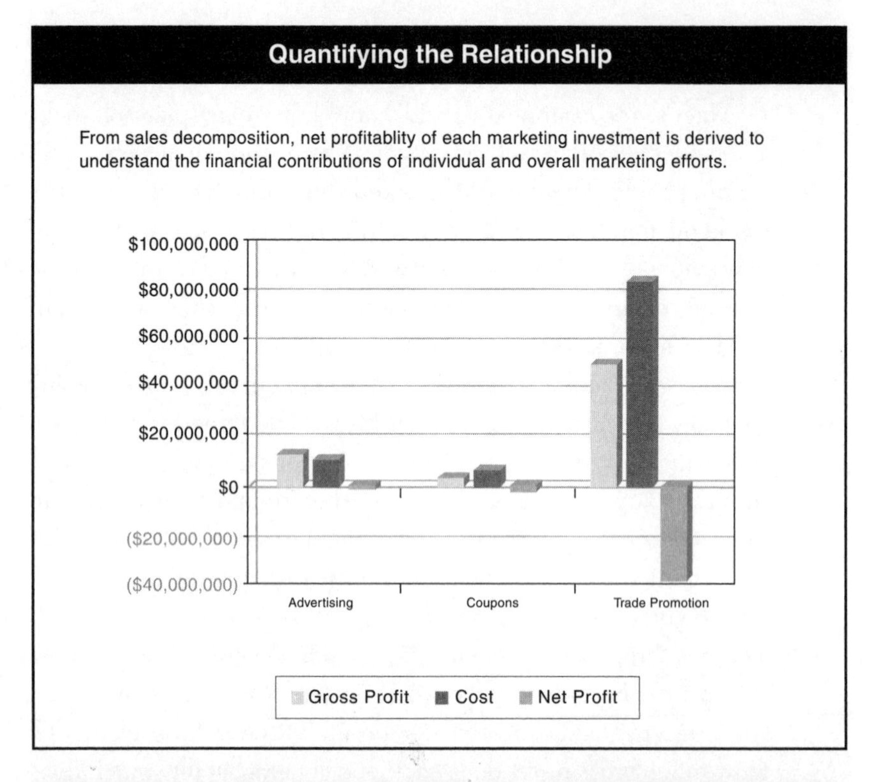

Quantifying the Relationship
From sales decomposition, net profitablity of each marketing investment is derived to understand the financial contributions of individual and overall marketing efforts.
$100,000,000
$80,000,000
$60,000,000
$40,000,000
$20,000,000
$0
($20,000,000)
($40,000,000)
Advertising
Coupons
Trade Promotion
Gross Profit
Cost
Net Profit

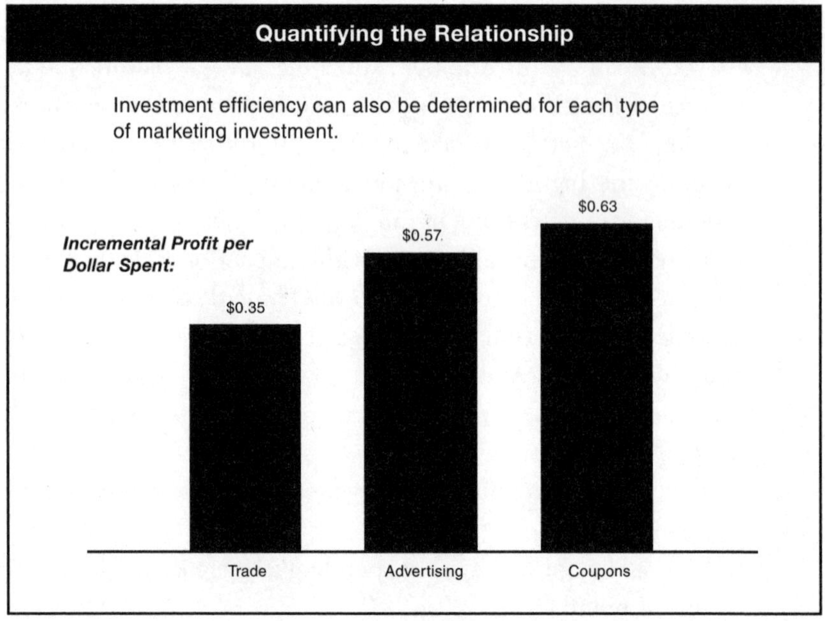

Quantifying the Relationship
Investment efficiency can also be determined for each type of marketing investment.
Incremental Profit per Dollar Spent:
$0.35
$0.57
$0.63
Trade
Advertising
Coupons

- How should the brand invest to extend brand users into new categories (for the same brand)?

Of course, your business objectives may be very different from these. But whatever they are, go back through the steps you just went through and recalculate everything with each individual objective instead of your overall brand.

Don't Even *Think* About Lowering Prices: Managing Value vs. Pricing Concessions

Everything Communicates

In my book *The End of Advertising as We Know It,* I introduced my theory that everything communicates, and I mean *everything*: your radio, print, and television ads, the way you package your product, your spokespeople, your promotional materials, the way you treat your employees and the way they in turn treat your customers, your annual reports, your promotional materials, the articles that get written about you, the events you sponsor, and even the way you handle unexpected business successes and failures. In short, *everything you do communicates something about your brand to your customers and prospective customers.* It all influences the way people view your company and your products, and it all influences whether or not anyone will buy what you're selling.

Well, guess what? Even the prices you charge for your product or service communicate something about your business—especially if you're having a sale—and they can be an important part of your marketing strategy. But how do you set those prices? Do you have a strategy (besides keeping even with your competitors), and do you actively manage your prices (besides lowering them)?

Sadly, most companies don't manage their prices at all. Actually, the problem runs deeper than that: Most companies don't even know what their prices are! Over time, companies have gotten into the habit of slapping rebates, promotions, and financing options onto their base product price, and they've cut so many deals with each channel and middleman that their true "take-home" price is a complete mystery to everyone. Always able to smell an opportunity, customers take advantage of this kind of pricing undermanagement to negotiate even better deals. Meanwhile, the competitors hear that prices are lower but aren't sure by how much. So, just to be safe, they drop their own, which triggers an insane downward spiral. We've seen this same scenario play out in industry after industry. And firms have no one to blame but themselves: They've trained their customers to respond to buy-one-get-one-free deals, super sizes, and "slashed" prices. Why buy clothes in July when there's a Memorial Day or Back to School sale right around the corner? And a growing number of people are exchanging holiday gifts well after Christmas so they can take advantage of all those after-Christmas sales.

The lesson here is that prices go one way: down. So think long and hard before you lower them—even temporarily. Temporary breaks have a nasty habit of becoming permanent. Your competitors will see your lower prices and drop theirs, not knowing about your plan to raise them again after a while. But once the other guys have lowered their prices, you'll have to lower yours again just to stay ahead of them and you're right back in that spiral.

General Motors' heavily marketed "zero percent financing" has hurt all of the major U.S. manufacturers. None of them had the guts to stand firm against GM, and they've all been paying for it, literally, ever since.

When I ask otherwise intelligent CEOs why they pay so little attention to a marketing element that actually *is* their top-line revenue, I usually get one of the following answers:

- Management apathy. "Things seem to be going pretty well right now, why upset the applecart?"
- Sales force resistance. "My sales guys don't really know how to sell the benefits of my products. It's easier for them to make pricing concessions than to sell value."
- It's the competition. "The other guys did it, so we have to. If we don't, they'll eat us alive."

- Poor pricing capability. "Managing pricing is too hard to do. It's too analytical, and there are too many scientific tools to master. My sales force is out there making deals and building relationships. They can't crunch numbers."
- Myths. "We think that the law requires us to offer the same price to everyone."

It's too bad that managers are so reluctant to manage their pricing, because it's a critical driver of marketing profitability. Actually, pricing has more impact on profits than any other factor. For a consumer products business that earns 7 percent in net operating profits, a 1 percent improvement in realized pricing drives a 14 percent increase in profits. At the same time, reducing prices by 5 percent means that you have to increase your volume by 20 percent just to stay even.

Retaking Control

Pricing is a lot more manageable than most people assume. But before we can start talking about that, we have to understand exactly what pricing means and where it comes from. And the best way to do that is to work backwards. The chart on the next page illustrates all of the factors that nickel-and-dime a $2.25 list price all the way down to a "take-home" price of $1.13.

Pretty horrifying, isn't it? And it only gets worse. A whole slew of other expenses (see the chart on the next page) eat up most of that $1.13 take-home price, leaving a take-home margin of only $0.13. Of course, the factors that make up your prices are unique to your company and your industry. But suffice it to say that if you spend some time on this, you'll be amazed at how many expenses you can come up with—and you have to analyze and track every single one of them. Once you've compiled all this data you'll be in a position to determine how you can manage them better.

▪ ▪ ▪

I have to admit right here that this is going to take some work. But rest assured, it'll be worth every minute you spend. One of my clients went

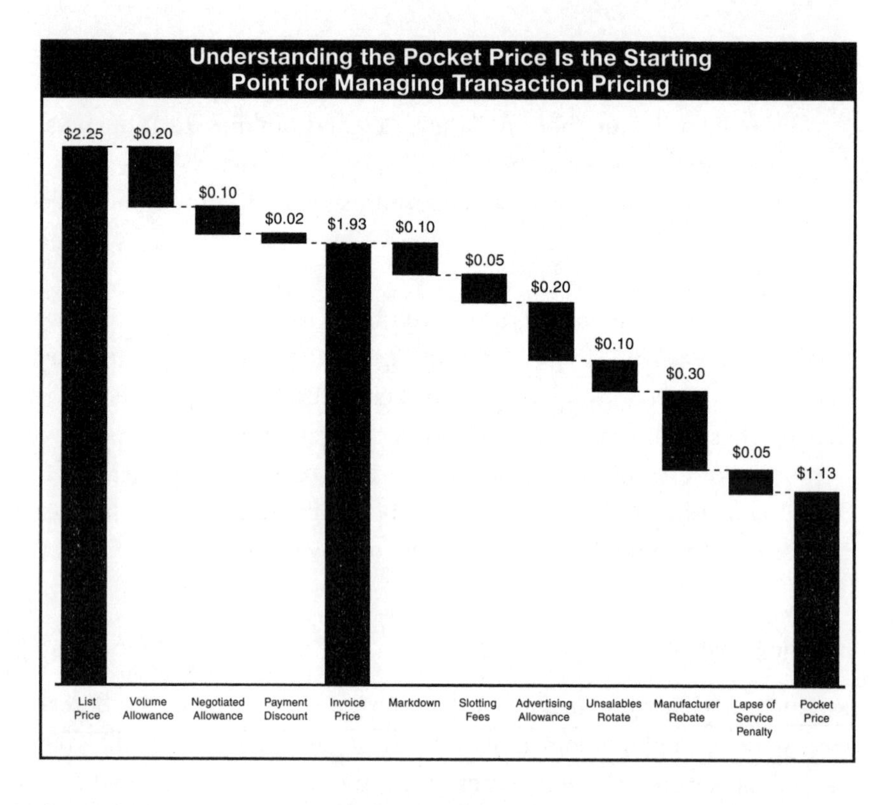

through this process and identified a number of problem areas. When they analyzed the various allowances they gave customers, for example, they found that they were being incredibly inconsistent. Smaller customers were often receiving allowances that were as high as those granted to large customers, and similarly sized customers often got very different allowances. They also found that the criteria used to grant allowances varied greatly by region.

As a result of all this analysis, our client made some major changes in their pricing strategy, going from simply managing pricing to managing value. Here's what I mean:

- They aligned their programs to their business objectives. Discounts were made more consistent by linking them to customer factors such as volume and financing terms. That meant that prices were higher for customers that wanted more credit, since they obviously had no other financing options. They also started tying commissions paid to brokers to certain volume and market-share objectives.

- They improved their discipline. They established—and stuck to—maximum allowance levels based on customers' volume and payment history. They also stopped giving early-payment allowances to customers who didn't meet the criteria, and they started charging interest on late payments.
- They reduced and/or recovered some of their costs. Instead of charging the same for freight regardless of region, they started charging fees that more accurately reflected prevailing local shipping costs. They were also able to reduce their billing and collections costs by restructuring and outsourcing those functions.

Not All Customers Are Created Equal

As you might guess, even though the client was thrilled by all this, not all of their customers were—especially the ones who ended up with bigger invoices. In many cases, though, the customers who complained the loudest were the ones who did the lowest volumes with the client and who contributed the least amount (in some cases, *negative amounts*) to the company's profits. The same kind of scenario plays out with every kind of industry and with every size company, from GM to the corner grocery store.

In summary, there are tons of ways to generate organic growth and build your business; cutting prices isn't one of them. Let me leave you with some dos and don'ts that are key to achieving success in putting together a pricing strategy and managing it:

Do	Don't
Remember that pricing communicates, so be sure to always tie it back to your brand strategy and your core essence.	Optimize pricing alone without considering what it says about the brand.
Be fact based and analytically driven. And never forget that pricing is more science than art.	Focus on recovering costs and out-negotiating (read "ripping off") your customers.
Focus on creating value and sharing it fairly with customers for what you and they bring to the table.	Make pricing so confusing that customers think you're charging more than you are and competitors drop their prices because they can't tell that you aren't.
Make sure everyone understands clearly what you are charging for and why. If you don't understand what your "take-home" price is, no else will either.	Use your gut or any rule of thumb that no one remembers any logic for.
Look forward. Set prices keeping in mind how you expect end users, customers, and competitors to react in the future.	Look backward, focusing only on "cost plus" data and on prior experience that may not matter today or tomorrow.
Know that only true profits matter, net of price-volume trade-offs and any offsetting discounts, rebates, and terms.	Consider any element of the pricing mix/profitability without taking into account how it will affect other linked drivers.
Be pragmatic. Adopt a less elegant solution if you can implement it more effectively.	Launch initiatives that your sales force and managers don't buy into.
Build a pricing capability. Commit to the program, give people the tools, training, and incentives, and hold them accountable.	Build a pricing model (and shrine to the analytic elitists) that would be phenomenal—if only anybody understood it and used it.

4

Renovate Your Business Destination

I know it sounds painfully simple, but the truth is that you have to know where you want to go before you can get there. The most successful brands didn't get where they are by accident—their path has been carefully planned. Sure, there were plenty of adjustments along the way, but the overall point-A-to-point-Z vision remained essentially the same throughout. At the same time, brands without a clear destination ended up jumping reactively from one opportunity with no consistent strategy. Before you can get anywhere, you have to figure out where—and what—you are first.

You may think that you already have a destination statement—a lot of companies I talk with think so. But you're probably wrong. For the most part, the "destination statements" that I see on company Web sites or in annual reports are more affirmations of where the companies *are* than descriptions of where they want to be. And that's a big mistake. So even if you think you *have* a destination statement, I strongly suggest that you read on anyway. At the very least, you might learn how to make your statement more effective.

Assessing Your Situation

Let's face it: If your company were operating at peak performance and everything were fine, you wouldn't have bought this book. So at this point take a deep breath and think honestly about your current circumstances and everything—good and bad—that you're facing. And be honest with yourself. Don't try—as the Singer Sewing Machine Company did—to convince yourself that your business is headed in one direction when it's really going the opposite way. Singer began selling sewing machines back in 1851, and over the years they completely revolutionized the industry. In your mother's generation there was a Singer machine in almost every home. But do you know anyone who's bought one recently? Probably not.

Today, Singer sells over $160 million in goods every year, which would sound pretty impressive if you didn't know that in the mid-seventies their sales were over $2.7 billion a year. In 2000, they filed for Chapter 11. The world changed a lot over the past 150 years, but Singer didn't. Instead, its business destination remained the same. Today, they're trying to pick up market share from their competition and they're expanding into new countries (extending a lot of commercial credit along the way), but they're going after a steadily shrinking market. Singer missed its chance to take the Singer brand name aggressively into other household products. And although they're licensing the name to third parties, the returns are a lot lower than they would have been if only they'd kept their eyes on what they had and where they wanted to go.

Since every company's situation is unique, I can't give you any specific rules for what to look for when you're appraising yours. But let me give you a few examples of how this kind of assessment might look:

Miller Beer

Miller was in a tough spot a few years back—a brand crisis defined by lack of relevance and hipness. But it wasn't always that way. Miller had a fantastic positioning: "If you've got the time, we've got the beer," which conveyed the idea that Miller was a very special reward. That idea was resonating so strongly with consumers that Budweiser introduced their own "You deserve it" slogan: "This Bud's for you." Miller apparently felt there wasn't enough room in the market for two beer rewards, so it completely abandoned "Miller Time," effectively letting Bud reposition them as a generic. After all, consumers thought, if Bud's a reward, everything else, including Miller, is pretty ordinary. Meanwhile, Corona was motivating consumers by selling an attitude and connecting with them on an emotional level even though they had far inferior intrinsics.

In a category with strong "badge" credentials, not enough consumers had any great desire to be associated with what Miller represented anymore—not because it said anything bad, but because it just didn't say anything at all. Miller was no longer a fully dimensionalized brand, and they were unable to deliver any emotional benefit to the consumer. They realized that the only relevance they had left was "beer at a price"—not a strong place to be.

A Major Cable Company

One of our clients, a major cable company (which I'll call MCC), saw its situation somewhat differently. Consumers have more choices than ever for entertainment, and the competition—especially satellite TV—was growing aggressively and positioning MCC as yesterday's technology, old and inferior. The pace of technological change and the increase in competitive products and services isn't going to slow down. People are always looking for the latest and greatest gadgets. On the other hand, trends like nesting and recentering as well as the recession and post-9/11 anxiety were having an impact on consumers and their habits and attitudes, bringing families closer together.

Overall, the opportunities facing MCC were huge, but to take advantage of them the company was going to have to do some major repositioning work: Consumers didn't perceive the MCC brand as particularly different from any other entertainment option. In fact, many people view cable as a utility, right up there with gas and electric. In addition, MCC lacked strong relationships with their customers, the kinds of relationships that build loyalty and help protect against competition.

You get the point, right? Okay, now that you know where you are and what obstacles you're facing, you can start figuring out how you can get where you want to be. The first step is to come up with a destination statement.

The Destination Statement

In rough terms, a destination statement—as you might expect—articulates where you want to end up as a business. More specifically, you'll need to articulate how you want the consumer to think, feel, and act in relation to your company and your brand. Finally, your destination statement must express the outcome you want to achieve in the marketplace—where you want to be, not where you are.

A destination statement isn't something you and a few of your buddies can just throw together over lunch. It's going to take a lot of work and a lot of thought. Before I get into the specific ingredients, let me give you a few actual examples of what the end product might look like:

- A major elevator manufacturer: "We are the leader in the business of transporting people short distances horizontally and vertically."
- A leading newspaper: "We will actively engage all readers so that they turn to our paper as a must-read every weekend, and more frequently during the week, because it makes a real difference in their lives."
- A leading beverage company (okay, it's Coca-Cola): "We are the world's most preferred and consumed commercial beverage."
- A software company: "We are the preferred, industry-leading integrated supplier of knowledge, programs, technology, administration, guidance, and continual improvement that enables customers to extract maximum value from their most desired consumers, more efficiently and effectively than any other option, through strategies and actions that are optimized for the individual consumer."
- A top recruiting firm: "We are the preferred search firm for clients who need to recruit C class candidates rapidly (including CFOs and CEOs) to accomplish their growth objectives. We do this . . .

– By developing a deep understanding of our clients' business needs and the requirements of the role they are asking us to fill;
– By leveraging our unique process of intensive firm-wide collaboration, which is proven to deliver a larger pool of high quality candidates faster;
– By packaging and projecting the opportunity to the industry's top prospects more effectively than anyone else to ensure that we help our clients 'close the deal.'

As a result, we will grow our share from 9 percent (in 2001) to 15 percent of searches (by 2004) at current margins while preserving our culture and the quality that we deliver to our clients."

As you see, destination statements can vary in length and detail. But in working with our clients we've found that the best destination statements address the following questions (you don't have to articulate each answer in your statement, but you should definitely know the answer before you come up with your final draft):

1. How do we define our business? What business do we want to be in on a long-term basis?
2. Who are our target consumers? Who should we sell to, directly and indirectly, now and in the future?
3. What do we want them to think? What explicit, tangible attributes and benefits will customers ascribe to our brand?
4. What do we want them to feel? What are the intangible, higher-order benefits and attributes we deliver?
5. How do we want them to act? What do we want customers to do as a result of their thoughts and feelings?
6. What do we want as a result? How will our company benefit from all of this over the long term?

To put this into more realistic terms, let's use Nike as an example. Here's how they'd answer these questions:

1. How do we define our business? Running shoes, athletic shoes, apparel, equipment.

2. Who are our target consumers? Competitive male runners, as well as numerous targets representing multiple athletic, fitness, and fashion markets.
3. How do we want them to think? Cutting-edge design by world-class athletes that will provide me with world-class performance.
4. How do we want them to feel? That I am cool (and performing better) because I wear Nike.
5. How do we want them to act? Choose Nike first when considering athletic apparel and equipment.
6. What do we want as a result? Nike will be the biggest sports brand in the world.

Better yet, here's how a leading cable company answered these questions:

1. How do we define our business? Leading and growing provider of in-home entertainment, communication, and information services.
2. Who are our target consumers? Current customers; multichannel video consumers using competitive services; key constituencies such as employees, communities, regulators, etc.
3. What do we want them to think? We have the best technology and the best service at the best overall value; that only we deliver what you want when you want it and how you want it.
4. What do we want them to feel? The cable company brings me the best now and in the future; I trust them to simplify things for me; I feel that the company cares about me as a customer.
5. How do we want them to act? They sign up for new services and use services more; they disregard competitive offerings and promotions.
6. What do we want as a result? 20% CAGR [compounded annual growth rate] in customer value; highest penetration in the industry on all products and services offered; significantly reduced churn, especially digital and hi speed.

Keep in mind that it's entirely possible for companies to have more than one destination statement, depending on who your customers are.

Elysia, for example, wanted to be a leading operator of funeral services. Their overarching destination statement is fairly simple: "Elysia is the consumer-preferred partner for transition into, and beyond, the final stage of life." Consumers now perceive two choices: the old-fashioned, outdated way of managing this process, or the Elysia way. Elysia is credited with redefining, in positive, enabling ways, how people manage the process of living, dying, and surviving.

However, Elysia has four distinct constituencies: patients, caregivers, partners, and investors. How the company tailored parts of its destination statement to each group is shown on page 78.

Dimensionalizing Your Destination

Your destination (and the statement that articulates it) must be specific enough to guide the decisions you make. It also has to become the cornerstone of your corporate philosophy, painting a clear picture, for every person who directly or indirectly touches the end consumer, of who you are, what you believe, where you're going, and what drives you on the journey. And finally, it has to lay out clearly—from the consumer's perspective—how they interact with you, how they think about you, how they feel about you, and the role that you play in their lives. For example, Delta Air Lines' destination statement used to be:

> "To become the #1 airline in the eyes of our customers, flying passengers and cargo from anywhere to everywhere."

That was okay as far as it went, but we felt it wasn't clear and crisp enough—it didn't do enough to tell each employee what she or he must do today and tomorrow to move toward a better future, individually and for the company. So we suggested that Delta rephrase its statement to make it more precise and to put it in simple terms that expressed the customers' perspective. I recommended to Delta something more like this:

	Patients	Caregivers	Partners	Investors
How do we want them to think?	- Elysia is the enlightened choice - It is a better way - The simplest and smartest choice - Overall better value (not cheapest price) - It has the capability to meet any need	- Elysia makes difficult, confusing choices easy - Elysia makes it possible for all of the decision makers to reach agreement without stress and disagreement	- A professional, high quality company - An efficient way to reach customers and a smart way to keep my business in the forefront of the industry - The best access to a more consistent stream of customers than through my own sales development means	- Elysia is the way to participate in an investment that has all the upside of a start-up with less of the risk - These guys really know their stuff and have their act together - The business model and the value proposition are both very strong, and the potential is significant
How do we want them to feel?	- I feel Elysia has my best interests at heart - They are really looking out for me - I can trust them to do what's best for me and my family - Elysia is caring and sensitive - Elysia is a friend I can count on when I need one the most	- Elysia takes the pressure off of me - I feel better equipped to handle a very trying time knowing they are around - I can rest assured that the patient could not be in better hands	- I am participating in the future of my industry - Elysia is a leader and I like to be associated with leaders - I feel good delivering better value to patients and their families - My success is tied to Elysia's success, so I am motivated to make Elysia successful - I can trust Elysia	- I have to be involved in this - I will regret it if I'm not
How do we want them to act?	- Select Elysia to manage my affairs as I age and to help my family and loved ones when I'm gone - I refer all of my friends and family to Elysia to meet	- They did such a good job with the patient during life, I want them to handle everything associated with the death as well - I will call them for help - I will refer them to my friends	- I choose to do business with Elysia whenever the opportunity presents itself - I have entered into a long term relationship with Elysia - I deliver products and services to Elysia's quality standards	- I will invest in Elysia

> "Wherever Delta flies (and wherever it may fly), I want to fly Delta. And I'm even willing to pay more to do it."

Much, much better. Don't let the short-but-sweet quality of Delta's statement fool you. Those twenty-three words were the product of digging a lot deeper into three important areas:

- The brand's internal compass
- The visceral response sought from consumers
- Delta's expected improvements

Delta's internal compass provides the brand's direction to make sure all areas of the business are aligned with a common goal: in this case, to make Delta consumers' airline of choice. At a time when low-frills competitors like Southwest were offering the cheapest prices, Delta took a firm stand with its destination statement to avoid a price war. Delta knew it had to give consumers a better experience than the competitors—an experience consumers would pay extra for.

■ ■ ■

Let's take a look at the chart on page 80 to see how Miller Beer used this process to dig itself out of what would have been an early grave.

The Brand's Internal Compass

Direction

The overall destination for the Miller brand should ideally be relevant for all the brands Miller currently markets and all the future brands it may introduce. It must clearly and telegraphically define the long-term

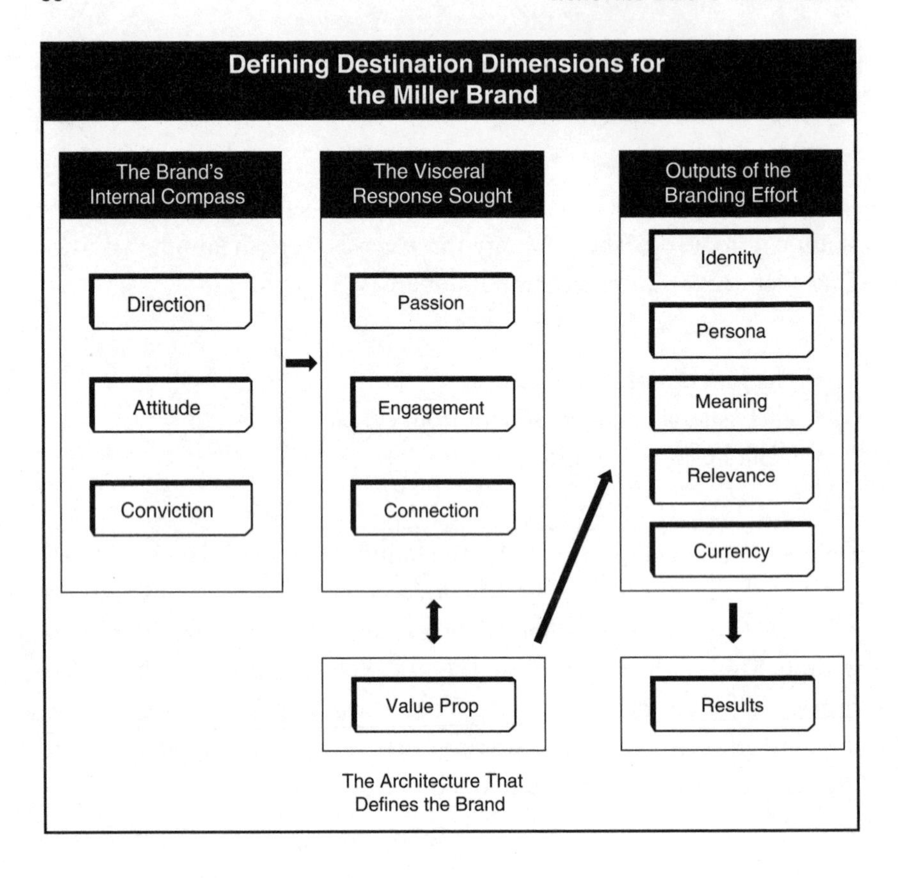

direction Miller should follow, and in turn inform and guide decisions regarding:

- How employees are recruited, evaluated, and rewarded
- How distributors are incented and motivated
- How trade customers are invested in
- How consumers are targeted and motivated

The destination also has to be based on differentiation—the company can't justify investing in a destination that moves Miller toward a place that is already occupied by an entrenched competitor. The destination has to be sustainable, not just a target that can be reached only momentarily, followed by a backslide. And finally, it must be something all of your employees and service partners will fully support.

Attitude

This is an important dimension in Miller's destination because successful brands in this category all have an attitude. And since the Miller brand has been beaten down for quite a while, it needs to adopt an attitude that matches its aggressive destination. Here's what that attitude might look like:

- Miller is a fighter. We don't back down.
- Miller is a winner.
- Miller is always upbeat and optimistic.
- Miller has a confidence that borders on cockiness, but is never obnoxious.
- Miller has infectious enthusiasm.
- Miller is different. We don't do what typical "beer" does. We're the opposite of a category generic. In fact, we're the most distinctive brand in the category.

Conviction

This is important to the Miller destination because in order to succeed, the Miller brand needs concrete beliefs it can live by, such as:

- The strength of our brand is a sustainable competitive advantage.
- We are the premier consumer marketing organization.
- We have successfully migrated from being a "business of brands" to brands as businesses.
- We have moved from fighting for consumers' attention to winning their minds, hearts, and wallets.

The Response

Passion

This is important because consumers don't currently feel passionate about Miller, and without consumer passion it's going to be impossible to kick-start and sustain the long journey back to a position of brand strength. Here's where passion comes from:

- Consumers care about the brand and feel that it's "theirs." If something related to the brand changes, they notice, and they want to be consulted, or at least notified.
- They feel so strongly about the brand they are willing to fight for it.
- If access to their brand is denied, they are upset and won't stand for it. If that means the bar or restaurant or supermarket doesn't offer their Miller brand, they will take their business elsewhere before settling for an ordinary beer.

Engagement

This is important because Miller is wallpaper today, essentially selling generic private-label beer in the "light" and "cold-filter" categories. You can't achieve a meaningful, sustainable relationship with customers without engaging them. Here's how we want that engagement to look:

- First, they really notice us, as they've never noticed us before.
- Their consumption occasions are not mere "beer" occasions, they are *Miller* occasions.
- And as such, to them the rest of the category becomes wallpaper, and Miller is the proprietary brand.

Connection

Engagement leads to connection. And once we effectively connect, we can start building consumer relationships that are worth investing in because they are built upon something substantial. As a result, when Miller consumers describe their relationship with the brand, we don't want them just to describe product attributes and functional benefits. Instead, we want them to say:

- Miller understands me and speaks to me.
- Miller is my brand.
- Miller fits with who I am and what I am all about.
- I feel the brand, and it feels right.

Changes You Hope to Generate from Your Efforts

Identity

This is an important dimension of Miller's destination because right now, Miller's identity is either out of date or nonexistent. They're the old brand, the other guy's beer. Identity means having:

- A clear, distinctive brand.
- A consistent message that is easily translated to each brand that carries the Miller name.
- A message that our target consumers want to be associated with.

Personality

This is important because when it comes to personality, Miller doesn't have one. Traits that Miller wants people to associate with its personality include:

- Being distinctive.
- Being bigger than beer.
- Embodying a strong, attracting quality.
- Being relevant with young category opinion leaders as well as the mainstream masses.

Meaning

In a highly competitive market, consumers are demanding a value proposition that means something more than just “beer.” Miller needs to broaden its meaning to include:

- Miller means *my* beer brand.
- Miller means a clear, multidimensional value proposition that makes sense to consumers at a functional and emotional level.
- A meaning that is easy to understand and communicate.
- A meaning that is unique and ownable in the category.

Relevance

Relevance drives regular use. A brand that lacks it will be nothing more than an occasional fling for consumers. Miller must be relevant:

- To motivate purchase.
- Daily, not just occasionally.
- Whenever a beer brand purchase decision is being made.

Currency

Social currency is an important dynamic in the beer category. It’s also something that Miller lacks. Miller must remake itself into a brand (and individual products) that:

- Every employee is proud to make.
- Every distributor is proud to sell.
- Every trade customer is proud to feature.
- Every consumer is proud to purchase, drink, and share with friends and guests.

Desired Net Results

The net result of all of this is that the Miller brand is a winner in every sense of the word. Commitment, support, partnership, purchase, and consumption are the gold standard in the beer category. And no matter how you measure it, Miller will have a dominant stature among employees, distributors, trade customers, and consumers.

Here's the new destination we proposed to Miller:

> "Miller is a *distinctive* brand (not a generic beer) that has reestablished itself as the *definitive* brand that *sophisticated and mainstream* consumers alike choose to consume for the majority of their beer drinking occasions, due to a value proposition that *engages, excites, and connects* with them like no other brand."

Value Proposition: Getting You from Here to There

A clearly defined destination leads to more effective business objectives, guides the development of the marketing strategies, and ultimately drives success in the marketplace. But if I had to sum it up in a sentence, I'd say that the real goal of destination planning and articulating a concise destination statement is this: Having a clear destination will clarify what your value proposition is and how to improve it.

Why is that so important? Because your value proposition is the catalyst that will propel your brand and business to their destination. But what, exactly, is a value proposition? Well, think of it this way:

At the end of the day, all that matters is what your brand means to your target customer and, in turn, how the customer acts on that meaning. And what gives your brand meaning is your answer to the customer's most important question: "What's in it for me?" In five words, that's your value proposition.

To be effective, your value proposition must operate on the three distinct levels that we discussed in Chapter 2:

- Product attribute
- Functional benefit
- Emotional benefit

Put another way, your value proposition must have the power to move consumers up the value chain. Let's go back for a minute to the cable company example I introduced earlier.

Today, MCC answers consumers' "What's in it for me?" question in a fairly traditional way: They offer price and programming value and local customer service. Nothing special. What MCC needs to do is give consumers more, and more distinctive, value—value that other companies can't or don't offer. So the next time consumers ask "What's in it for me?" they'll get answers such as those on the next page.

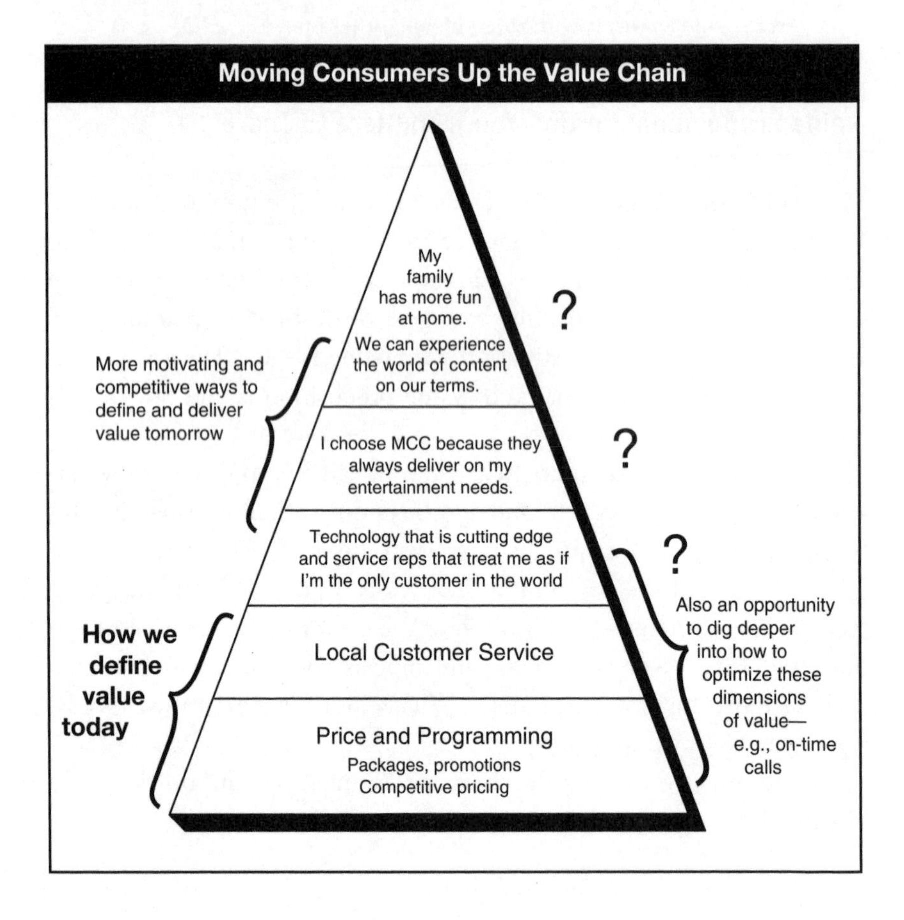

- I get cutting-edge technology and service reps who treat me as if I'm the only customer in the world.
- MCC always delivers on my entertainment needs.
- MCC gives my family and me a way to experience the world on our terms and have more fun at home.

By putting an emphasis on higher-order benefits, MCC is changing its value proposition from the expected to the unexpected and from the undifferentiated to the differentiated.

Although the entire destination planning process may seem complicated (and, honestly, it can be), going through it often yields some unexpected—but usually very valuable—results. A major mining firm decided that it wanted to be the preeminent provider of materials to the building and construction industries. But they quickly saw that although they were highly respected in mining, they didn't have the supply-chain and distribution skills they would have needed to succeed. They wisely

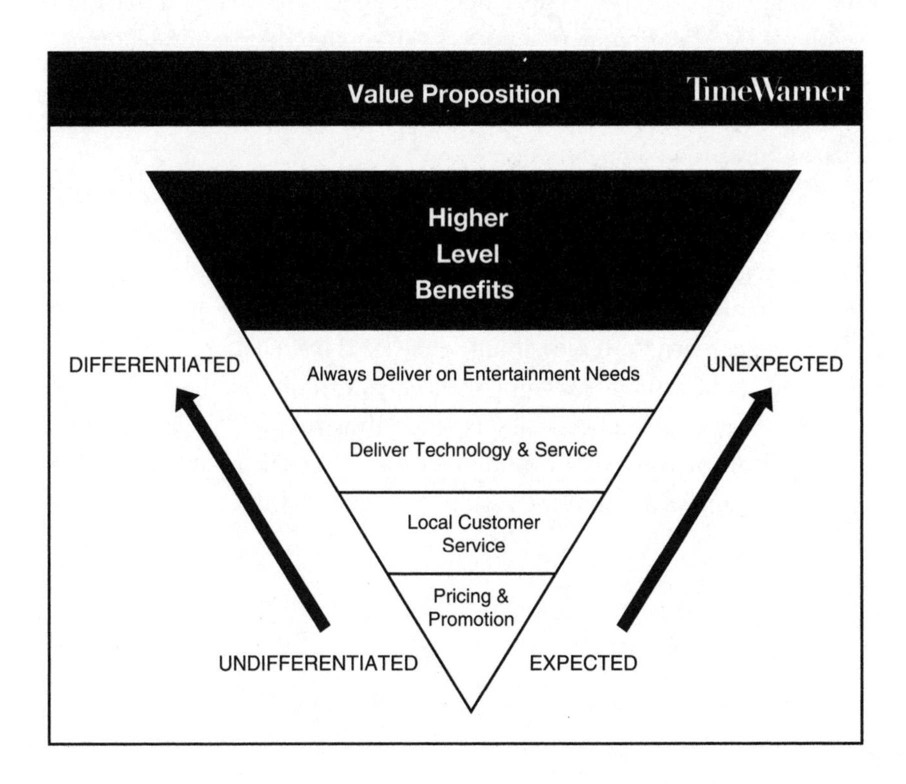

abandoned the project, realizing that it would have been an unprofitable and distracting detour from their destination and where they wanted to go, which was to sell more of their mined products.

Another client, the executive recruiting firm I mentioned earlier, made a major change to their destination. They'd originally wanted to be the preeminent purveyor of executive CEO and CFO talent. But they came to realize that their value proposition would be far more relevant and valuable to their target clients if they could offer top HR talent as well.

Summing Up

As you've seen, understanding and being able to articulate where you want to go are critical to your overall renovation plan. Don't be afraid to take some risks; aim high, for where you *want* to get, not simply where you can get easily. At the same time, be very careful that you don't develop your destination in a vacuum. Even though destination planning, by definition, deals with the future, it has to be firmly rooted in the present, based on what you currently have and do, including your assets, infrastructure, and competencies.

Most important, though, your destination must be consistent with your core essence. As you remember from the previous chapter, your core essence is defined by your customers and noncustomers alike, *not* by you. In all the excitement of coming up with an ideal, perfect-world plan, it's very easy to forget about whether those customers and noncustomers will actually let you go where you think you should be. You may have the competencies, assets, and infrastructure, but if your destination is inconsistent with your core essence, you'll end up innovating instead of renovating, and the results will be disastrous.

5

Renovate Your Competitive Frame

Do you really know who all your competitors are? I'm willing to bet that you don't, and I'm not just being cocky. The reason I say that is that I've never—and I mean *never*—met a CEO or manager who did. How is that possible? Easy. When most people think of their competition they think of their industry rivals, other companies in the same category or that offer similar products or services. But that's only part of the story.

Your *real* competition is the entire set of viable alternatives to your product that compete for your customers' money and time. That's the *competitive frame* that I introduced back in Chapter 2, and it includes a lot of things you might never have considered. Let me give you one example that may help clarify what I'm talking about.

When foreign cars first started trickling into the U.S. auto market, GM, Ford, and Chrysler (the companies we used to call the Big Three automakers) yawned. They saw only each other as competition and didn't believe for a moment that imports could ever hurt them. Just a few decades later, Toyota is number three in the American market and Chrysler isn't even owned by an American company anymore. Underestimating imports was a mistake that the Big Three will be paying for for years to come.

On the other hand, Outback Steakhouses could easily have defined their competitive set as only other sit-down family restaurants. But the recent introduction of a take-out menu expanded their competitive set to include drive-throughs and other fast-food places. That put Outback in the running for a much larger share of all family meals. Boston Market did something similar when it started selling a line of inexpensive frozen meals in grocery stores. Sales have been good, largely because Boston Market is now a serious player in a whole new category.

Sometimes competition comes from the least expected places. When Coke first got into the Russian market, we spent a lot of time researching our competitors. And what we found shocked us. Our biggest competitor wasn't Pepsi, or some local or regional soft drink. And it wasn't Stolichnaya or rubbing alcohol. It was the city bus! Many Russian consumers simply didn't have enough disposable income to buy a Coke *and* take the bus home from work, so they had to choose one or the other. Actually, the situation was a little broader than that. Our competition in Russia was essentially *everything*. And that had a tremendous impact on all of our marketing efforts in the former Soviet Union. Rather than being able to compete on taste and refreshment as we did in the rest of the world, we had to convince Russian consumers that Coke was a good value for the money, that when it came down to a choice between a Coke and a McDonald's hamburger or a candy bar or an ice cream cone or a magazine or some other nonessential thing, Coke was the best—and most satisfying—investment.

Another good example is the gradual evolution of the entertainment industry. Remember the good old days when you could watch Cronkite at seven, Disney at eight, and then maybe settle in with *All in the Family* or *M*A*S*H* before listening to Johnny Carson's opening monologue? And remember all those movies of the week, the ones the networks made a huge deal about—a year after the films had been in the theaters? Then all of a sudden VCRs appeared and we could rent movies at Blockbuster and watch them instead of one of the regular shows. Today, there are too many choices even to keep track of: Rent or buy a video or DVD, subscribe to TiVo, online downloads, video on demand on cable, go out to a movie, watch people eat maggots on a reality show, or, if things get really desperate, read a book (or listen to a book on tape).

Where I'm going with all this is that the definition of "entertainment" is far broader than most people assume, and *time* is a very important—and often overlooked—competitor. It's about more than CBS's eight o'clock program walloping NBC's in the ratings. But the networks keep deluding themselves into believing that they're competing only with the other networks. They don't even consider all the things I mentioned above. Pretty dopey. The networks have the same blinders on when it comes to evaluating their competitors in the news sector. They keep looking at each other and maybe CNN. But what about *USA Today* and *The New York Times* and *The Wall Street Journal?* And what about Reuters, *The Drudge Report, Slate,* and the hundreds of other online options that can tell you what's going on all over the world while Tom Brokaw and Peter Jennings are still sleeping?

For a long time, McDonald's and Burger King thought they competed only with each other. Taco Bell was Mexican food and not even on their radar. But when Taco Bell came out with 49-cent tacos, prices became a factor to consumers, and all of a sudden they started to take Taco Bell seriously. Although this may seem to contradict what I said earlier about low price being a lazy marketing strategy, it really doesn't. What Taco Bell was doing in this case was redefining fast food as not only good quality and great taste, but quantity—you could afford to buy more of it, thanks to their low prices. That approach worked well for Taco Bell, which was a new player in the category. But McDonald's was selling *value*. And when they responded by introducing a 99-cent burger, they changed their own value proposition to *volume* and lost a huge amount of business. (Interesting, while Taco Bell's approach worked well in the short run, it's ended up hurting them in the long run. They've been plagued by problems for the past few years, partly because they're perceived as cheap bulk food.) And while I'm talking about McDonald's, what's the competition for their ever-popular Happy Meals? They think it's Burger King (or maybe Taco Bell). But I think it's Lunchables.

Of course, not all companies fail to consider nontraditional competitors. When Campbell's started running special ads during snowstorms, they realized that they could sell more soup by offering themselves as a winter competitor to sitting by the fire or shoveling snow or reading a book or fixing leaks in the room. And when Gatorade started pitching itself as a way to replenish lost fluids after the flu, it was broadening its competitive frame and competing to a certain extent with cold and flu remedies.

And look at what Avon did. For years they sold makeup only through individual sales representatives. When they saw that consumers were buying cosmetics online, they came out with an online catalog. And when they realized that women were buying competitors' products in department stores and drugstores, they launched a line of cosmetics to be sold in select stores. The traditional Avon Lady is still important, but adding online and in-store product lines has helped Avon broaden its competitive frame and capture more sales.

The Focus Trap

The big problem that most companies make when it comes to competitive frame—and actually just about every other aspect of their business—is that they fall into the trap of thinking about themselves instead of about their customers. A business-focused company asks "What other businesses are like mine?" A consumer-focused company, however, asks "What other choices do my consumers have?"

Defining Your Frame

How you define your competitive frame will have a direct impact on the size of the opportunity, the diversity of the consumers and competition, and the benefits you'll need to offer to compete effectively. Defining your competitive frame very narrowly may seem like a safe thing to do, but it's usually a huge mistake. That's exactly what icebox manufacturers in the early part of the twentieth century did, though. They considered themselves ice storage companies and felt that they competed with other ice storage companies. The railroads thought they were competing with other railroads and got completely obsoleted by trucks and airlines. The same thing happened with Fuller Brush, which defined its competitive frame as door-to-door hairbrush sales. Had the icebox manufacturers and Fuller Brush broadened their competitive frame just a little bit—to something like "cold food preservation companies" and "door-to-door grooming products companies," respectively, they might still be in business.

And let's not forget about Montgomery Ward, which got its start in 1872 with a one-page sales sheet and a promise of "everything for family, farm, and home" at a good price, satisfaction guaranteed. Ward's grew quickly into a huge mail-order catalog business and then, following JCPenney's lead, got into retail stores. But being a follower instead of a leader eventually caught up with them. They lost market share to more forward-thinking broad retailers such as Wal-Mart and Target and lost the specialty markets to niche marketers such as Bed Bath & Beyond, Williams-Sonoma, Best Buy, and Office Depot. In 2000, after 128 years in business, Montgomery Ward was forced into bankruptcy and had to liquidate its two hundred fifty stores.

Ward's is hardly the only company that's squandered a huge name brand. Smith Corona, for example, has been synonymous with typewriters since 1886, but that's not worth much these days. When personal computers hit the market in the 1970, Smith Corona's competitive frame got blown apart. But instead of adapting as IBM did, they put their blinders on and kept manufacturing typewriter products that were obsolete the day they shipped. To make matters worse, Japanese companies came out with cheaper, fancier typewriters that captured most of what was left of Smith Corona's share of a disappearing market. Today, the company is in bankruptcy and no longer even produces its own machines, instead slapping their label on imports.

▪ ▪ ▪

The bottom line is that the broader your definition (provided it's consistent with your core essence), the more purchase occasions and the greater wallet share you'll capture. Take Electrolux. The company had always been associated with clean floors, but business was fading. They talked to their customers and found that they wanted something more than just clean floors. So Electrolux changed its name to Aerus and broadened its focus to "healthy living"—a concept that included clean floors.

As I discussed back in Chapter 2, some companies have enough equity and relevance that they can expand their franchise into completely new categories. Companies like these are all over the place, and you'd better watch out. They may not look like competitors right now, but they could be back to eat your lunch tomorrow.

Arm & Hammer is one of these companies. By all rights, Arm & Hammer should be a commodity—they even put instructions for how to make the product on their Web site! Years ago, the company started as "baking soda for recipes." Since then it's expended into "odor fresheners," "pet products," "deodorant," "dental care," and much more—all manifestations of "pure and natural cleaning ingredients." If you work for any household consumer products company, you're probably competing with them, or you will be soon.

Your product may not be as versatile as baking soda, but you can learn a lot from how Arm & Hammer broadened its competitive frame and extended its brand and made a lot of money in the process. When Celebrex first came out, it competed in the "arthritis drugs" frame. After a while it very successfully moved into the far larger (and far more profitable) "drugs-that-help-restore-free-movement" frame. And a guy named Stu Leonard, who used to run a small store that sold cheese and milk products, transformed that store into one of the most successful specialty food store chains on the East Coast.

Most of the traditional grocery chains have expanded their frame from "supermarkets" to "supercenters," which has enabled them to upgrade their value proposition by offering their customers conveniences such as in-store banking, prepared foods, longer hours, and gourmet private label products, all of which also produce a lot of revenue for the stores.

I know I've been illustrating my points with examples of large companies, but everything I'm saying applies equally well to small businesses. If you run a neighborhood pizza restaurant, you may define your competitors as "other local pizza restaurants." But if that's where you left it, you wouldn't be in business very long. When Domino's started delivering in your market (which you know they'll do sooner or later), you'd suddenly be facing huge competition with regard to both time and convenience—even if you made a better pizza. You're also competing against cheap frozen pizzas in grocery stores that have enabled pizza-eating families to cut out the delivery man. And on the high end, you're competing against California Pizza Kitchen's high-end pizza parlors and frozen pies. You're also competing against local Chinese, Thai, and Italian restaurants, which all offer relatively inexpensive food for families who don't want to cook. And when the Super Bowl rolls around you'd better believe that you'll be going head-to-head against chips and dip too. Bottom line: Run your business aggressively to take on a variety of competitors, or you'll rapidly lose sales.

One of the great examples of broadening competitive frames is Gold Bond. Back in 1991, Jeffrey Himmel bought the company, which was then a small regional brand with only about $1 million in annual sales. Because the product, powder, included zinc and some other skin-soothing ingredients, Himmel positioned Gold Bond as an upscale alternative to traditional talcum powder—a completely new category. Every time he felt a competitor breathing down his neck, Himmel added another dimension to his competitive frame. Over the course of a few years, he introduced a baby powder, an anti-itch cream, and an extra-strength version of the original Gold Bond, each time expanding the company's competitive frame into more and more categories. More recently, Gold Bond has come out with foot care, first aid, and skin lotion products. In 2003, the company posted sales of nearly $48 million, coming from a wide range of products and categories.

Take a look on the next page at the choices United Artists has for how to define its competitive frame.

Starbucks has a similar constellation of choices. They started off competing within the "coffeehouse" frame, looking for a way to collect a few dollars for a cup of coffee that cost less than a nickel to brew. But then they shook up the business by creating new competitive frames and installing themselves as the only competitor. They redefined the coffee business as a social experience, offering a place where you can hang out with your friends and get gourmet cappuccino, espresso, latte,

What Is the Competitive Frame?

The definition of the competitve frame will have a direct impact on the size of the opportunity, the diversity of the consumers and competition, and the benefits needed to compete effectively.

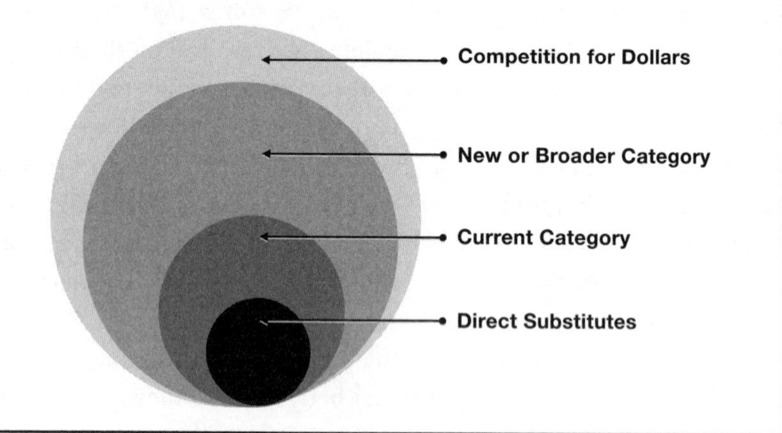

The Competitive Frame Has Also Changed

- What else are your movies competing with?

Possible Competitive Frame Definitions

Disposable income

All entertainment options

All movies and television programs

All theatrical movies

Your theatrical movies

or whatever, just the way you want it. They even created their own language and became the only people in town to offer a "double decaf grande half-caff skim," whatever that means.

The company has grown at an incredible clip—I've actually seen city streets where there are two Starbucks on one block. They've gotten so big that their ubiquity is in danger of turning into sameness and lack of differentiation.

At the same time that they've been trying fend off new entrants into the social, "my-coffee-my-way" competitive frame, Starbucks has simultaneously been expanding its competitive frame beyond the coffeehouse and right into people's homes. It started with bagged coffee in grocery stores as a challenge to traditional brands such as Folger's and Maxwell House. Then, thanks to a sweet distribution deal with Pepsi, they introduced Frappuccino in a bottle, which they have positioned against other morning beverages and late-afternoon treats. Finally, the new Double Shot pits Starbucks against such other high-caffeine beverages as Mountain Dew and Red Bull. Even with all these new competitive frames, Starbucks has practically saturated the U.S. market, so they're expanding overseas. If they're going to make it there, they'll have to broaden their competitive frame once again and create a compelling new coffeehouse experience. This may involve competing more on food and offering more than just scones and muffins in the morning.

In a way these challenges are similar to those faced by candidates running for president. A lot of them start off competing locally, in fairly small competitive frames. Almost nobody outside the South had ever heard of Bill Clinton or Jimmy Carter before they launched their campaigns. After a while, the candidates divide into two groups and compete nationally against a few others in either the Republican or Democrat frame. Once a winner emerges from each frame, they both have to expand into the national frame, and they have to make sure that their value proposition—what they can offer that no one else can—is relevant not only to their party but to at least some people in the other party as well.

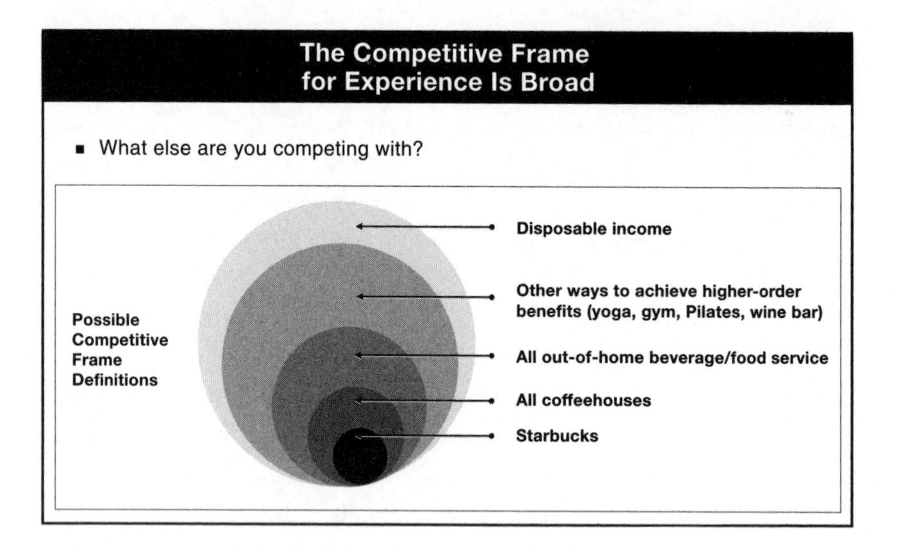

How Am I Different?

By definition, a brand is very different from a commodity, which is a product or service that is perceived to be completely undifferentiated from other similar products or services. Typically, the only determinant of a commodity's value is price. Quality is assumed to be identical unless you tell consumers otherwise and give them a compelling reason to pay more.

Differentiation, on the other hand, is where value is created, and it's what separates you from the pack. It gives customers a clear message about why they should purchase your product over your competitors'. The driving philosophy behind differentiation is the belief that customers do not buy sameness (even with commodities, consumers will differentiate on the basis of who's cheapest). The only way to build brand equity and drive sales volume is through offering consumers relevant emotional benefits. Don't believe me? Try grocery shopping in a country where you aren't familiar with any of the local brands. You'll have a pretty tough time making up your mind about what brands to buy.

Offering relevant emotional benefits is exactly what Aspen/Snowmass, one of the top resorts in the Colorado/Utah market, needed to do. Because of years of traditional ski resort marketing that featured generic functional skiing benefits, most skiers didn't perceive much significant difference between Aspen/Snowmass and any of the other resorts, including Breckenridge and Vail. They'd all become interchangeable, which encouraged skiers to choose largely on price.

Before we go on, I want to introduce something very important: my model for how brands are adopted.

- Price of Entry. Before you can even show up on a potential customer's radar, you've got to get into their consideration set (the group of companies or brands they'll consider buying from). And the only way to do that is to come up with a price-of-entry proposition, which is a fancy way of saying that you have to meet some basic requirements before anyone will pay attention to you. Sometimes these requirements are tangible, other times intangible. Sometimes the consumer is conscious of using them to make a purchase decision, sometimes not. But the one thing that's always true about price of entry is that the bar is always being raised.

  Remember when American Airlines launched their frequent flyer program, American AAdvantage? At the time, customers loved the new product and did more flying on American so they could earn points. But today, loyalty programs are everywhere and you don't even need to get on a plane to earn miles (or hotel stays or meals or whatever). These programs are expensive to run and don't generate much new loyalty anymore, but they're part of the price of entry, and not offering one would be the kiss of death.

  In Aspen/Snowmass's case, the price of entry is having great Rocky Mountain skiing, access to several different mountains, short lift lines, plenty of snow, and a ski school. As nice as these attributes are, they won't help you bring in business. But missing any one of them would guarantee that you'd lose business.
- Differentiation. Being different from your competitors is what separates you from the pack. It's what motivates people and can influence their decisions. But as important as it is, differentiation by itself doesn't drive sales. The differences have to be relevant before that

can happen. A/S can boast a special ambience, great people, and culture; but most of the other resorts have something similar. What Aspen/Snowmass has that no one else does, though, is the town of Aspen, which offers a number of nice attributes: It's an authentic ski town, it has something for everyone, and it's famous for being luxurious, exclusive, and world class. Besides its attributes, Aspen also has several important functional benefits: There's so much to do in town that visitors can have as much fun off the mountain as they do on, and just being there feels like a self-indulgent reward.

Promoting the town and the Aspen experience is about more than just winter and snow; it extends to other times of the year as well, and includes concerts, competitions, festivals, and exhibits. By looking at their competition as more than just "Colorado ski resorts," Aspen will continue to find new ways to extend the brand and reap the rewards.

At the same time, it's important to remember that not all differences are positive. The town of Aspen is also known as being expensive, hard to get to, and snobby—differences that could potentially drive people away. As they say in Mexico, those are the fleas that come with the dog. Aspen/Snowmass's challenge is to identify ways to leverage and translate the favorable attributes of the town that appeal to a broader, more moderately wealthy audience. To do so, they'll need to manage the dialogue more creatively and proactively by strongly accentuating Aspen's positive attributes.

- Preference. This is the Golden Fleece. If you can get your customers to prefer your product or service on the basis of more than just the product itself, you've got it made. Earning your customers' preference can propel your brand to leadership in its category faster than any other factor.

  Aspen/Snowmass's attributes are that it's harder to get to but well worth it. It also has some of the highest service ratings in the industry. Overall, it just might be the best ski resort there is. But again, that's not enough. Functional benefits (and points of difference) include great snowfall, ideal ski conditions, fast lifts, lots of restaurants, and an ability to put together a completely unique package of entertainment. We're getting better. But what really moves Aspen/Snowmass from *different* to *preferred* are the emotional benefits: You feel you've gotten away from it all, you can get in several epic runs every day, it's just plain fun, the Aspen name all by itself is kind of thrilling, and you know you'll never be bored.

Never forget, though, that preference is a perishable commodity; you must constantly refresh consumers' minds about the things that make you unique, why those things are important, and why they should buy your brand over someone else's. Not doing so can be expensive.

The chart below offers a graphic summary of the entire brand adoption model:

Recommended Aspen/Snowmass Brand Architecture

	Price of Entry Ideal Rocky Mountain Skiing	**Differentiation** Exciting Aspen Skiing Town	**Preference** Ultimate Ski Vacation Experience
EMOTIONAL BENEFITS			▪ Epic runs every day ▪ Get away from it all ▪ Just plain fun ▪ Most exciting
FUNCTIONAL BENEFITS		▪ Fun on and off mountain ▪ Reward for a chaotic life	▪ Great snowfall and conditions ▪ Offers total package
BRAND ATTRIBUTES	▪ Less crowded slopes ▪ Access to 4 mountains	▪ Authentic ski town ▪ Fame and reputation ▪ Is for everyone	▪ Harder to get to but worth the rewards ▪ Highest service ratings ▪ Best ski resort there is

Telecommunications in Europe: A Case Study in Establishing Preference

The mobile telecommunications sector in Europe has been growing at an incredible clip, increasing by more than 300 percent since 1997, when cell phone penetration was about 14 percent. In 2001, market penetration stood at about 70 to 75 percent, and in 2004, it's expected to reach 80 to 85 percent, at which point the growth curve will plateau. As fantastic as that kind of growth may look on paper, there is a down-side: There are essentially no more new consumers out there. Nearly everyone who will ever have a cell phone already does.

If this development hasn't already thrown everyone in the telecom industry into a tizzy, it will soon, because it's going to require a profound change in the way they do their marketing. With fewer and fewer first-time customers coming into the market, the focus has already begun to shift from driving penetration and competing for new customers, to competing for *existing customers* and increasing their usage. Long-term survival will be a function of how successful companies can be in reducing customers' switching behavior (churn).

At this point, mobile phone users in Europe have a number of options. In fact, some people we spoke with said there are so many options that they have no clue where to start. Worse than that, consumers see very little difference between competitors. Functional benefits such as coverage, reliability, customer service, and having the latest technologies are perceived as almost interchangeable. So are emotional benefits, such as feeling that the provider is trustworthy, friendly, approachable, and likable, understands customers' communications needs, and helps them solve problems.

What I've just described is the "perfect storm" of marketing, and the result of this kind of undifferentiated market is churn. Nearly a quarter (23 percent) of all mobile telecom users have changed service providers at least once. Why? Well, it's not what you'd think. Price was the number one reason that both contract and prepaid customers switched. Surprisingly, satisfaction didn't even make the reasons-for-switching top ten list. In fact, 80 percent of customers who jumped ship said they were "very satisfied" or "quite satisfied" during the time they had service.

So how can companies survive in this environment? Clearly, reducing prices provides a Band-Aid—it'll work for a while, but then the competition will match the reduced prices and profits will ultimately suffer. The only solution is to establish brand preference and reduce churn. To give you an idea of just how important this is, let me use the case of Vodafone, one of the major players in the mobile telecom market in Europe.

Vodafone has about 122 million customers worldwide, and their churn rate is between 1 and 2 percent monthly or 15 to 20 percent annually. (Put differently, they pick up about 2.5 million customers each month, but lose just about as many.) Assuming that everyone else's churn rate is about the same (which it is), Vodafone is playing a zero-sum game, picking up over the course of a year roughly the same number of people that it loses. Here's where the importance of preference comes in.

If Vodafone can find a meaningful way to differentiate the brand and drive preference, fewer "at-risk" existing customers will leave. And given that each percentage point represents more than a million customers, reducing the churn rate from 20 percent a year to 19 percent could have a significant impact. At the same time, creating preference for the brand will enable Vodafone to capture—and retain—a larger percentage of the competitors' at-risk customers. It will also allow the company to ease away from low, commodity pricing because, as I've said, differentiation can command a higher price. The problem is that Vodafone's competitors will eventually match Vodafone and cheap, commodity prices will return.

There is another option. Mobile service providers have typically viewed their competitive frame as mobile communications. What if they expanded the frame to include all phone communications? Or better yet, what about all communications of *any* kind—cellular, fixed-line, face-to-face, e-mail, and others? Vodafone has done exactly this, and now offers Internet access, e-mail, text messaging, fax services, games, and entertainment. Overall, they're working to make the cell phone an essential part of everyone's communication, from the gossipy teen to the frequent-flying exec.

Throughout the rest of this book I'll tell you more about how companies—whether they're as big as Vodafone or as small as your local dry cleaner—can retain customers. But for now, let me leave you with this: The dividends earned by doing so are huge, and you'll see them immediately.

When Differences Aren't All They're Cracked Up to Be

Ordinarily, when you move into a new competitive frame, you want to make sure that you offer concrete points of difference that satisfy consumers' needs and wants. Typically, these points of difference will come in the form of attributes and/or benefits. Then it's a question of whether your company can actually deliver those attributes and benefits and how well you deliver them as compared to the competition.

But be careful. Sometimes being *too* different can actually hurt you. Dove has been a major force in the "soap for delicate skin" frame for decades. Expanding into the "dishwashing liquid" business probably seemed like a natural extension—especially when they pitched the product as softening your hands while you do the dishes. But going from "soap for delicate skin" to "dishwashing liquid" didn't work out too well because people who buy dishwashing soap are primarily concerned with clean dishes. (Interestingly, Palmolive, which was already in the "dishwashing liquid" frame, was able to move into the "dishwashing soap for people with delicate skin" frame by having Madge the manicurist soak people's hands in it in her nail salon.)

Dove recently launched an aggressive expansion campaign that, if it's successful, will dramatically expand their competitive frame. They did extensive research that showed that current customers (most of whom are female) are extremely likely to try Dove shampoo and conditioner. The company went a step further, creating branded hair care, deodorant, body wash, and skin lotion—essentially everything a woman could want in order to keep clean. Overall, they're spending well over $100 million to advertise these products, and they're including coupons, discounts, and free gifts to increase trials and sales. Of course, trying is one thing, buying regularly is something else entirely. But if they're successful, they'll be extremely successful.

▪ ▪ ▪

If you're planning to move into a different frame than the one you're currently operating in, you'd better make sure that your brand has enough relevance in the new space that consumers will let you play. If your offering is too different from everyone else's, you'll never be able to compete on an equal footing with the folks who are already in that space. Philadelphia, for example, has done an excellent job of extending its frame by competing not only as a cream cheese, but also as a substitute for butter on your morning toast. But if the Philadelphia people were to discover that their cheese has an incredible capacity to block ultraviolet light, it's pretty doubtful that anyone would see Philadelphia as a relevant alternative to their usual SPF-30.

In the mid 1990s, Tombstone Pizza was faced with this kind of situation and handled things exactly right. Tombstone (owned by Kraft) had defined their competitive frame as "the frozen pizza business," which was roughly a $2 billion sector at the time. But then-division president Betsy Holden had the idea of expanding the frame to "all pizza eaten at home, including take-out and delivery"—a $17 billion sector. Naturally, getting into that bigger market meant being perceived as an equal or better alternative to the fresh, delivered pizzas which dominate that market. So they tinkered with their recipes (to make them look and taste better) and their packaging and came up with DiGiorno, which they pitched as "It's not delivery, it's DiGiorno." It's also been a fantastic success.

When Expanding Isn't Enough: The Case of Microsoft's Xbox

What happens if you decide that expanding the frame isn't enough, that you want to take your brand into a completely different competitive frame? The simple answer is "Be damned careful." It can be done, but it's not for the faint of wallet. Typically, the better known a company is in one area, the harder it is to convince consumers it can succeed in another area. Let me take you through an example of how Microsoft got into the game console set.

At first glance you might think that Microsoft wouldn't have any problem at all leveraging its enormous credibility in technology to compete with Sony and Nintendo. But you'd be wrong—the company actually faced a number of significant challenges:

- No credentials in console gaming. Unlike Sony, whose entertainment credentials were enough for consumers to accept the PlayStation, Microsoft's credentials in software didn't translate into hardware. When we interviewed experienced game players, they said things like "I can't even think of Microsoft making a game system" or "Games just aren't Microsoft's thing." The company's expertise in PC games wasn't worth much, since many people felt that PC games were slow, boring, and unsophisticated.
- Microsoft's corporate image didn't fit with the category's image. Microsoft was perceived as being for work and school ("I just see it as typing and word processing"), while PlayStation was perceived as for play. A lot of players agreed that "you wouldn't go to PlayStation for help with your homework, but you would go to Microsoft." People also saw Microsoft as boring and PlayStation as fun. ("Microsoft and PlayStation are two different things. When you turn on a computer you don't jump for joy.")
- Performance concerns. People were suspicious about Microsoft's reliability, and they worried that the system freezes and "blue screens of death" would ruin their game-playing experience.
- There are already established competitors. Sony's PlayStation and Nintendo had already staked out distinct positions in the market, and players were satisfied with—and very loyal to—their current brand.
- The true product possibilities are vague. Microsoft built the product with so much flexibility for future development that some consumers (and members of the media) saw Xbox as a "Trojan horse," a way to sneak into living rooms a Microsoft that would eventually take over home entertainment. The problem with this perception is that when consumers don't understand something about a technical product, they usually keep their wallets closed.

Those obstacles would have been enough to get most other companies to shut up shop and head back to what they do best. But Microsoft did have some positives that it felt outweighed, or at least counterbalanced, the negatives:

- Money, money, money. People believed that since Microsoft had the deep pockets to do anything it wants to, it wouldn't come out with a cheap or flawed system. In fact, Xbox actually won a number of design awards.
- Connectivity. Web-based gaming is seen as a big part of the future, and consumers felt that Microsoft's Internet credentials could give it an edge.
- A general technology halo. Although Microsoft isn't a technology innovator, it's still recognized as having technological expertise. And while computers aren't seen as being directly related to game consoles, people believed that the general technological know-how would translate.
- Partners. Microsoft hired the best developers and used their names and established reputations to create games that consumers had to have, whether they played on a Microsoft system or not.

Having weighed the positives and the negatives, Microsoft decided to go ahead with the Xbox introduction. Their goal was to be the worldwide leader in gaming consoles, but they knew that if it was going to happen at all, they'd have to be patient. They acknowledged that console gaming wasn't a natural extension of the Microsoft brand, but they felt that by coming across as confident (but not cocky or arrogant) they could ultimately get where they wanted to go.

Their first step was to introduce Xbox and establish it as a serious part of the competitive set. The next step was to position Xbox in a way that clearly differentiated it from its competitors. That positioning was supported by three pillars:

- Future technology today. They focused on a proprietary chip, which they pitched as providing the most realistic graphics available and allowing the player to achieve previously unimagined potential.

- Killer titles from the best game developers in the world. Here they played on their software expertise, designing a high-performance platform with game developers in mind so they could immediately deliver the best game experience. They promised exciting titles in every genre—action, sports, racing, and fighting—and a twenty-four-month schedule of new game releases.
- Leading-edge online gaming tomorrow. To emphasize the state-of-the-art positioning, they designed the system around broadband technology, promising that the minute the customer was ready to get rid of his dial-up modem, Xbox would be there with the ultimate online gaming experience, including online gaming sites and downloadable games.

Whether Microsoft's strategy was right or wrong is hard to say right now. Xbox is still losing money, it's perceived as somewhat short on content, and PlayStation is still number one—by a large margin. But Xbox is a major competitor and the potential is there. And there's a good chance that the "Trojan horse" theory is at least partially right: Xbox could help broaden Microsoft's competitive frame into a wider range of home entertainment products.

Conclusion

At the end of the previous chapter I talked about how important it is to keep your core essence in mind as you renovate. The same applies here.

Think of your core essence as an anchor and your competitive frame as the line that attaches the anchor to your corporate boat. With your core essence firmly anchored, you can move around quite a bit, generating opportunities—not just any opportunities, though, only the ones that have a good chance of success. At some point you'll run out of line and you'll have a choice. If you don't try to go further than your anchor will let you, you'll be renovating and you'll be fine. But if you cut the line, you'll be innovating. You'll lose track of your core essence and float around aimlessly.

6

Renovate Your Segmentation

In the simplest terms, the objective of segmentation is to group markets, customers, or consumers in order to maximize profit. Traditionally, it's done by dividing consumers into neat, predictable groups that are based on demographics (race, age, occupation, gender, education, marital status, geographic location) or psychographic factors (lifestyle, political affiliation, interests) or behavior (hobbies, frequency and quantity of purchasing behavior). But whatever factor (or combination of factors) is used, the assumption is identical: that everyone in each group will behave the same way—reading the same magazines, watching the same television programs, eating in the same kinds of restaurants, and so on. Theoretically, then, each group will respond to different kinds of promotions and advertising, and you'll be able to target consumers more efficiently by creating products and messages that are more relevant to them and better meet their needs.

Your company may already do customer segmentation, and you may be perfectly satisfied with the way things are going. But read this chapter anyway and keep an open mind, because renovating your segmentation in the way I'm suggesting will make you a lot of money. It will also keep you from going after "ghost customers" who won't buy your product even if they match your target's ideal age, gender, geographic location, and marital status.

On its face, the traditional segmentation model makes perfect sense, and it's one of the most commonly used strategic applications in marketing research. Information is sometimes a little expensive, but it's incredibly easy to get—you can order it from Nielsen or one of dozens of other companies that provide such data. For smaller companies whose pockets aren't deep enough to hire Nielsen, the same kind of information can be gathered fairly inexpensively by surveying current and potential customers in your local area.

If you think about it, though, traditional segmentation isn't really segmentation at all—it's actually more of a way of organizing consumers into groups that you can easily characterize and identify. Organization is all about the past—looking at historical data and trying to use it to predict future behavior. And as it's done today, it doesn't produce results. Oh, sure, it groups consumers neatly, but not in ways that can actually influence your marketing actions. It tells you who people are, but not why they buy. It tells you *where* they are, but not what to do with them to increase profitability. Organization provides few if any opportunities to grow your brand's volume and make it more relevant to consumers. And it does little or nothing to tell you what's going on right now or what you need to do to improve your offerings in the future.

There are, of course, some companies for which traditional segmentation is exactly the way to go—at least part of the way. *Cosmopolitan* magazine, for example, is absolutely right to segment based on gender, while *Black Entertainment* is right to segment based on race. But both of these companies could benefit from the kind of segmentation I'm going to talk about in the rest of this chapter.

Two people who are in the same demographic group—say, two thirty-five-year-old men with MBAs who make $150,000 a year, are married with two kids, and drive BMWs—could have very different cell phone usage patterns. One might use his phone to get the latest sports scores and to check his home e-mail account while he's at work. The other might use his phone to receive pictures from his wife or text-message grocery shopping lists. Trying to pitch the same calling plan to those two guys—even though they have a lot in common—would be a waste of time and money.

Probably the worst thing about traditional segmentation is that it's like a parasite that completely takes over the host organism. Once you've started organizing your markets by gender, age, income, behavior, etc., your whole business will change. You'll have to hire sales and marketing people who have expertise in selling to those groups. You'll come up with products and features that you think will appeal to those groups. And you'll pay your ad agencies to come up with commercials aimed at women, or left-handers, or whatever—the very same overly broad groups that all your competitors (who got their segmentation data from the same place you did) are working, so bye-bye competitive advantage.

A Whole New Kind of Segmentation

When you segment your market using traditional methods, you get segments that are:

- Meaningful and mutually exclusive. Each segment should be different enough from the others that it's unique. Plus, each customer should belong to one—and only one—segment. And keep in mind that customers can—and will—move from segment to segment as their circumstances change.
- Measurable. Each segment should be clearly definable and have a quantifiable market share.
- Substantial. Each segment must be able to produce enough volume and profit to justify an investment in new offerings or new marketing approaches.
- Attainable and actionable. You must be able to design a separate value proposition for each segment, and you must be able to reach that segment in order to sell to it.

No question, these factors are essential. But they're not enough to help you achieve profitable volume growth. If you want growth, you have to allocate your resources to the segments that produce the highest profits. And the only way to rank your segments in terms of potential profitability is to assess them in terms of their current contributions to volume, their potential to make future contributions to volume, and the costs associated with realizing that incremental volume.

Clearly, the old ways of doing things just don't cut it anymore. What we need is a completely different approach, one that allows you to segment your market based on the values, attitudes, and behaviors that shape demand, as well as the attributes and benefits that will *increase* that demand.

Well, it just so happens that that approach to segmentation exists: It's called *demand-based segmentation* (catchy, don't you think?), and it's a three-step process:

1. Identify your most valuable customers. This is a radical departure from the old organizational segmentation methods, which are focused on getting new customers. Demand-based segmentation is about giving existing customers reasons to buy more. As we've discussed elsewhere, roughly 80 percent of your business comes from 20 percent of your customers. You'll get that 20 percent to buy more by segmenting those existing customers based on their usage. Create an ideal customer profile and start thinking about ways to increase consumption. Your research at this stage should also help you segment consumers by their attitude toward your company. In politics, attitudinal segmentation looks like this:
   a. Hard Opposition. These are the voters who will come out and vote against you in a blizzard. In business, they are unconvertible loyalists of the competition, the vegetarians who wouldn't eat your steaks if you paid them. You must write them off.
   b. Soft Opposition. These are consumers who are currently not in your brand franchise, but aren't loyal to any one competitor. In your market, they may constitute a large number of consumers, but winning them to your brand is going to be very hard and very expensive.
   c. Undecided. In politics, a campaign will do whatever it takes and spend whatever it costs to move the undecided on election day. Essentially it amounts to buying votes. The same thing is done in business all the time, of course. It's called "renting share" with costly price promoting that wins tempo-

rary consumer volume, but not their loyalty. In other words, it makes them loyal to the bribe, not to the brand.

d. Soft Support. A political campaign is constantly trying to move these soft loyalists to hard loyalty. That's because soft supporters can't be counted on to vote, even though they may like your candidate. In business, these are consumers who may like your brand and use it occasionally, but not often enough. Moving them to greater loyalty is efficient (most studies show they're about six times cheaper to attract than the undecided or soft opposition to your brand). And it's highly effective in building profitability. Microsoft focuses its marketing strategies on its brand franchise, its installed base. Bill Gates calls this movement of soft support to hard support "the annuity stream."
e. Hard Support. These are your strong loyalists. They're pure profit, so protect them at all costs. These are customers who love your brand so much that they'll keep buying even if it requires paying a premium or they can't find it in the first place they look.

When it comes to highly targeted customer segmentation, credit card issuers are at the top of the heap. You probably get one or two preapproved card offers every week, and you probably drop most of them right into the shredder without even opening the envelope. But the fact that you're getting those offers at all is an indication that they've got an amazing amount of information on you.

Since the banks issuing the cards will be lending you money, they build detailed risk and response models that will increase their back-end profitability by coming up with the profile of the perfect cardholder. Then they pay credit bureaus such as Equifax or Experian to find people who fit that profile. And they get a lot for their money: where you live, where you moved from, how much money you make, your marital status. They also know where you shop, how often you travel and where, and what other credit cards and lines of credit you use.

As an individual, I find that pretty scary. But as a marketer, I'm impressed by the way these banks do their homework and come up with a highly targeted program, including initial interest rate, balance transfer offer, annual fee, and rewards program. And although you may toss out some of those offers, their segmentation is so good that there's a good chance that one of these days you'll bite.

Ritz-Carlton is another company that thoroughly segments their target customers. In 2002, Ritz-Carlton's worldwide occupancy rate was 67.3 percent, up from 2001 levels. That's a very high rate for the hotel industry in general, but particularly impressive in the luxury sector. Because they target people who are in the top ten percent of income, it would have been easy to identify prospective guests as "upper-income individuals who travel frequently" and leave it at that. But they also incorporate consumer behavioral and attitudinal preferences and individual needs. And they tailor their offering to each consumer group to make sure their messages have the most impact.

When targeting large corporations for off-site events and team-building programs, Ritz emphasizes their large conference facilities or private boardrooms. When targeting couples for weddings, honeymoons, and anniversary celebrations, they focus on the service, food, spa, and other amenities. And when they target families, they emphasize Ritz Kids Clubs, which will take care of the children while mom and dad go shopping. And for the vacation traveler, it's antiques, fishing, and Pilates.

A few years ago the *Chicago Tribune* hired Gallup to do some segmentation for them. Gallup analyzed the *Trib*'s subscriber database and came back with a breakdown by "loyal" (that is, "hard") and "soft supporters." We approached the *Tribune* with the idea that adding an analysis of reading-behavior-based segments would help them reduce churn, improve the return on their marketing spending, and increase circulation.

The first thing we did was to cluster prospective *Chicago Tribune* readers into groups based more on actual "consumption" (i.e., readership) rather than demographics. We came up with three separate segments:

- Avid *CT* readers
- Loyal *CT* readers
- Soft *CT* readers

Each of these segments was further broken down into "exclusive" and "nonexclusive" categories, depending on whether or not they read other newspapers besides the *Tribune*. Within each segment, demographics were almost irrelevant—age, income, and education varied widely. But the behavior of *Tribune* readers in each of those segments was very similar. By segmenting this way we were able to model various *CT* benefits and features to see which would drive greater frequency of use among each segment, thereby reducing attrition.

As you can see from the chart on the next page, there are 510,000 "soft," nonexclusive readers of the *CT*. We hypothesized that they read the paper once a week. There were also 1,185,000 "loyal," nonexclusive readers of the *CT* who, we hypothesized, read the paper 3.5 times per week. Taken together, these two groups account for more than a quarter of the population of the entire Chicago area.

2. Segment the opportunity. That means segmenting consumers based on their response to specific benefits, products, services, promotions, and other inducements. By design, demand-based segmentation defines the marketing levers that are the most effective and that you can use to target and sell to each segment. In short, it makes segmentation actionable! If you can identify your daily users and understand why they buy, you can turn them into three-times-a-day users. The segments you form will be based on usage frequency and perceptions of the benefits your brand offers. You then create a demand curve that illustrates the relationship between usage and benefits (see below). Finally, you need to forecast increases in usage by influencing the perceptions of the brand and of the products used.
   a. What specific products and/or services will increase consumption?
   b. What is the probability of increased usage due to specific products?
   c. What amount of increased usage can be expected?

As you can see, the total demand curve for mobile phone usage is actually comprised of multiple demand curves. The demand

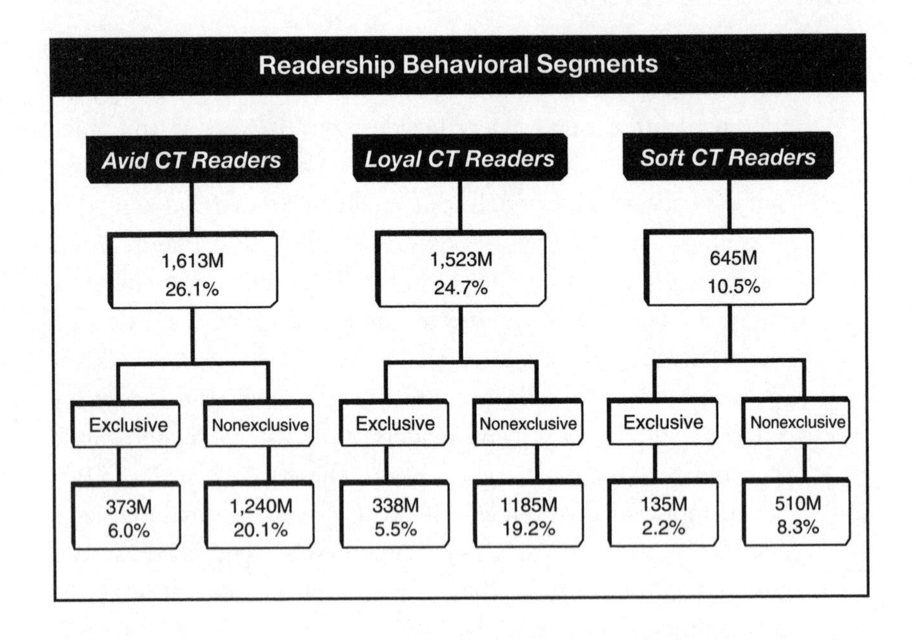
Readership Behavioral Segments
Avid CT Readers
1,613M
26.1%
Exclusive
Nonexclusive
373M
6.0%
1,240M
20.1%
Loyal CT Readers
1,523M
24.7%
Exclusive
Nonexclusive
338M
5.5%
1185M
19.2%
Soft CT Readers
645M
10.5%
Exclusive
Nonexclusive
135M
2.2%
510M
8.3%

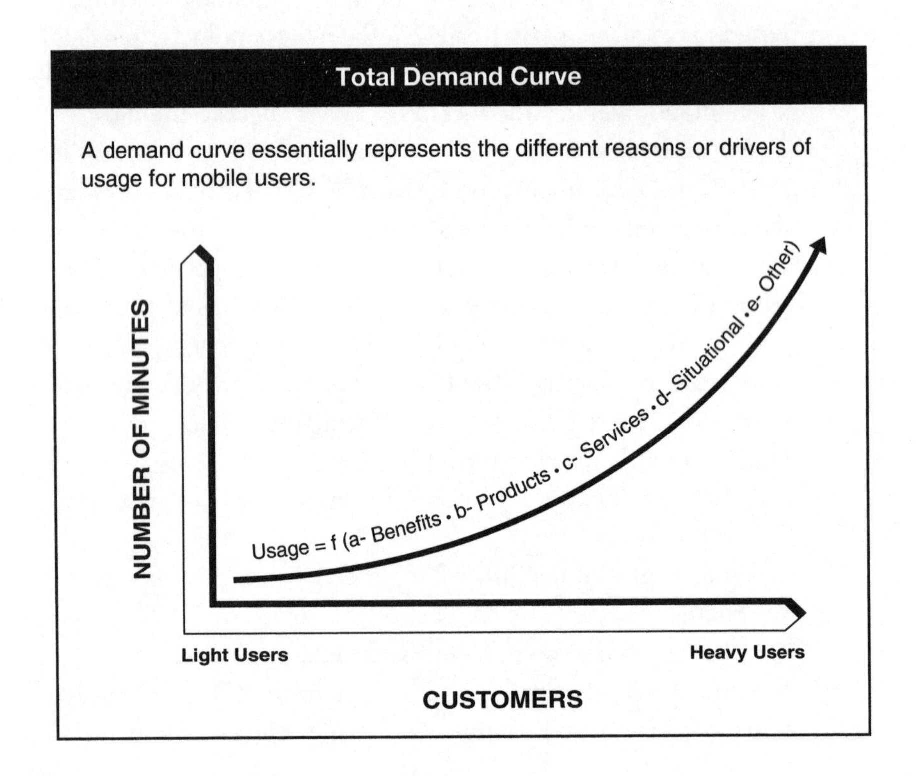
Total Demand Curve
A demand curve essentially represents the different reasons or drivers of usage for mobile users.
NUMBER OF MINUTES
Usage = f (a- Benefits • b- Products • c- Services • d- Situational • e- Other)
Light Users
Heavy Users
CUSTOMERS

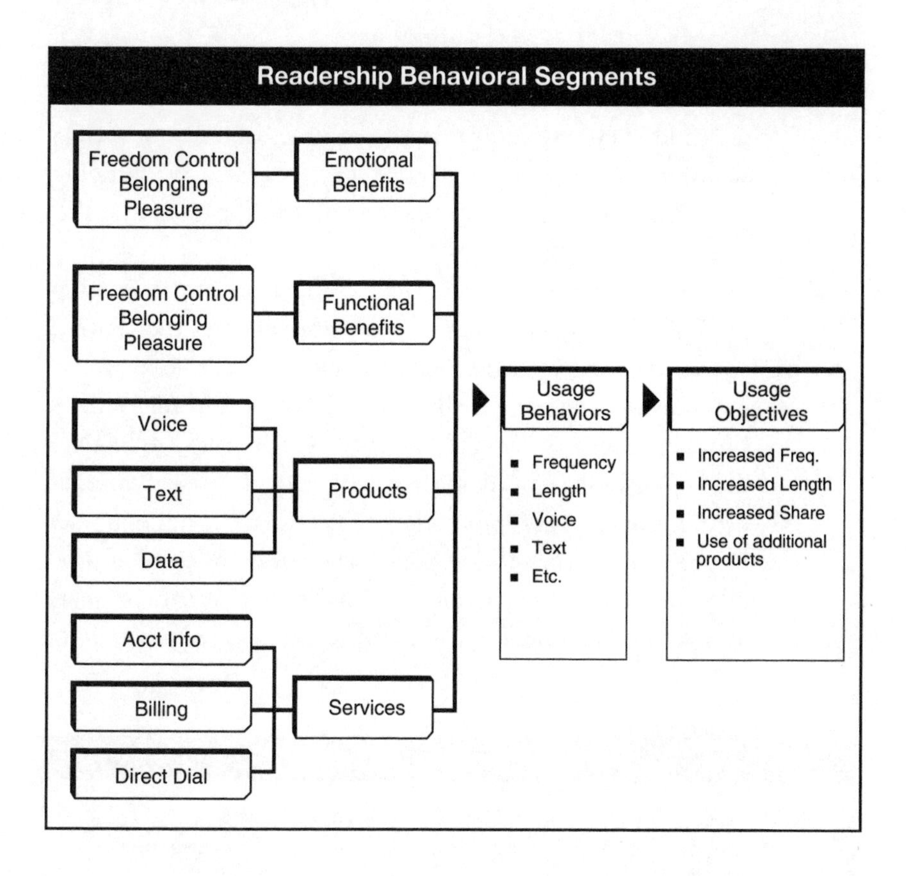

curve for different groups of consumers will reveal the leverage points that will drive incremental usage. The segmentation will be driven by opportunities to increase usage and revenues. It will produce a framework of opportunities rather than a structure of the market. As such, it will guide all marketing strategies (e.g., communication, products, services, and distribution.)

3. Segment the occasion. There are two particular occasions that deserve special discussion:
   a. Purchase occasions. Growth in this area comes from penetrating additional places where the decision to make a purchase is made. Penetrating additional purchase occasions helps you differentiate from competitors. You become relevant to customers at times that the competition is not in the consideration set. Enterprise used this kind of segmentation to

create a whole new niche in the rental car business. Instead of focusing on airports and downtown locations like Hertz and Avis and everyone else, they concentrated on a few specific occasions when people needed to rent cars, in particular when their own vehicles were stolen or in the shop and they needed to be picked up.

b. Communication occasions. Many companies also miss an opportunity to understand the many different ways they have of communicating with their customers. For example, churches hardly leap to mind when thinking of places to advertise movies. But Mel Gibson's *The Passion of the Christ* saved millions of marketing dollars by doing advance screenings at churches, distributing 250,000 promotional DVDs, and conducting 300 *Passion* "summit meetings." Before the movie was even released, churches had reserved almost $10 million worth of seats. Thanks to a combination of these alternative communication

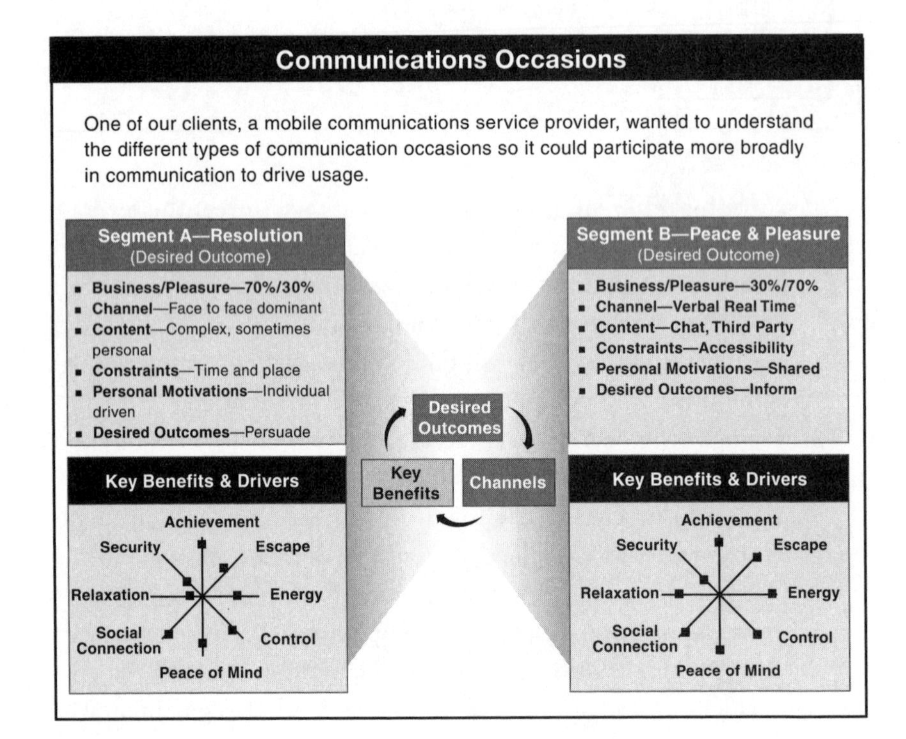

> occasions and a huge amount of controversy, the movie generated $125.2 million in its first five days. Only two other movies made so much money so quickly: *Lord of the Rings: The Return of the King* and *Star Wars: Episode 1* both had bigger openings, but they spent way, way more on advertising.

We helped one of our clients, a mobile communications service provider, to segment their communications occasions so it could more effectively use communications to drive usage.

A Closer Look at Demand-Based Segmentation: Borders

My company did a project for Borders not long ago. Borders was struggling, trying to find its footing in the shadow of its primary competitor, Barnes & Noble. Because books are a commodity—and a multibillion-dollar industry—any brand preference or loyalty can significantly drive profitability. However, neither chain has done much to give consumers a compelling reason to chose one store over the other. Each is strong in a different region of the country, and each has a somewhat different personality. But neither one generates much customer loyalty, because most potential customers don't see any real differences between the two; people who actually shop in brick-and-mortar bookstores tend to pick the closest or most convenient one. Currently, most bookstore advertising emphasizes highly discounted new releases. Any differences that come up can be copied by the competitor overnight.

Consumers have a wide range of reasons to go into a bookstore. For example, many people come in just to browse and leave without buying anything, while others find what they're looking for but then go home and buy it on Amazon for less. In order to help Borders bring more people into the stores and sell more books, we had to come up with profiles of typical book buyers—whether they buy at B&N, Best Buy, or Amazon.

We segmented the general book-buying public into five segments, each with very distinct motivations and shopping behavior.

As you can see, traditional demographic segmentation might have been of some use here, but the demand-based factors are far more

	Knowledge Seekers	Information Seekers
Occasion	27%	15%
Reasons for Shopping	• Wanted to learn about a particular topic • Wanted to treat myself • Wanted to do something good for myself • Wanted to find something new • Looking for a comfortable and relaxing activity • Wanted to be intellectually stimulated	• Looking for a particular item • Needed information on a particular topic • Wanted to learn about a particular topic • Wanted to add something to my collection or library • Wanted to improve myself or others • Wanted to find something new
Shopping Behavior or Strategy	• Purchases item for significant other and children • Spends 2+ hours • Likes shopping at Best Buy • Equally likely to shop on weekdays or weekends • More likely to shop in the afternoon than the evening • Spends an average of $50.80	• Likely to purchase for friend, family members (parents, siblings, other), or children • Spends 30 minutes to an hour • Shops both Borders and B&N • Shops with spouse or friends • More likely to shop on weekday than weekend • Spends an average of $31.10
Departments They Visit	Evenly distributed throughout the store	Business Finance Cookbooks History Self-Help Reference

Seekers of Something New	Entertainment Seekers	Gift Seekers
14%	14%	14%
• Looking for a particular item • Wanted to treat myself • Wanted to add something to my collection or library • Wanted to find something new • Wanted to go shopping • Wanted to check out something I had heard about	• Wanted to treat myself • Looking for a comfortable and relaxing activity • Wanted to find something new • Wanted to be entertained • Wanted to do something good for myself • Wanted to have inexpensive fun	• Wanted to buy something someone wanted • Was looking for a particular item • Wanted to buy something someone needed
• Likely to shop by themselves or with children • Likely to spend 2+ hours • More likely to purchase items for friends • Likely to shop Walden Books • Twice as likely to shop in afternoon as evening • Evenly distributed between weekday and weekend • More likely to come by themselves • Spends an average of $28.20	• Purchase for themselves • Most likely to shop later at night • Most likely to shop Books a Million • Most likely to have shopped with friends or family • Like to browse, not looking for anything specific • Lowest average spending at $9.70	• Likely to shop with significant other • Likely to spend an hour or less • Spends an average of $22.70
Best Sellers Fiction Mystery Romance Gifts & Stationery Under-Index in Computer, Finance & Business	Café Fiction Music Mystery Romance	Finance Nonfiction Reference

	Knowledge Seekers	Information Seekers
Occasion	27%	15%
What They Tend to Buy	Books Movies Music Food/Coffee 74% make a purchase	Books 81% make a purchase
Demographics	• Large household, at least two kids under 18 in home • Income over $100K	• Mostly caucasian and black • More likely not to have children in the household • More likely to be single, widowed, or divorced • Income over $100K
Other	• 21% usually shop at Borders; 35% B&N • 54% are very satisfied	• 26% usually shop at Borders; 40% B&N • 59% are very satisfied

valuable. If you know what motivates each group, what time of day they're most likely to be in the store, where they'll be browsing, and what services they want, you'll be able to tailor special promotions and displays that have a higher chance of success.

An Even Closer Look at Segmentation: Aspen/Snowmass

With its 1.4 million skier visits every year, Aspen/Snowmass accounts for about 10 percent of the entire Colorado/Utah ski resort market. This places Aspen/Snowmass right up there with some of the biggest-name resorts, including Breckenridge and Vail, each of which also has about a 10 percent share of the market. But Aspen/Snowmass (A/S) has a lot of unused capacity which, if better utilized, could substantially increase its market share.

Seekers of Something New	Entertainment Seekers	Gift Seekers
14%	14%	14%
Movies 77% make a purchase	Food/Coffee Movies Books and music 87% make purchase	A little of everything More music 78% make purchase
• Mostly Caucasian and Hispanic • Oldest segment with 26 percent over age 55 • Income of $80K–$100K	• Mostly caucasian, Asian, and "other" • More likely to be single, divorced/widowed • Youngest segment. 36% between 18–34 • Lowest income, with 44 percent reporting less than $20K • Highly educated, 52% having at least a college degree	• Mostly caucasian, black, and Hispanic • Age 25–54 • 49 percent have at least a college degree • Income $80K
• 21% usually shop at Borders; 35% at B&N • 55% very satisfied	• 26% usually shop at Borders; 36% B&N • 43% very satisfied	• 24% usually shop at Borders; 36% B&N • 55% very satisfied

One of A/S's objectives was to increase its occupancy rate to 95 percent. In order to do so, they'd have to attract an additional 443,000 skier visits each year. For A/S that's a pretty aggressive goal—a 31 percent increase—especially given the soft economy. But those same 443,000 skier visits would be only a 3 percent increase of the overall Colorado/Utah market. Not something A/S could accomplish in one or two years, but certainly achievable over the long term.

A/S had fairly limited resources to devote to marketing, and I suggested that they focus on attracting and retaining the most likely and valuable customers. Based on their firsthand experience and knowledge, A/S gave us a list of three potential target consumers:

- Affluent couples and singles
- Younger, less affluent couples and singles
- Snowmass families

These segments may have been entirely valid, but we felt they were too limiting, too much based on demographics, to be useful. What we really needed was a better understanding of the needs, motivations, attributes, and perceptions that made our loyal return consumers different from our less loyal customers. The object was to identify and recruit more skiers that fit our core consumer profile, and other types of skiers who would find our value proposition motivating. We felt that if we could do that, we'd be able to differentiate and position A/S more effectively versus other competitors in the Colorado/Utah market.

By digging deeper into what motivated consumers to ski and visit ski resorts—particularly Aspen/Snowmass—we were able to identify six distinct attitudinal skier segments:

- Aspen-Loving Families (19%). Wealthy, well-educated, middle-aged parents who have skied A/S before, have a work hard/play hard attitude, and who define value based on what they get.
- Empty-Nesters (17%). Wealthy, married, 50+, intermediate skiers, with no children at home, who ski cautiously and often with their spouse and who love being outdoors.
- Social Singles (15%). Single, middle-class, price-conscious skiers, who take lessons often and ski cautiously with friends to meet new people.
- Aspen-Avoiding Families (21%). Middle-class families that have not skied A/S, ski less often and do so cautiously, and are less interested in fitness or being outdoors.
- Active Skiing Dads (15%). Wealthier, well-educated, middle-aged, male parents who exercise frequently, have a work hard/play hard attitude, and ski aggressively with their families.
- Young Aggressive Males (12%). Less educated, 18–24, single, male, hard-core skiers, who ski very frequently with friends and who prefer aggressive terrain and taking risks.

Based on A/S's data, we found that in the previous year, three segments, Aspen-Loving Families, Young Aggressive Males, and Empty-Nesters, accounted for 68 percent of Aspen/Snowmass volume. When we factored our own research into purchase intent, it became clear that those same three segments had the very real potential to grow to a whopping 91 percent of A/S skier days in the future.

Skier Segment	Segment Size	# Skiers	Avg Days per CO/UT Ski Trip	Avg # of A/S Trips per Year	Est. Previous A/S Skier Days/Year	% of Prev. A/S Skier Days
CO/UT Destination Skiers	100%	1,831,830	4.99	0.17	1,500,628	100%
Aspen-Loving Families	19%	353,212	5.17	0.22	403,229	27%
Young Aggressive Males	12%	221,672	4.52	0.35	355,427	24%
Empty-Nesters	17%	319,108	5.47	0.15	254,716	17%
Aspen-Avoiding Families	21%	384,878	4.64	0.11	192,245	13%
Active Skiing Dads	15%	272,825	5.19	0.10	143,076	10%
Social Singles	15%	280,134	4.88	0.11	151,936	10%

Our analysis clearly showed that those three segments represented the greatest targeting opportunity for A/S. We weren't suggesting that they abandon their other segments, just that they focus especially sharply on the three biggies. Had A/S relied only on their traditional demographic segmentation, they never would have uncovered these insights and would have done a lot of inappropriate and ineffective marketing.

What Consumers Say vs. What They Do

Obviously, being able to segment a market the way we did with Borders and Aspen/Snowmass requires asking a lot of questions. But sometimes you have to take people's answers with a grain of salt. The fact is that people aren't always completely aware of why they behave the way they do, and there's often a huge difference between the attributes and benefits someone feels are important and the attributes and benefits that will make them take out their charge cards.

One of the best examples of this involves more healthful foods—the stuff our arteries and waistlines want us to buy but that we walk right by to get to the tastier (and less healthful) versions. It all comes down to taste. People know they should eat better, and in survey after survey they swear they will—as long as it tastes the same. That's actually a pretty safe bet, because most of the time the low-fat version isn't as good. You might call this the Parental Guilt Syndrome. When you ask parents what kind of snack they bring their child to eat after school, most say carrots or celery or something wholesome like that. But when the minivan doors open, all you see are empty Fritos packages and Slurpee cups.

Another example might be British Airways asking people about the new 180-degree flat seats in first class. If they were to ask me and my cowriter whether completely flat seats are a good idea, both of us would say yes. But if you ask us whether it would make us more likely to fly British Airways, you'd get very different answers. In my case, the answer would again be yes. I fly first class a lot, and being able to sleep on a plane and wake up refreshed is extremely important to me. But it wouldn't make any difference to Armin at all because he hardly ever flies first class anyway.

We call the disconnect between words and action a conflict between *stated importance* and *derived importance*. Graphically, it looks like the chart on page 127.

The quadrants of the graph have the following meanings:

- Important: These tend to be price-of-entry things. They're required, but by themselves won't drive purchase for the brand. At the same time, since everyone offers them, if Borders doesn't, they risk not even being considered. For Borders, they include factors such as:
  - Superior service (The staff engaged me in a courteous manner, the store personnel were knowledgeable about the store's products, the store had employees who were easy to approach.)
  - Relevant content (It had the books and music I find interesting.)
  - Value (I feel I got a good deal.)

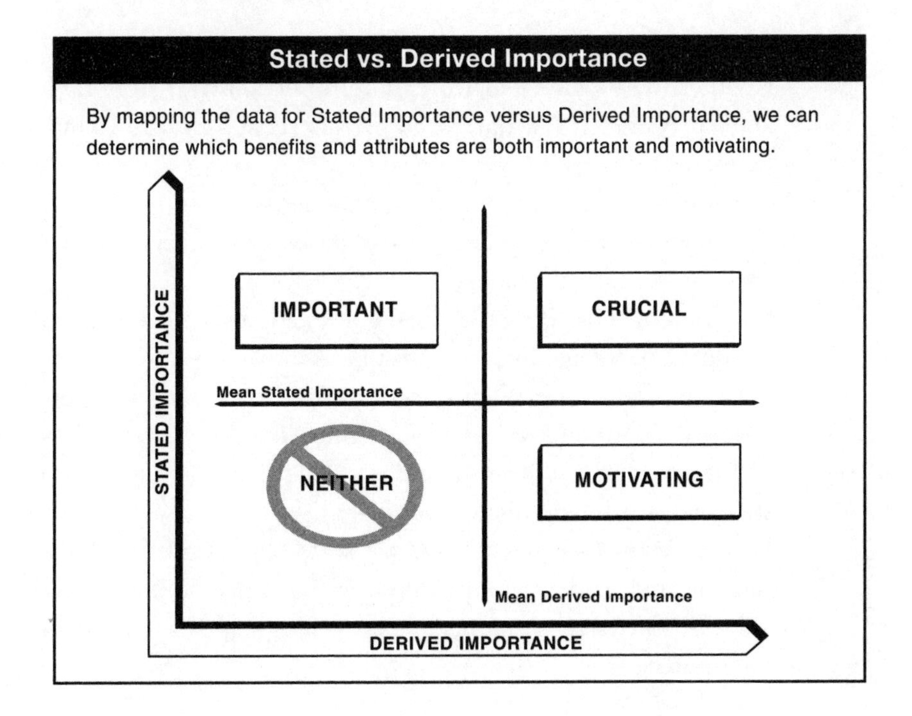

- Crucial: Consumers perceive these things to be important and they motivate behavior. Because they have the most leverage with consumers, they're core focus areas and give Borders a way to differentiate itself. As a result, they should be central to Borders' operational and communication platform. These include:
  - Confidence (I feel certain that I bought the right item.)
  - Significance (I felt like a valuable customer.)
  - Productivity (I feel I spent my time in a worthwhile manner.)
  - Comfort (This is a pleasant, relaxing place to be.)
  - Convenience (The store's easy to get to, there's plenty of free parking, and the store layout and design make it an easy place to buy books and music.)
  - Selection (The store has a wide range of products to choose from.)
- Neither/disregard: These elements add no value to your brand strategy. Consumers don't think they're important and they don't motivate purchase.

  - Personal preference (Since my kids are grown, I don't care about whether there's an extensive children's section with story time and a play area; for Armin, however, that section could be a major motivator.)
- Motivating: These elements drive the behavior you seek, but they're too low in stated importance to have a critical mass impact by themselves. For example:
  - Loyalty programs (Barnes & Noble has a loyalty program called Readers Advantage, but since you have to pay a fee to join, it's not clear that it actually inspires any loyalty; Borders has purposely not introduced a loyalty program like this because they feel it wouldn't significantly increase sales and it might end up shrinking an already-small profit margin.)
  - Events (Many consumers want a store to have events like book signings and reading groups; however, most people have never attended one of these events and they have no plans to do so in the future.)

With Aspen, our interviews showed that functional benefits like "great snowfall" and "shorter lift lines" were the most important concerns in all of the target segments, as was "highest ratings in friendliness and personalized service." Psychological benefits such as "pamper and indulge" and "stays on the edge of the sport" weren't important at all. Overall, emotional benefits were rated to be much less important, but among them, "is for everyone" was rated highest.

Here's what we found when we then correlated this *stated importance* with the attributes and benefits that consumers said were driving their intent to visit A/S next season:

- For Young Aggressive Males, "on the edge of the sport" and "has the feel of adventure" were highly motivating.
- For Empty-Nesters, "for the whole family" was highly motivating, while "for everyone" hardly registered.
- For Aspen-Loving Families, "just plain fun" and "fame and reputation" were the most motivating.
- "Great snowfall," "shorter lift lines," and "highest ratings in friend-

liness and personalized service" were simply price-of-entry factors for all three segments—important but unmotivating.

These results were fascinating and underlined the importance of going the extra step and correlating customers' stated likes and dislikes with purchase intent. Ultimately, by doing a detailed demand-based segmentation of the market, we were able to make several concrete suggestions:

- Aspen-loving families should be Aspen/Snowmass's top priority. They are the low-hanging fruit who find the brand appealing and should be easiest to capture. While currently the greatest contributor to A/S skier days, more than half of this segment has never skied at Aspen/Snowmass before, and only 13 percent have skied there in the last five years. They are less price sensitive and much more interested in the social currency aspects of ski vacations, such as "telling stories afterwards" and "meeting new people."
- Young aggressive males should be A/S's next priority, since they are currently the second-largest contributor to current skier days and ski more frequently than any other segment. These guys have skied equally often at Vail over the last five years and so, with consistent targeted efforts, might be converted to A/S loyalists. At the same time, this segment is much more motivated by the "harder to get to," "on the edge of the sport," and "has the feel of adventure" benefits of A/S than other segments. They're also much more compelled by Aspen Mountain and Highlands, and much less by Snowmass and Buttermilk. Targeted marketing and communications for this segment should focus on the younger, edgier, more-aggressive benefits and attributes of the Aspen mountains and town.
- Empty-nesters should be the A/S brand's third priority, since they are the most Vail-loyal and least Aspen/Snowmass-loyal of our target segments and thus may be a bit more difficult to capture consistently. However, they registered a 41 percent increase in A/S purchase intent when exposed to our functional and emotional benefits, suggesting that they could contribute up to 23 percent of future Aspen/Snowmass skier days. To capture them, A/S will

> need to leverage the benefits they are most motivated by, which include "great snowfall and ski conditions," "just plain fun," and "for the whole family." Targeted marketing and communication aimed at them should reflect their much lower interest in aggressive skiing and risk taking, along with their reluctance to try new resorts.

The benefits of demand-based segmentation are pretty significant. You'll be able to concentrate your resources on activities (products, advertising, etc.) that will generate the most significant increases in usage. You'll also be able to test-market—by asking people what would make them buy or buy more—*before* you introduce a product instead of after you've spent a ton of money designing and marketing something no one wants. Ultimately, you'll be able to give each segment that you choose to target the exact benefits they want.

7

Renovate Your Brand Positioning

Your brand's positioning is the overall image of your brand that you create in your constituents' minds. It clearly and concisely articulates what you want your target customers and consumers to think, feel, and do regarding your brand. Over time, managing your positioning well will give you control of your base volume and will free up some of those scarce marketing dollars for you to use to go out and get more volume. Although how you're positioned is summarized in a few sentences at most, when it comes to building a brand, there isn't a more important collection of words out there. Your positioning is your brand's DNA. It defines and guides everything that everyone associated with the brand does.

When I say everyone, I really mean *everyone*—not just the marketing people. The fact is that marketing is far too important to be left up to the marketers. Every single member of an organization should know the brand's positioning by heart and bring it to life in his or her day-to-day work. It's the strategic compass you have to use to measure every program, activity, or initiative that directly or indirectly touches the consumer. Anything that's inconsistent with the brand's positioning at best wastes resources, and at worst could inadvertently destroy the brand you're trying to build.

I hope I'm being clear: Positioning doesn't just happen by itself. It's a tough job that requires clear thinking, deep insight into your customers and consumers, and a thorough understanding of your competitors' strengths and weaknesses. It's also something that's easy to get wrong. But one way or another it *does* happen—whether you do it or somebody else does it for you. How you position yourself and your brand depends on every aspect of your advertising and marketing mix: your employees, your public relations, sponsorships, packaging, pricing. It depends on what you do and what you don't do, what you say and what you don't say, how you say it and how you don't. It depends on what your competitors say about you and about themselves and on what you say about them. In short, *everything* communicates.

Taking Control of the Dialogue

The key to good positioning is to take control of the dialogue you have with your customers and consumers early and never let go. If you don't, your competitors will, and that's something you never want to let happen, because whoever controls the dialogue controls the positioning.

Just think back to Bill Clinton's famous phrase from the 1992 presidential elections: "It's the economy, stupid." Every time Clinton said that, he was reminding voters that he was concerned about jobs, unemployment, welfare, taxes, and a whole bunch of other issues that were worrying them. But the best thing about "It's the economy, stupid" was that it positioned Clinton as the only one who cared. Other candidates tried to jump on the "It's the economy" bandwagon, but Clinton already owned that space, and people's response to the others was "We already know about the economy. Don't you have anything new?"

Eleven years later, actor Arnold Schwarzenegger did a masterful job of dialogue control in the 2003 election to recall and replace Gray Davis, the governor of California. Arnold consistently refused to answer any substantive questions about his views and participated in only one debate, but managed to take control of the dialogue anyway, leveraging his movie action hero persona to make it all about strength, size, and decisiveness—traits Davis was pretty short on. He made great use of the titles of some of his movies, telling voters that the election should be a "Total Recall," and that he was going to be the next "Governator." The few times he mentioned any issues, he emphasized the economy, which more than 80 percent of voters said was broken. His opponents tried to reposition Arnold by running with allegations that he'd harassed a number of women and that he'd made positive comments about Adolf Hitler, but voters had other things on their minds.

Still don't believe how much positioning matters in politics? Look at what happened to Howard Dean in the 2004 election—he's living proof that everything communicates. After coming in second in the Iowa caucuses, he tried to rally the troops and reinvigorate his campaign staff. But his whooping and shouting and listing of states came across as less than statesmanlike and essentially doomed his chances of winning the Democratic nomination.

One of the ways companies fail to control the dialogue is by confusing people. In 1999, Disney created the Go network and tried to position it as the ultimate Internet portal—*the* place to go on the Internet. They started by buying Starwave, a software company, and then spent $70 million for 43 percent of the Infoseek search engine. A while later they later bought the rest of Infoseek and rolled their ESPN, ABC, and Disney sites into the Go site. As icing on the cake, Disney added all sorts of other services, including online auctions, weather reports, news, product reviews, movie listings, and free email. They were so confident that Go would, in fact, go, that they created Go.com (later the Disney Internet Group) as a separately trading stock.

Very ambitious, wasn't it? You'd think that with Disney's money and brand behind them, all these properties together would enable the company to quickly make Go.com into exactly what they wanted it to be: *the* place to go on the Internet.

The problem was that consumers weren't looking for another portal; AOL and Yahoo! were enough choices. Instead of jelling into a cohesive brand, Go.com remained a collection of disconnected properties that lacked a unified meaning with consumers. When they wanted sports news, they went straight to ESPN.com; when they wanted regular news they went to ABC.com; and if they wanted to find out what was up with Mickey Mouse, they went to Disney.com. But no one went to Go.com.

Go.com never managed even to *open up* a dialogue with consumers, let alone come up with a value proposition that resonated with them.

Only twelve months after it launched, Go.com became gone.com. Disney refocused its Internet efforts on the ESPN, ABC, and Disney sites, which remain some of the most popular on the Web, letting Go.com languish as an "entertainment and leisure" site. They then entered into an agreement with MSN to launch Disney on MSN, a family-friendly site that truly does leverage Disney's core essence with families.

▪ ▪ ▪

Once the dialogue with consumers is open, managing it is a process that never ends. That was a lesson that the major cable company (MCC) I talked about earlier learned the hard way. As I mentioned in Chapter 4, MCC underestimated the impact that the economy and 9/11 had had on people's habits and attitudes, and they failed to realize just how fast the pace of technological change was moving. As a result, they were gradually getting repositioned as yesterday's technology. Their value proposition wasn't clear or well defined, and they had no meaningful, ownable points of difference—emotional or functional—that consumers could connect with. The default became price and promotion. MCC could have avoided some or all of these problems by consistently managing the dialogue with consumers, but they didn't.

In recent years Coca-Cola has also lost control of the dialogue with consumers and customers. There was the racial discrimination suit in 2000 which they settled for almost $200 million; that tarnished the brand. In 2001 Coke got into a joint venture with Procter & Gamble to develop and market innovative juice-based drinks and snacks on a global basis; that confused everyone and the idea was eventually scrapped. That same year they launched "Life Tastes Good," which didn't connect with consumers at all and has done nothing for the brand. In 2003 Coke (and Pepsi) were accused in India of selling drinks containing unsafe levels of pesticides. Coke responded by taking out ads denying the charges and telling people "There is no contamination or toxicity whatsoever in our brand of beverages." Not particularly reassuring. (Contrast that with Pepsi's rebuttal ads, which turned a potential negative situation into a positive branding event: "The safest thing you are likely to drink today is a Pepsi.")

In MCC's and Coca-Cola's cases, it's a question of proactively recasting the brands to regain control of the dialogue with consumers. With Microsoft, things are a little more complicated: They couldn't even think about positioning until they'd molded their wildly disparate properties into a brand.

One of the best examples of how to confuse consumers is Breck, which was one of America's first shampoos. For years, the face of the brand was the Breck Girl with the luscious, shiny, full, sexy hair. Brooke Shields, Christie Brinkley, Kim Basinger, and, yes, Martha Stewart, all got their start as Breck Girls. But in the 1980s the brand managers abruptly dumped the Girl, and sales just as abruptly dropped through the floor. So they brought her back. But in what I think was a silly bow to political correctness, they made her into the Breck Woman. Didn't help. So they dropped the price to 99 cents a bottle, turning a classy, upscale brand into something just a step up from generic. Not surprisingly, things kept getting worse. In the 1990s Dial bought the company, and the new managers introduced more than thirty variants—for dry hair, for oily hair, for combination hair, for dandruff. Today, the brand is on life support. But we'll see what happens. Jeffrey Himmel, the guy who turned Gold Bond into a major success (and who also brought Ovaltine back from the dead), recently bought the company.

Okay, now that you have a sense of what brand positioning is, let's talk about how to build it. As you might expect, it's a process that involves several steps, starting with:

1. Create a brand positioning statement. To do this you'll need to answer a few questions:
   a. Target audience. Whom are you trying to influence? Where are they? What are their needs? What past experience have they had with you and your competitors?
   b. Frame of reference. What is the frame of reference or competitive framework from the consumer's point of view? What are the relevant alternatives to your brand, and what differentiates you from your competitors?

c. Points of difference. What is the unique selling proposition for your product or service? How is it different from other brands in the frame of reference? What do you do better, differently, faster, cheaper, to create value for the consumer?
d. Support. Although you won't address this specifically in your positioning statement, it's important that you think about how you're going to support your points of difference and what you're going to do to make sure the things in the previous steps actually happen. This includes making sure that your employees are on board and that they'll consistently deliver on it.

Now before you flip back to the Business Destination chapter to check whether I'm repeating myself, take it easy. The destination statements that I introduced back there are very different from the brand positioning statements we're talking about now. A destination statement, for example, might be "I want to be the president of the United States," while a brand positioning statement for the same person might be "I'm the only candidate who truly understands and supports the inalienable rights of chinchilla farmers."

Let me give you an example of one destination statement that does an excellent job of putting the pieces together. This one was created for Motel 6 by the Richards Group, a Texas-based branding company:

> "For frugal people, Motel 6 is a comfortable night's stay at the lowest price of any national chain."

That's it, pure and simple, short and sweet. The target audience? Frugal people. Frame of reference? A comfortable night's stay. Point of difference? Lowest prices of any national chain.

Here's the destination statement for Merrill Lynch, which also nicely satisfies the three main requirements:

> "To a broad range of individuals and businesses, Merrill Lynch is the leading world-class financial services brand that delivers superior financial performance through its thinking (intelligence, advice, and guidance) and action (services)."

This statement lays out the target market (individuals and businesses) and the frame of reference (world-class financial services brand). It also includes the point of difference: superior financial performance through employees' thinking and actions. It's a clear road map for the business that employees can easily understand and communicate.

2. Test your brand positioning hypothesis. Marketing decisions are too important to be left to intuition. It doesn't matter what *you* think; all that counts is what consumers think. As I discussed in earlier chapters, you can buy data that will supposedly tell you what consumers think. But in my experience, there's no substitute for getting out there and asking questions.

   Near the beginning of the questionnaire we put together for Aspen/Snowmass, we asked respondents about their intention to visit different ski resorts next season. Purchase intent for Vail and Park City was much higher than for A/S across almost all segments. Given the diverse set of ski resorts with which it competes, we came up with the hypothesis that Aspen/Snowmass could achieve greater unduplicated consumer reach by distinctly positioning and targeting each of its four mountains toward somewhat different audiences, as opposed to its current consolidated Aspen/Snowmass brand. To test this hypothesis, we asked people about their purchase intent for each individual Aspen/Snowmass mountain. The result was that as a whole, purchase intent was higher for A/S as a whole than were the combined intents for each individual mountain. Our hypothesis was dead wrong.

   We tested a number of other hypotheses for A/S. Some were generated by us, some by A/S's marketing people. Interestingly, more than a few were completely contradictory. For example, A/S was sure that its commitment to environmental friendliness would be a major motivating factor. Turns out that most skiers didn't have any idea which resort was strongest in that area. Those who were aware appreciated A/S's commitment to the environment, but that alone wouldn't cause them to pick A/S.

   A/S also felt that its pricing structure was keeping skiers away, but we disagreed. Aspen/Snowmass could never be the least expensive destination in the area, and we hypothesized that a substantial segment of the skiing population would be willing to pay a premium for a superior total experience. Here's what we found:

- "Has packages to fit many budgets" was the single *least* motivating benefit statement tested.
- Only 12 percent of respondents who'd never skied at Aspen/Snowmass said that price was the reason. Twenty-five percent said they had no particular reason for not having done so.
- 63 percent of respondents strongly agreed that they defined value not in terms of how much they pay, but how much they get for the price they pay.
- Only 16 percent of respondents said they strongly agree that they don't ski as much because it's become more expensive.

Of course, we and A/S didn't always disagree. We both thought that having excellent service would be a major motivating benefit. However, it turned out that while good service is important, it's really a price-of-entry factor—the level of service at all of the resorts is universally high enough that it slips into the background.

As you can see, whether your hypotheses are right or wrong doesn't make any difference. What's important is what you learn from the process. By testing various hypotheses, it became clear, for example, that Aspen/Snowmass should stay away from discounting tactics and focus on building greater brand differentiation instead. It was also clear that although A/S should continue to provide high levels of service, it shouldn't do so at the expense of more motivating brand benefits. And significantly exceeding the service levels of other resorts wouldn't deliver much of a return on the investment.

3. Position Yourself. The basic rule of positioning is "define and deliver." Tell people who you are and then show them. Lather, rinse, and repeat as necessary.

   The *define* part of the basic rule gives you a lot of flexibility, although if you don't choose the territory you want to occupy, your competitors will do it for you—and chances are you won't like it. (I'll talk more about that in the next section.) Heinz, for example, defines excellence in ketchup as being thick and taking a long time to come out of the bottle. Whether that's actually true is doubtful, but it doesn't matter. Heinz said it was so, and then they played Carly Simon's "Anticipation" to underscore that good things come to those who wait. Milk Duds positioned itself as an alternative to the chocolate bar by emphasizing that since Milk Duds take a lot longer to eat (because they're made out of chewy caramel) you'll enjoy yourself for longer than if you just wolf down a Snickers. Hertz says you shouldn't have to wait in line to pick up your rental car. And they deliver by allowing #1 Club members to hop on the shuttle and go straight to their cars. Years ago, Prego positioned Ragú as a thin, watery spaghetti sauce that no one would ever use. To this day, no matter how many "Thick and Meaty" sauces Ragú comes out with, Prego is still seen as the cook's preferred option.

In the previous chapter, I talked about Borders and how they should be renovating their customer segmentation. When they've done that, they'll be able to develop a clear brand positioning statement that will differentiate the brand from Barnes & Noble and that will align everyone in the company.

Timex has consistently defined quality in watches as being able to "take a licking and keep on ticking." They took it to the next step by delivering the Ironman watch, one of the most successful products in the watch business. And they maintain their positioning of durability and endurance by sponsoring the Ironman triathlon.

Although it may be tempting sometimes to skip the *define* part and go straight to delivering, *don't*. The two pieces go together in that order: Define, then deliver. If you don't define yourself, someone else will, and you'll have a hell of a time trying to deliver anything because you won't know what the customers' expectations are. Ultimately, the goal is to define where you play, get into the consumer's competitive set, and then define yourself on the basis of your strengths and, hopefully, the weaknesses of your competitors.

In case you were worried, positioning isn't only for big companies with big marketing bucks to spend. Your local Yellow Pages is full of examples. Your neighborhood pizza shop defines his pizza as the freshest in the neighborhood and then physically delivers it to your house. The lawyer who advertises that he defends people on DUI charges is putting himself into a pretty crowded area, but he tries to deliver on his promise by telling you that he's got a 94 percent success rate or that he won't charge you for the initial consultation. And even you—yes you—are positioning your own personal brand when you're socializing, making a presentation, interviewing for a job, or arguing with the cop who pulled you over for going 45 in a 25 mph zone.

As an exercise, think about your own positioning statement. What traits are you trying to sell, and to whom? And just for fun, take a look at match.com or the personals section of your newspaper; they're filled with positioning statements.

Sometimes you can position yourself in several places at the same time. A tire dealer can position himself in the tire sales area and deliver lower prices or free tire rotation for life. At the same time he might also position himself in the auto repair area and deliver laser-guided alignment and brake jobs.

Wherever you position yourself, be sure not to get too comfortable. Consumers want to know that the product or service you're offering is at least as relevant to their lives today as it was yesterday. Our lives change, our needs change, our values change as consumers, but more importantly, our values change as people. And any time those values change, your brand has to reposition itself in front of consumers in slightly different ways, adding relevance to what the brand means. Actually, not only what it means in itself, but, more important, what it means in terms of the big questions consumers ask: "What is this going to do for me?" and "How is this going to make my life better?"

Madonna is one of the absolute masters of redefining customers' needs and renovating positioning to meet those needs. She's been the sex symbol, material girl, movie star, bad girl, serious actress, pop icon, mother, and, most recently, a children's book author who just published her first book in thirty languages and a hundred countries. By constantly renovating the positioning of her brand, Madonna gives her core fan base a reason to come back for more, offers nonfans a new reason to become fans, and keeps a constant stream of new competitors wondering how to keep up. Madonna's marketing skills look even more impressive compared to Britney Spears's. Britney is struggling, trying to transition from virginal teen pop idol to sex kitten; but Christina Aguilera got there first. It's not really clear anymore who's buying Britney's albums, although there's a good chance that a lot of people (okay, men) who don't like her music would buy a magazine with her (half naked) on the cover.

Think for a second about the Concorde—a classic example of lousy positioning followed by an absolute refusal to renovate. From the very beginning, the Concorde was positioned as an elite form of air travel, exclusively for the rich and famous. Businesspeople used it, but then Concorde got labeled as yet another example of extravagant corporate spending. Somewhere along the line, the Concorde should have been repositioned as an economical and efficient way to do business in London and Paris. Yes, it would cost a little more, but you'd get to your meetings fresh and ready to go, plus you'd be able to shave a few days off the length of a business trip.

Just to emphasize the point that positioning is everywhere and that everyone does it, take a look at how miserably the British monarchy has handled theirs. Without any real power, the monarchy has a tough battle to establish relevance with their "subjects," many of whom want to know what the royals are good for anyway besides charity work and selling tabloids. During the Second World War, the Queen Mother remained in Buckingham Palace during the German air raids. That made the British feel that she genuinely cared about them and sympathized with their plight.

Sure, the royals were different from commoners, but they had responsibilities and obligations that made them different, special, and worthy of respect.

Half a century later, few British subjects enthusiastically support the crown. Adultery, public feuds, divorces, and an expensive fire have turned the royal family into just another rich family that doesn't pay its share of taxes. Perhaps the biggest positioning blunder happened just after Princess Diana died. Instead of immediately letting the people know that she was as devastated as they were, Queen Elizabeth waited several days before saying anything, leaving them with the impression that she didn't really care.

Certainly a lot of the scandals plaguing the royal family lately are beyond the Queen's control. But she should have realized that even the way she does damage control affects her positioning in British society.

4. Position the Competition. Whether you realize it or not, every time you do something to position yourself, you're also positioning the competition. And of course, the same holds true the other way, which again highlights the need to stay constantly fresh. (Once you've identified your key competitors from Chapter 5, you'll know which companies to target.)

   You can position the competition actively or passively. Back in the late 1970s, Ronald Reagan repeatedly positioned Jimmy Carter as a man with no ideas by shaking his head and saying, "There you go again . . ." every time Carter opened his mouth. A few presidential campaigns later, Lloyd Bentsen positioned Dan Quayle as a man with no brains when he said "You're no Jack Kennedy." (Bentsen, unfortunately, also positioned himself with that remark as something of an insensitive bully.) When Oxy-Clean cuts a piece of stained fabric in two and shows how the half washed in Oxy comes out a lot cleaner than the half washed in Tide, they're positioning themselves as the best laundry detergent—and Tide as an inadequate also-ran. And every day, Subway uses its napkins to position McDonald's as a purveyor of fatty, unhealthful food by printing side-by-side fat-per-serving comparisons. Capital One does a great job promoting their "No Hassles Card's" low interest rates. Their commercials portray their competitors as monsters and barbarians who arbitrarily change interest rates and charge high fees. Without naming names, Capital One effectively positions all of its competitors as the bad guys. This last approach has been very successful for other companies as well, including Breyers Ice Cream and Wise Potato Chips, who've run commercials in which people read their all-natural ingredients and then struggle over the six-syllable, ghastly-sounding words on the competitors' labels.

Expedia, the travel Web site, is doing a good job of positioning their competition right now. Many consumers see travel Web sites as interchangeable, but Expedia is the only one that lets you choose the hotel you stay in. So they're positioning Priceline (where you can bid only on an area of town) and Hotwire (where you accept a price based on amenities, but not location) as much less flexible and somewhat risky. After all, wouldn't you rather know exactly where you were going to stay before you agreed to pay for it?

When we were working with Aspen/Snowmass, we realized that Vail was the primary competitor in the relatively flat ski resort market and that it was essentially a zero-sum game: Whatever Vail lost, A/S won, and vice versa. For that reason it was essential that in addition to positioning themselves as more relevant, A/S had to reposition Vail as *less* relevant. Skiers are already sold on the benefits of skiing, but they needed to be sold on the benefits of skiing at A/S instead of anywhere else.

When we examined the issue of accessibility, we found that A/S's location—farther from Denver than Vail, with a very small local airfield—reduced purchase intent by about 10 percent. We were able to turn that hurdle into a highly motivating advantage by positioning A/S as "harder to get to but worth it" because being farther away from the roadside resorts means less traffic—on the highway getting there as well as on the slopes. This was a benefit that was highly motivating to all target segments and enhanced A/S's overall positioning as "the ultimate ski vacation experience." Again, because of the zero-sum-game factor, positioning Vail (and other nearby resorts) as crowded and less fulfilling was a critical part of A/S's own positioning.

On the more passive side, there's positioning by implication. I do a lot of business in New York, and I gave my driver there a copy of one of the books I've written. Next time I saw him he said "Wow, I'll bet there are a lot of people who don't like you." He's probably right, but I asked him why he thought so. "You take such a strong point of view and you come down pretty hard on other people's." That, in a nutshell, is a kind of positioning. When I say I'm tall, I'm implying that everyone else is short. And when I make a public statement about my beliefs, I'm also making a public statement about everyone out there who happens to be wrong.

This kind of approach is especially good at narrowing your competitors to one or two undesirable traits. By positioning themselves as the thick, slow ketchup, Heinz is implying that everyone else's is watery and unacceptable. When Avis says "We try harder," they're saying that they'll do anything for you and that Hertz is lazy and unwilling to work for your business. And when Capital One advertises its low rates and fees, it's positioning all the other credit card issuers as thieves stealing money out of your pocket. One particularly good example has been Verizon's "Can you hear me now?" campaign. It's positioning competing cell phone companies as networks which inhabit the unreliable land of dropped calls and static. Having neatly positioned its competition, Verizon creatively and effectively leveraged these vulnerabilities to position itself as the national leader in providing clear networks.

Involuntary and Voluntary Repositioning

Be careful: Brand positioning statements—even the most perfect ones—are never foolproof. Sometimes events completely out of your control can dramatically change consumers' view of your brand, so you'd better have a contingency plan in place.

Let me give you a few examples of involuntarily repositioning. For many people, the Catholic Church, while it isn't a traditional brand, has stood for religion, holiness, and virtue for the past two millennia. But within just the past few years, things have changed. Allegations of sexual abuse hit the Church hard, and all of a sudden what had once seemed so holy was now tainted with scandal. Priests went from being direct communicators with God to something much less pious. Could the Church have kept themselves from getting repositioned? Probably not completely, but they certainly could have softened the blow by taking immediate action when the allegations first started surfacing. As it stands, the Church's value proposition is no longer as compelling to its consumers, whose trust in the brand has been badly shaken, and Catholicism as a whole may never fully recover.

Remember "Frankenfood"? In many parts of the world, people are adamantly opposed to scientifically engineered foods, even if they're more healthful, larger, more insect-resistant, or stay fresh longer. Several European countries have banned food containing GMOs (genetically modified organisms), and a number of the world's largest packaged foods companies woke up one morning to find themselves on international boycott lists. Many of them have been scrambling to promote their foods as safe, but brands like Nabisco and General Mills suffered significant negative publicity, and many Europeans still boycott their products. Even General Mills's seemingly wholesome Cheerios fell under suspicion. This has opened up the door for smaller food companies who are positioning themselves as GMO-free.

A lot of pharmaceutical companies are getting involuntarily repositioned or will be soon. Eli Lilly, for example, positioned its Prozac brand as *the* treatment for depression and leveraged that positioning into $2.7 billion in sales. But in 2001, the moment the patent ran out, generic companies flooded the market, taking Prozac's positioning and 90 percent of its sales with them. According to the Office of Generic Drugs, by 2010 over $20 billion in annual drug sales will go off patent. More recently, Claritin and Prilosec are facing enormous pressure as their active ingredients have become over-the-counter medicines.

Your company can be repositioned by changing technology. I already talked about Singer sewing machines and Smith Corona typewriters, which have become essentially irrelevant in today's world. But other industries are also being threatened by technology. Travel agencies, for example, now have to compete with low-overhead online travel options. Consumers now do their own research and book their own tickets, rental cars, hotels, even meals. A lot of consumers see agents as nothing more than middlemen who can easily be cut out to save a few bucks. If I worked for an agency, I'd start developing a new set of skills right now, because the handwriting is already on the wall.

Companies can also be repositioned by behavior, whether it's the CEO having a public affair or a mail clerk putting talcum powder in an envelope and telling his coworkers it's anthrax. Some of these repositionings may be fairly minor, but any time one of your employees harms or threatens a customer or causes a public scandal, your brand will suffer. Allegations of racism by employees at Denny's led to expensive lawsuits and extremely negative publicity. And in 2000, 171 people came down with *E. coli* bacteria at Wendy's restaurants.

And think of how one lousy journalist repositioned *The New York Times,* one of the most important and respected newspapers in the world for the past century. Their slogan—"All the news that's fit to print"—does a great job of positioning the *Times* as providing only the very best, and everyone else as providing who knows what. Then in 2003 there was the Jayson Blair scandal, in which it came out that one of their up-and-coming reporters was plagiarizing, lying, and just plain making up stories. To their credit, the *Times* jumped on the case right away, running a four-page apology followed by the resignations of two high-ranking editors. Had they tried to ignore the scandal in the hope that it would all blow over, the paper might never have recovered.

As I said earlier, individuals have positioning. And if they aren't careful, that positioning can change in a hurry. Back in the 1950s, Jerry Lee Lewis was almost as popular as Elvis. But marrying a thirteen-year-old cousin repositioned him as something of a letch. O. J. Simpson's brand became pretty worthless after he was tried for the murder of his ex-wife and her friend, even though he was acquitted. And basketball superstar Kobe Bryant recently lost many of his sponsors when he was accused of rape, before he was even charged, let alone convicted.

Perhaps the most effective involuntary repositioners are large-scale disasters that are completely unexpected. Airlines are particularly vulnerable to this kind of repositioning. TWA, for example, never fully recovered from the 1996 crash of Flight 800. But plenty of other sectors can be hit hard too. In 2002 there were several major outbreaks of mysterious bacteria on cruise ships. Hundreds of passengers got sick and hundreds more canceled their trip. The 1990 *Exxon Valdez* oil spill changed the Exxon brand into a symbol of environmental concerns.

And of course the September 11 terrorist attacks in New York and Washington, D.C., repositioned more than those two cities' tourist industries. Just think of the George W. Bush brand on September 10, 2001, the day before the terrorist attacks. He had an approval rating of 45 percent or so. In marketing terms, we'd say that consumers of the Bush brand were giving him only a 45 share of the market, based on the criteria Americans had for rating presidents. One month later, though, Bush's approval rating had hit 92 percent. Lazy marketing says that the public changed its mind about him, but that's not true. What changed were the criteria by which we evaluated him. Before September 11, no one who was asked to rate a president would have considered how well the president would rally the nation or how tough he'd talk if we were attacked by terrorists. But after September 11, those became the most important criteria, far overshadowing his tax cut plans, education reforms, or Social Security. Bush was repositioned as a president tough on terrorism.

Similarly, before invading Iraq in 2003, Bush positioned himself as trying to save the world by ferreting out Saddam Hussein's weapons of mass destruction. But as time went on and no weapons were found, Bush's tough-guy positioning came back to bite him in the butt, allowing the media and his political opponents to reposition him, rightly or wrongly, as a president who played fast and loose with the truth.

McDonald's and a bunch of other fast food companies are quickly being repositioned as dangerous. Although most people laughed when they heard about the first lawsuit against McDonald's brought by an obese guy, more followed. In one of the most recent, a federal judge threw out the case of two teenage girls who claimed that McDonald's made them obese and caused other health problems. And yet the judge referred to Chicken McNuggets as "a McFrankenstein creation of various elements not utilized by the home cook" and wondered whether a reasonable consumer could know that McNuggets were made from "so many ingredients other than chicken and provided twice the fat of a hamburger."

So all of a sudden McDonald's and a lot of others (including Coke) are running scared. Lawyers are hoping for a repeat of all the lawsuits against the tobacco companies. School boards are canceling partnerships with Coke and Pepsi, and other companies, like Kraft, are promising to introduce smaller portions and cut back their marketing to children. Similarly, Frito-Lay now fries most of its chips in less fatty oils and has expanded its line of baked products. Even the FDA is getting involved, requiring that labels now disclose trans-fatty acids on all packaging. Given how bad trans fats are for you, that's essentially like forcing manufacturers to include "poison" in their lists of ingredients.

Some companies are acting quickly to reposition themselves in light of these big external changes. McDonald's has said it's cutting back on the trans fats, and it's introduced some salads. And at least one restaurant chain has started a joint venture with Weight Watchers to add low-cal/low-fat meals to the menu. The ones who do a good job of repositioning will get through this thing okay. The ones who don't will disappear.

The same kind of thing happened in the spring of 2003 during the SARS epidemic. Because the World Health Organization was required to reveal where cases of SARS had appeared, every new WHO statement positioned a new city as infected with SARS. Naturally, an "infected" rating would almost instantly destroy that city's tourism industry. One of those unfortunate cities was Toronto, Canada, which wasted no time in trying to regain control of the dialogue and re-reposition the city as healthy and clean of the deadly virus. They've been doing everything they can to support that "healthy and clean" positioning, including having the Rolling Stones put on a benefit concert! A few months later, when they got caught in the massive blackout that took out most of eastern Canada and the United States, Toronto's reputation was hit once more and tourism dropped off again. But they didn't waste a minute, immediately confirming that actors Nicolas Cage, Nicole Kidman, Denzel Washington, and Meg Ryan would attend their International Film Festival.

Voluntary Repositioning

So far I've been talking about involuntary repositioning. But there are times when the motivation to reposition comes—or should come—from within. When it comes to brands, the old adage "If it ain't broke, don't fix it" doesn't work, and if you're going to keep ahead of the competition, you're going to have to be constantly tinkering with things *before* they break, adjusting your message and your image to your customers' wants and needs.

But does this mean that your brand is always at the mercy of your customers' whims? What if you want to change direction completely? Whenever I get a client who asks about this, my answer is usually the same: While remaking your brand may offer some attractive advantages, such as bringing in new customers, it also involves alienating your base, the core customers who support your brand right now. So if you're going to completely rework your brand, you'd better have a pretty good reason for it.

One great example of voluntary repositioning is TNN, the cable television station now known as Spike TV. In 1983, the station launched as The Nashville Network, hoping to appeal to country music fans. In 2000, Viacom bought Nashville out, changed the name to The National Network, moved the station to New York, and changed its focus from country to mainstream. Unfortunately, it never caught on very strongly with viewers. In 2003, it relaunched yet again, this time targeting young men with Gen X sports like Slam Ball and edgy cartoons like *Stripperella.*

Miller Lite has recently been on a repositioning campaign that I find very interesting. Without changing the product attributes at all, they've managed to change the image of their product. As I mentioned back in Chapter 4, Miller Lite had mothballed their "Make It Miller Time" promotion and turned the brand into a commodity.

But as it turns out, Miller Lite has fewer carbohydrates than the rest of the light beers out there, which gives it a significant competitive advantage and should make it the drink of choice among Atkins-diet-obsessed people trying to cut back on carbohydrates. Miller Lite's new slogan is "Fewer Carbs. So you can have a beer to wash down that beer." This continues to leverage the core essence of "tastes great, less filling," but also offers a new incentive to buy.

Of course, repositioning your brand isn't always something you do because you want to. Sometimes it's essential to your brand's success. Marlboro cigarettes, for example, were originally positioned as a cigarette for women—they were actually made with red tips "to conceal those telltale lipstick traces." It wasn't until 1963 that Philip Morris introduced the Marlboro Man and repositioned the cigarette as the manliest thing out there. And Saturn started off positioning itself as a top-quality, U.S.-made car. After a while, though, it changed its positioning to emphasize the relationships Saturn builds with its customers.

How and when you reposition your brand is strictly a function of knowing your brand's destination and keeping your eyes focused on that target. That's something politicians do incredibly well. Their brand destination is to get elected, and they'll do pretty much anything they need to do to get there. Sometimes that means changing their methods and tactics and even their message. Of course I'm not advocating lying to your customers or making promises you don't intend to keep. What I am saying, though, is that there's no guarantee that what worked in the past will get you where you want to go in the future. But if you keep your brand's destination and positioning statements in mind, you'll always be able to stand up and say "Hey, I made a mistake" or "Hmm, that tactic didn't work, looks like we need a new one."

Finally, it's critical to remember the role of core essence in any repositioning. Bayer, for example, is almost synonymous with aspirin, and they've had a tough time persuading people to buy their nonaspirin products. Can Johnnie Walker sell gin? I don't think so, but they could sell single malts and maybe prepared cocktails in cans. And could GE sell small appliances? Maybe, but which ones would work with GE's core essence?

Don't Forget About Pet Rocks

Renovating your positioning can be an essential component of business success, as long as you don't get obsessive about it. Your ultimate goal is to sell more stuff to more people . . . (you know the rest). To a great extent, being able to do that is based on having repeat customers. But if you change your positioning too often, you'll end up as little more than a fad that people buy once and never come back to. Companies in food, consumer goods, and fashion do this kind of thing constantly. Eventually people are going to get sick of fat-free foods and they'll just buy bigger pants. And they'll stop buying disposable products that waste natural resources and fill up landfills.

Remember when everybody wore Izod alligators? Keds? Esprit? It's been awhile since any of these brands was part of pop culture. And look at the endless parade of jeans brands that went from teen girls' "must have" to zero sales almost overnight: Jordache, Gloria Vanderbilt, Z. Cavaricci, Get Used, Guess, Gap. Today it's Seven and Juicy, but I expect that those won't last any longer than the others did. It's truly the minority of fashion companies that can renovate their positioning enough to stay relevant but not so much that they end up disappearing.

Entertainment generates a lot of fads, too. Look at *Who Wants to Be a Millionaire.* It started off as a once-every-few-weeks show, then a few times a week, and then almost every night. Eventually we all got sick of it and pulled the plug; too much of a good thing is never that good. Remember when every kid played with a Cabbage Patch Kid (1983), Tickle Me Elmo (1996), and Beanie Babies (1997)?

The fad problem develops when companies refuse to acknowledge changes in consumer tastes. The world may be a certain way today, but it probably won't be that way tomorrow or the day after or next year. Instead of leveraging their core essence to adapt to new consumer preferences, too many brands fantasize that consumers will always like them. These guys should learn a lesson from Barbie, Lego, and Crayola—a few children's brands that have been consistent sellers for generations because they constantly update their positioning and relevance while staying true to their core essence.

5. Avoid Virtual Consumption. The ultimate goal of positioning, just like the goal of everything else that you do in business, is to drive consumption. But be careful: Not all types of consumption are created equal. There's one kind, *virtual consumption,* that you want to watch out for.

   Never heard of virtual consumption? Well, you'd better listen up, because it could kill your business. Virtual consumption is when customers' actions don't match their stated preferences. And believe me, it happens a lot.

   My coauthor is something of a Porsche fanatic. He has Porsche books all over the house and a Porsche screensaver on his computer. He can even identify the model and year of a Porsche driving by from the sound of the engine. And if the Gallup Poll people were to stop him on the street and ask what his favorite car brand is, there'd be no doubt—all they'd have to do would be to look at his Porsche T-shirt and baseball cap. But Armin doesn't own a Porsche, and he's probably not going to buy one any time soon. What he's already bought, though, is Porsche's value proposition: He thinks Porsches are great-looking cars, fun to drive, and he loves the feelings he gets when he drives a friend's Porsche: important, prosperous, and good about himself. But never forget that there's a huge difference between buying the value proposition and buying the product.

   Virtual consumption happens when companies use name recognition and consumer awareness instead of sales as markers of success. Ninety percent of companies out there do this. They say, "Gee, look, 100 percent of the people know who I am. Ninety-three percent say I'm their favorite brand, 85 percent say I'm a very likable brand." And then they can't figure out why they have only a 15 market share. Well, you know, unfortunately, love doesn't pay the rent. It's all too easy to have very high levels of irrelevant brand awareness or high levels of irrelevant likeability—awareness and likeability don't motivate people to buy.

   Television ads are especially good at generating virtual consumption. In some cases, the more successful the commercial, the more virtual (and less real) the consumption. During Apple's famous "think different" campaign, the company's market share declined and the company had the lowest revenue per ad dollar in the computer industry. It was basically the same thing for Taco Bell's Chihuahua commercials, and Budweiser's "Wassup" series. And that's why I killed two of the most popular Coke ads of all time: "Mean Joe Greene" and "I'd Like to Teach the World to Sing." Both were wildly popular, but neither one helped sell more Coca-Cola.

There are two cures for virtual consumption. First, you need to change the way you define consumption: It means "sales," not name recognition. Second, and most important, you have to renovate your brand's positioning so you can offer consumers a value proposition that's relevant to get them to buy once and keep coming back.

A Case Study

I want to take a minute here to talk about a company that's currently being eaten alive by virtual consumption: Starbucks.

Back in 1960, coffee had a 70 percent market penetration—people drank an average of 3.2 cups of coffee per day. By 1988, penetration was down to 50 percent and daily consumption was down to 1.67 cups. Everyone was about ready to give up the coffee category for dead: The theory was that newer, younger consumers didn't want hot beverages, didn't like the taste of coffee, and didn't have time for a drink that has to be consumed slowly. Then along came Starbucks, which turned the whole thing on its head.

Starbucks repositioned the whole category. No more boring "Coffee, please." All of a sudden, it was about gourmet blends, double mocha cappuccino, espresso, latte, and tables where you could hang with your friends or plug in your laptop and pretend to work. And they repositioned coffee itself, from a drink that might give you a morning boost to a way to excite the senses, discover the world, and indulge yourself. And they positioned themselves as the company that could deliver on consumers' newly reignited passion for "my coffee, my way, dammit!"

The results were amazing. The category was completely revitalized and the downward consumption trend was completely reversed. In 1999, penetration was up to 76 percent and daily consumption was up to 3.5 cups—both higher than they were in 1960. Even the size of the servings is up: 33 percent of cups are bigger than eight ounces. Back in 1988, when the category was left for dead, Starbucks had only thirty-three stores. Today it's nearly five thousand.

Starbucks is far and away the dominant player in their category. Sixty-three percent of category users identify Starbucks as their primary specialty coffee shop. More than half (56 percent) say they visit Starbucks several times a month or more. And 88 percent intend to visit Starbucks as much or more often in the next twelve months as they do currently.

While these numbers tend to confirm Starbucks' dominant position, our research also suggests that the company may be at risk of losing its unique reason for being. Many category users believe Starbucks no longer provides a unique, differentiated experience: 57 percent say that being able to get their coffee customized exactly how they want it is available from multiple brands; 44 percent say the same quality of coffee available at Starbucks is now available from other brands; and 43 percent say that the things they like about Starbucks—the things that make Starbucks special to them—are increasingly available elsewhere.

What's especially worrisome is that long-term Starbucks customers are more likely than newer customers to agree with the above statements. Overall, 46 percent of long-term Starbucks customers say that, more than ever, the things that used to make Starbucks special to them are available at other places, versus 31 percent of newer customers. This suggests that Starbucks may be losing some brand equity—and its premium position—among its core, established customer base. If that trend continues, it's all over.

For consumers who indicated that over the next twelve months they would visit Starbucks less frequently than they currently do, the main reason for cutting back was price. Although this should raise some red flags at any time, it's especially disturbing in the current economy, when consumers may be less willing to pay a premium if they don't believe there's a difference. Clearly, pricing is an area where Starbucks is particularly vulnerable. And the situation will get worse if consumers' perceptions of Starbucks' uniqueness doesn't improve.

What Starbucks needs to do is completely renovate its brand positioning to keep it current with—or ahead of—customer needs. They did it once, and they can do it again. The first step might be to do something to improve the quality of their baked goods.

8

Renovate Your Customers' Brand Experience

Okay, answer me this: What business are you in and what, exactly, are you selling? Got your answer? Well, whatever you said, you're wrong. The truth is that even though you might think you're selling a product or a service, you're actually selling an experience. And when it comes right down to it, that experience is often the only significant thing that separates you from your competitors.

In most cases, experiences rarely have anything to do with the products themselves, no matter how hard the companies who offer them try to make the connection. Apple, for example, promises—and delivers—an easy, fun customer experience and sleek design. But there's a lot more than that to the Apple experience, which is really more about the feeling of belonging to an exclusive group. It's kind of like owning a Harley-Davidson motorcycle. Harleys certainly aren't the most comfortable or fastest or best-designed bikes out there. And most Harley owners don't even ride their bikes as much as Honda or Kawasaki owners do. But that isn't what matters. The reason people buy a Hog is for the Harley experience: outlaw, "ride to live, live to ride," Hell's Angels, made in America, wind in your hair, American classic, and, of course, that distinctive Harley sound.

The real reason that products in and of themselves have become almost afterthoughts is because technology has advanced to the point where almost any company can come up with a copycat product and have it on the shelves in forty-eight hours. A couple of years ago, for example, Procter & Gamble introduced the Swiffer WetJet, a complete, easy-to-use floor-cleaning system that even came with prediluted cleaning solution. But Clorox immediately came out with the Ready-Mop, which was essentially the same thing. Only seven months after the WetJet was introduced, P&G had cut the price in half. The same kind of "Me too!" marketing is happening hundreds of times every day.

This is all very interesting, but for me, the big question is why experience has become the new basis of competition in so many categories. Back in 2001, we did extensive consumer research and found that after 9/11 consumers started placing a lot more emphasis on family and relationships. That insight enabled us to help our clients position their products and services better in order to tap into consumers' changing values.

We recently redid our consumer research and found that although 9/11 has become a less painful memory, and most people's lives are back to normal, there are some lingering effects. Consumers told us that on any given day, if they had to choose between making more money and taking things a little easier, they'd go with easier. They also told us that the brands and products they find most appealing are the ones that make their time more enjoyable, *not* the ones that save them money.

Time, it seems, has become the new currency. And its scarcity has made consumers more conscious, more discriminating, and more aware of the "present tense" than they ever were before. For that reason, product benefits and attributes aren't enough anymore. Today's consumers want experiences—experiences they can feel, experiences that will change their emotions, their attitudes, and maybe even their lives.

That may sound a little overwhelming, but simply being aware of this shift in consumers' wants is great news for your company. Being able to compete on the basis of experiences expands your competitive frame and gives you more opportunities to deliver value and to differentiate yourself from the competition. Think for a second about British Airways and Southwest Airlines. BA sells "British Comfort," while

Southwest sells "no frills transportation by air." Two very different brands, delivering two very different . . . experiences. Still, both of these companies have expanded their core proposition to include the process of exploring, deciding, buying, using their products. Here are a few more examples of what I mean:

Technically, Saturn may be selling cars, but what they deliver is a straightforward car-buying *experience*. Barnes & Noble sells books, but delivers a multisensory book-buying *experience*. And Starbucks sells coffee but provides an exceptional coffeehouse *experience*.

Experiences can sometimes be service-based. The Ritz-Carlton, for example, knows that the experience they provide is the key to success, and they continually monitor guests' changing preferences to ensure that they always get the best experience. Two recent additions are "luggageless travel" (which allows frequent guests to leave clothing at the hotel between visits) and "flight bites" (carry-on meals for guests who are on the way to the airport). Ritz also puts all of its employees through extensive customer interaction training and gives each employee the authority to resolve problems on the spot. The company has also set up a database with information about each guest's previous stays. As soon as they found out I used to work for Coke, they no longer put Pepsi products in my in-room refrigerator. And every time I check into a Ritz hotel—no matter where—my radio is always tuned to the kind of music I like. That's the kind of customized experience that keeps me and thousands of other people coming back—and paying a premium for the privilege.

Any company, large or small, can provide a similar level of service-based experience. The only rule is that every single employee—from the guy who cleans the toilets to the CEO—absolutely must know and fully support the company's core essence and business destination. No exceptions. Those two things are at the heart of customers' experience.

Experiences can also be retail-based. Nordstrom is famous for the pampering department-store experience; Sharper Image creates unique, fun, and engaging customer experiences at each of its stores, and so do FAO Schwarz and Niketown. IKEA, on the other hand, creates an absolutely frightening experience, offering reasonably nice stuff for reasonably good prices, but laying out their stores so that it takes twenty minutes just to find an exit. How they manage to make you feel claustrophobic in a space the size of three football fields amazes me. Still, I have to admit that the poor IKEA experience doesn't seem to stop people from spending a good part of their income there. Just goes to show you that consumers will sometimes endure less-than-optimal experiences to get a good deal.

Experiences can be product-based. When you buy Tartar Control Crest, factors such as taste and how your breath smells are important. But so is what happens at your next trip to the dentist. If the hygienist has to chip the tartar off your teeth with a chisel, you're going to chuck that tube of Crest in the trash as soon as you get home.

Condoms are another product where the customer's experience is critical. Condoms were basically a commodity—used to prevent pregnancy and disease—and consumers didn't see much of a difference among brands. But Durex found a way to pull itself away from the pack. Recognizing that the contraceptive and disease-preventing attributes of condoms were the price of entry, they began offering sensation-enhancing bumps, sensation-dulling anesthetic, and other features designed to increase customers' experience of the product, and by extension, of sex itself. Sales are on the rise, and consumers can choose based on the experience they want.

Overall, the experience you offer is likely to be a combination of product attributes, service, retail environment, and every single other point of contact you have with consumers: your advertising, promotion, marketing, public relations, and sponsorships; your Web site, packaging, and employment policies; how your receptionists answer the phone, and how your top executives behave at parties.

It's important to keep in mind that you can't control every aspect of consumers' experience with your brand. Your Rolling Stones experience, for example, includes the concerts you went to, the songs you like and the ones you hate, the albums you bought, the people you made out with while listening to their music, articles about the band, and your amazement that Keith Richards is still alive after all the drugs he's taken. What's important, though, is that over the last thirty years or so, the Stones have stayed true to their core essence of "classic rock and roll" and continually renovated the experience they offer. As a result, their new albums still go platinum and their concerts still sell out, partly to people who weren't born when the Stones first hit the charts.

Some companies have recognized the importance of the experience they create in their customers' minds and how everything they do contributes to that experience. Starbucks' CEO, Howard Schultz, once said: "The advantage Starbucks has over other brands is that our customers see themselves inside our company, inside our brand—because they're part of the Starbucks experience." United Airlines' attitude toward customer experience is very similar: "The sum of all impressions, good or bad, that have an influence on our customers' experience. Every service experience, product, program, or piece of communication that we generate serves to build or break the United brand."

At Universal Studios theme parks (and Disney's as well), even the employees' uniforms contribute. Giant cartoon characters and adults dressed in animal prints and safari hats bring you into the fantasy experience instead of letting you simply observe it. And the U.S. Army has recently started virtual skydiving and Humvee rides, climbing walls, and even interactive video games to give prospective recruits a chance to test-drive the Army experience before they "buy" it.

For the most part, though, most companies just don't get it. They measure success in customer satisfaction levels, but they don't realize that 80 percent of people who switch brands were actually satisfied with the brand they switched from. The only way to build loyal customers is to deliver experiences that create value *beyond* satisfaction. Consumers are looking for experiences which complement their lifestyle and brands which say something about their aspirations.

But I Am a Product, Not a Place

Sometimes, when I discuss these points with clients, I get very puzzled looks. "How can my brand deliver an experience," they ask, "if I'm not in a service or retail environment where people have a chance to interact with the brand?" In response I often ask them to think about turkeys—specifically, Butterball turkeys. Butterball, I tell them, is not a brand. It's a branded experience.

Just think about the last time you had a whole turkey at home. It was probably a holiday or celebration of some kind, and you were probably surrounded by family and friends. Someone—maybe you—prepared the turkey using some secret-family-stuffing recipe, put it in the oven, basted it, cooked it, carved it. Everyone else smelled the bird, anticipated eating it (or maybe shuddered at the thought of eating turkey leftovers every day for the next week). All in all, it was a very interactive and multisensory experience. Unless the meat was rancid, though, the bird itself had almost nothing to do with the experience. At the same time, though, it was absolutely critical.

The Retailer's Challenge

In the retail segment, low margins create a need for meaningful differentiation, greater loyalty, and increased traffic. The problem is that within most segments, retailers offer essentially the same products and services. But that doesn't stop them from assaulting consumers with an amazing variety of competitive brand messages.

Today more than ever, retailers have to find a way to deliver an in-store experience that redefines their value proposition and delivers added value to customers. In our experience, the following five factors will determine whether a retailer will be able to do that:

1. The ability to understand the customer's overall value equation.
2. The ability to develop "ideas" that deliver against that value equation.
3. The ability to leverage the store's brand equity *and* the equities of the major brands it sells to add value to the shopping experience.
4. The ability to define the brand experience to multiple constituencies (including customers, employees, investors, and suppliers).
5. The ability to execute the programs and ideas using existing competencies and hard assets.

Recipe for Experience

My colleague Dave Singleton says that trying to define "experience" is like shooting at a moving target. There are so many different kinds of experiences that it's almost impossible to pin down. But after thirty years of marketing experience I've come up with the following guidelines. An experience can:

- Offer easy access
  - You don't have to work too hard to get what you want.
  - You can decide on the spur of the moment.
- Be a social, shared experience.
  - I can tell someone about it.
  - I derive pleasure from seeing someone else enjoy it too.
- Be interactive.
  - You can touch it, feel it, move it, shape it.
  - It gives you immediate feedback.
- Be unexpected.
  - It surprises you.
  - It's not what you expected (in a good way).
- Be personalized.
  - It can be customized to you.
  - It's not the same for everyone every time.
- Remove the negatives.
  - It can distract you.
  - It makes the time go fast.
- Be dynamic.
  - It can be interrupted.
  - It can be improved, or not.

Although those definitions are helpful, they really only tell you what an experience might *look* like. Let's take a few minutes to talk about what an experience is actually *made* of. Basically, it's a five-part progression:

- Intrinsics. Physical elements that are integral to the experience.
- Intention. What the consumer needs or wants from the experience.
- Interactions. The actions, communication, and behaviors.
- Impact. The tangible results.
- Impressions. What the consumer is left with.

Let me give you a couple of real examples of how this works. The Starbucks brand experience offers:

- Intrinsics. Quality gourmet beans and Starbucks lifestyle accessories.
- Intention. Connection and personal indulgence.
- Interactions. Starbucks vocabulary (double decaf latte grande) and personalized beverages delivered one at a time by "bohemian" employees.
- Impact. The tangible results. You feel refreshed and revitalized.
- Impressions. Sensory excitement, a sense of affiliation and of having found a personal oasis.

	Dealerships: The Driving Superstore	Service
Intrinsics	• Solutions to your driving needs • A multitude of products, services, and brands	• Clean, laboratorylike aesthetics • Technology to keep my car running like new
Intention	• Enjoy driving • Enhanced, hassle-free ownership	• Peace of mind • Prolonged value • Confidence in quality
Interactions	• On-site access to experts • Not focused on "the deal"	• Focused on me and the car • Professional, organized, and efficient • Maintenance experts, not just mechanics
Impact	• Better driver • Better owner • Better customer	• Increased car value • Greater trust in the dealer and the brand
Impressions	• Dealership is a destination • Partnership • The "Home Depot" of driving	• "The service department helps me manage my investment"

Depending on your product or service, you might be offering different experiences to different consumers, or different experiences to the same consumers but at different times. Above is an analysis my company did for one of the Big Three car companies, illustrating how important it is to provide different experiences at the dealership and service department levels. In fact, it's the experience with the dealership that will make the service experience possible: A bad dealership experience means no car sale, which means no service.

Losing the Experience: McDonald's

Part of my company's business development strategy is to look for companies that have made costly marketing mistakes and offer to help them find solutions. McDonald's is one of those companies. McDonald's is a huge brand with nearly universal name recognition and market penetration. Although that's an enviable spot to be in, it's also a tough one—when you're the biggest, everyone else is always trying to eat into your market share, and it's a constant struggle to keep doing the things that made you a success in the first place.

We'd been tracking McDonald's for the past few years and felt that part of their problem was that they'd been so focused on the *what* (value pricing, Dollar Menus, etc.) and the *how* (operations, expansions, acquisitions, etc.) of their business that they had neglected their customers' *experience*. For consumers, the McDonald's brand is more than Ronald McDonald, it's more than the Big Mac or fries, more than the company's ads or its frequent Disney movie product tie-ins. The truth is that on some level consumers see, feel, touch, smell, hear, and taste McDonald's. Or at least they used to. McDonald's brand positioning was undefined, they'd given up control of the dialogue with consumers, and customers had noticed.

Before even making the call, I had our research people do some preliminary investigation. Here's some of what we found:

When we asked consumers to describe their most recent McDonald's experience, 38 percent said they were "just glad to get in and out as quickly as possible." Twenty-one percent said they "enjoyed it," 12 percent "didn't feel anything," and 9 percent said they "felt relaxed and comfortable."

The answer to that and a few other questions told us that for a lot of people, an essential part of the McDonald's experience is speed—if they're feeling rushed they know they can get their food quickly and get back to whatever they were doing. Interestingly, being able to get in and out quickly is part of consumers' experience with other brands as well. But more consumers told us that they were "glad to get out quickly" of McDonald's (38 percent) than either Blockbuster (24 percent) or the dry cleaner's (22 percent).

The problem with speed as a critical component of the experience is that while helping customers get in and out quickly and efficiently is great for the customer, it's hard for McDonald's to build relationships with customers who are always rushing off somewhere else. As a result, whatever connections you do have naturally weaken over time.

To test that hypothesis, we asked people to describe their relationship with McDonald's. Although more than a third (35 percent) said it was "like being with a member of the family or a close friend," exactly *half* said it was like "an old friend I used to know and miss," "an old friend I rarely see anymore," an "old friend I don't care about," or "someone I've never known that well."

Going even further, when we asked people which companies they have the best relationships with, only 6 percent said McDonald's—below local banks (51 percent), local movie rental stores (17 percent), Internet service providers (15 percent), and even local dry cleaners (7 percent).

All told, that wasn't particularly good news. And things got even worse when we asked people to describe McDonald's in human terms—as if the restaurant itself were a person. Almost a third said that McDonald's seemed either like "an impersonal corporate executive" or like "someone who's a little out of touch with his friends."

We felt that in order to renovate the experience it offers its customers, McDonald's would first need to reconnect with its customers. So we asked people to tell us the things that were most important to them. Here's what they said:

• Family	53%
• Personal Happiness	14%
• Financial Security	11%
• Enjoying Life	9%
• Health	9%
• Professional Advancement	3%

Plenty of companies appeal to consumers through one of these channels and provide experiences that capitalize on them. Sometimes, of course, elements of these experiences overlap. When banks, for example, say they're helping people realize their dreams, they're really offering "personal happiness" and "enjoying life." When video rental stores say they're providing fun and togetherness, it's really about "family" and "enjoying life." And when ISPs claim to bring the world to you, they're trying to deliver "personal happiness." But the big question facing McDonald's was "What value does McDonald's deliver?" Unfortunately, not enough people could answer that question.

Based on our preliminary research, we had a strong sense of what McDonald's consumers were thinking and feeling and what would make them act. We then put together a rough outline of how we felt consumers would describe their McDonald's experience:

- McDonald's is *the* preferred place to relax, refuel, and recharge. McDonald's is the smart choice over all other "relax-and-recharge" choices because the food, the people, and the environment give *me* and *my family* exactly what *we* want, when we want it, the way we want it. McDonald's delivers value to our family.
- I *feel* comfortable at McDonald's and I get energy from being there. I know the experience will be easy and the food will be what I know and expect and enjoy. When I walk through the door everything feels familiar and I am glad to be back. When I leave McDonald's, I feel *good* (about myself and others) and can't wait to come again soon.
- As a result, McDonald's is an *anticipated routine*. It is an integral part of my life, one that never fades to the subconscious, but one that a part of me looks forward to each and every time I go.

Unfortunately, McDonald's doesn't quite get how its core essence influences its customers' experience. Take their new "Be Active" meal pack, which is supposed to provide a healthful experience by giving customers pedometers (so they can track how much they're walking), a nutrition booklet, a salad, and a bottle of water. Sounds great, except for one thing: People who are truly concerned about how much they walk aren't going to eat at McDonald's. Plus, their Crispy Chicken Bacon Ranch Salad has more fat and calories than a Quarter Pounder. The bottom line is that McDonald's core essence keeps it from competing in the health space and makes trying to offer a healthful experience practically impossible.

One Company That Does It Right: Wal-Mart

With annual sales of $270 billion, Wal-Mart is the world's largest company. It has nearly thirty-five hundred stores today and plans to increase that to five thousand by 2008. Despite its massive size, Wal-Mart gives customers the kind of positive experience that most other companies can't even come close to. To a great extent, that experience is driven by the company's core essence: Everyday low prices on everything you need.

There's no question that the company has plenty of detractors—people who are convinced that Wal-Mart is some kind of corporate antichrist, destroying local communities, putting mom-and-pop stores out of business, and lining their own pockets in the process. But the fact is that people buy anything and everything from Wal-Mart, and they're fiercely loyal to the company—something Target, Kmart, Sears, Kroger, and the rest of the players in the competitive set are fiercely envious of.

To get an idea of what Wal-Mart is doing right—and what, by extension, everyone else is doing wrong—let's examine how they have addressed the five *I*'s we discussed earlier. Keep in mind that what you're going to read may sound a little like an infomercial—but it's not. To be honest, I don't shop at Wal-Mart. But everything I'm telling you below comes directly from our research, and we believe it paints a very accurate picture of exactly what's involved in creating a memorable—and profitable—customer experience.

- Intrinsics
  - The core elements. The most basic building blocks of the Wal-Mart experience are its low prices, wide selection, and convenient location. Together, these core elements give customers a clear frame of reference and create several key expectations: that they can buy more for less, that they don't need to shop anywhere else because Wal-Mart has it all, and that other places have higher prices and less to choose from. All of these factors are crucial to—but can't completely explain—Wal-Mart's success.
  - The ties that bind. In a very real way, Wal-Mart's customers have reached an agreement with the company before they even enter the store, and it's all about the "everyday low prices" guarantee. Customers know they don't have to shop around for a deal or a sale; they know they're going to get a good, fair price—probably the best price around. People we interviewed felt that many of Wal-Mart's competitors offer the *opposite* of everyday low prices: constantly changing prices; inflated prices, marking prices up and then having a sale to make it look as though they're offering a good deal; and the lingering feeling that if you aren't getting it on sale, you're paying too much.
  - Shoppers' insurance. Wal-Mart's unconditional, no-hassle return policy sends a clear message to customers that the company is seriously interested in their happiness and satisfaction and that they'll never make a mistake at Wal-Mart.
  - Wal-Mart extends a hand—and makes a good first impression every time. Those friendly greeters at the front door are Wal-Mart personified, and the experience continues through the shopping trip: helpful, smiling employees directing customers to neat, well-organized, well-stocked displays.
- Intention
  - Learning and discovering. Shoppers feel that Wal-Mart shows them and teaches them what they need to know. People we

spoke with valued Wal-Mart's expertise. And whether it was books, toys, video games, or plants, they felt that in every department they were getting the widest selection, the newest, most up-to-date products out there, and products unavailable anywhere else.
  - Providing solutions. People feel that Wal-Mart can meet their needs. They feel confident that they can come into the store and walk out with everything on their shopping list. It's also a place that's fun to go—alone or with the family—even when you don't need anything.
- Interactions
  - All the store's a stage . . . with characters and props that create a story. The customer plays the lead, the employees and the products are the supporting cast. And the atmosphere in the stores sets the mood. Shoppers told us that the Wal-Mart blue brightens their mood and that the friendliness of the employees rubs off and makes the overall experience more enjoyable; they don't feel rushed to get through the checkout line, and the layout and organization of the store make it a very efficient place to shop.
  - Wal-Mart speaks—with messages that communicate the basics, that engage customers, and that make decisions easy to reach.
- Impact
  - Consistency. Although Wal-Mart stores are huge, customers rarely feel as though they're in a warehouse. In fact, they say that shopping there feels like being in a small store—the ease of finding things, the high level of customer service, and the comfort and familiarity of the store design.
  - Trust is a two-way street. Consumers trust Wal-Mart and Wal-Mart trusts its customers. Customers feel confident that they're getting good quality, trustworthy advice, and the best prices. In return, Wal-Mart lets them return anything they aren't satisfied with, any time, no questions asked.
- Impressions
  - Wal-Mart is an expert. There are knowledgeable people in every department who can explain alternatives and help customers who don't have the necessary expertise to make decisions with

confidence. And if an employee can't help, he or she isn't embarrassed to find someone else who can solve the problem.

- Expertise personified. When we asked people to describe Wal-Mart to us as if the store were a person, the most common answers were:
  - Doctor. You go in with a goal and you usually leave with exactly what you need.
  - Teacher. Wal-Mart is always teaching their customers about saving time and money under one roof.
  - A trusted relative. Shopping at Wal-Mart feels relaxed and enjoyable, and you know you're going to be treated fairly even if you don't know something.

To sum it all up, Wal-Mart provides a customer experience that is full of contrasts, completely consistent with its core essence. That allows Wal-Mart to continually renovate customers' shopping experience, which ultimately drives sales and creates strong loyalty. Here's what it looks like:

Wal-Mart is for one thing and everything:

- Wal-Mart will have it.
- Wal-Mart can do it.

Wal-Mart is for me and for us.

- I can get it all done at one place.
- We can do it together.

Wal-Mart shopping is boring and exciting.

- I know exactly what to expect.
- And I will probably get more.

Wal-Mart shopping is low risk and consistent reward.

- I cannot make a mistake.
- I have confidence that I will come out ahead.

Wal-Mart is a big store that feels small.

- Lots of merchandise.
- Lots of help and enough expertise.

Okay, So How Do You Create a Meaningful Brand Experience?

Let's get this out of the way up front: There's no silver bullet. If you're looking for a quick, painless way to define and deliver a brand experience, you'd better think again. The process of successfully changing a brand from a collection of mere benefits into a true experience can be complicated, but it's well worth it.

There are three basic steps:

- Define. You need to delineate the brand, its target, and the benefits it provides.
- Translate. Use consumer touch points to help translate the brand into experiences.
- Deliver. Deliver on customers' expectations, react quickly, and continuously measure the impact of your efforts.

Because they're so important, let's look at these three steps in greater detail.

1. Define the Brand

   The first step in defining the brand is to have a firm grasp of your *competitive frame* and your *competitive set*. We talked about this a lot in Chapter 5, but to give you a quick summary, the competitive frame is basically the standard your customers use to evaluate things. It's the bare minimum that they'll accept in terms of product attributes, service, and so on. The competitive set is the group of alternatives to your product or service. I can guarantee you that if you want to define and deliver a positive brand experience, you'll need to be intimately familiar with both.

The second step is to understand your *brand architecture* and *value proposition*. If you don't, you'd better stop right now and figure them out. In the simplest terms, brand architecture and value proposition are what's behind every single point of contact between your brand and consumers. This includes advertising, in-store communication, and contact between your employees and customers. Understanding your brand architecture will enable you to identify key consumer functional and emotional benefits and the most effective touch points.

The third step is to assess your *brand capacity*. As shown in the graphic below, this is a function of your brand's ability to meet the performance goals of the business, to withstand competitive pressures or attacks, and to create sustainable value to customers in the longer term.

In summary, defining your brand provides the foundation you'll need to translate it into value-added experiences that will keep your customers coming back.

2. Translate the Brand

Back in Chapter 6 (Segmentation) I talked about the process of gathering customer insights. The most productive insights

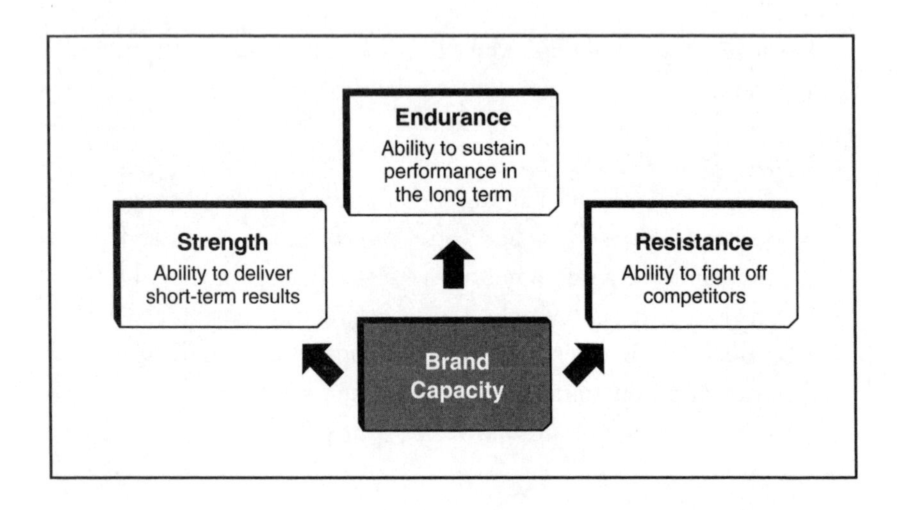

usually come from a combination of *core motivations* and on-site observations (where possible). Core motivations are the deeply rooted reasons why the customer uses your products or services (e.g., satisfactions and/or motivations associated with work, home, leisure time, etc.). These insights form the basis for making meaningful connections between the brand and the customer.

Integrating your insights into your customers' motivations, needs, attitudes, behaviors, and other relevant characteristics with your brand's architecture will reveal a number of ways to deliver that all-important experience to the customer.

3. Deliver the Brand Experience

   Each of the options you identified in the previous step should be individually assessed to determine whether it has what it takes to actually deliver a unique brand experience. At the same time, come up with a reasonable time frame within which you'll be able to develop and execute the option. (See the graphic below.)

   You should also write what we call *activation frameworks and briefs*. These clarify the target customer, the shopping situation occasion, the key need and/or motivation addressed by the program, and the specific benefits the experience will ultimately deliver. The exact format and content of the frameworks and briefs

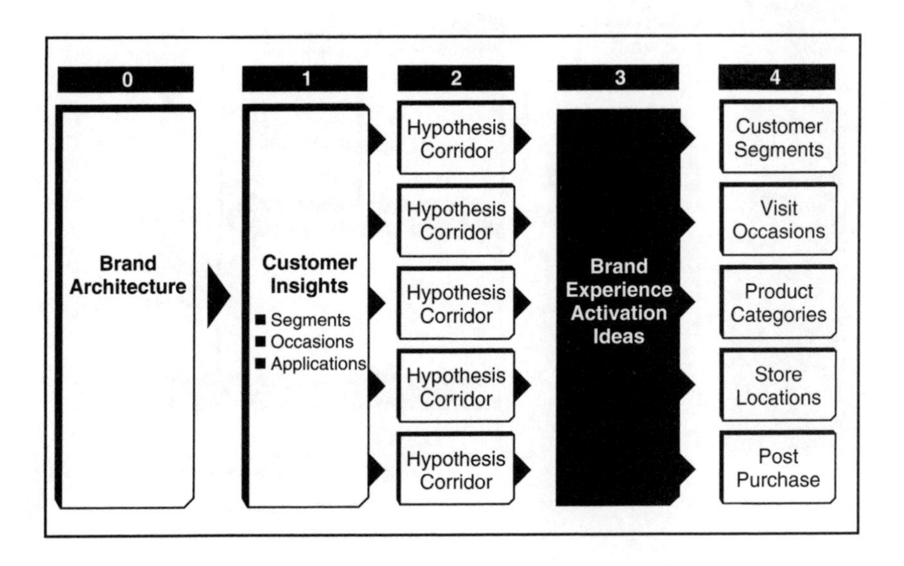

will depend on the nature of the experience you're trying to deliver. Nevertheless, they must always provide explicit explanation and direction to ensure that everyone involved in the delivery of the experience understands the whys and hows of the program.

The fourth step in this three-step process (I know three-step processes should be limited to three steps, but this last one is less of an actual step and more of an overall way of life) is to continually test, modify, and refresh your customers' experience. This means going back through steps one and two every once in a while and fine-tuning them to make sure that the experience you're providing is still what your customers want and need. Doing regular reviews like this will also give you an opportunity to test new ideas before you implement them on a large scale.

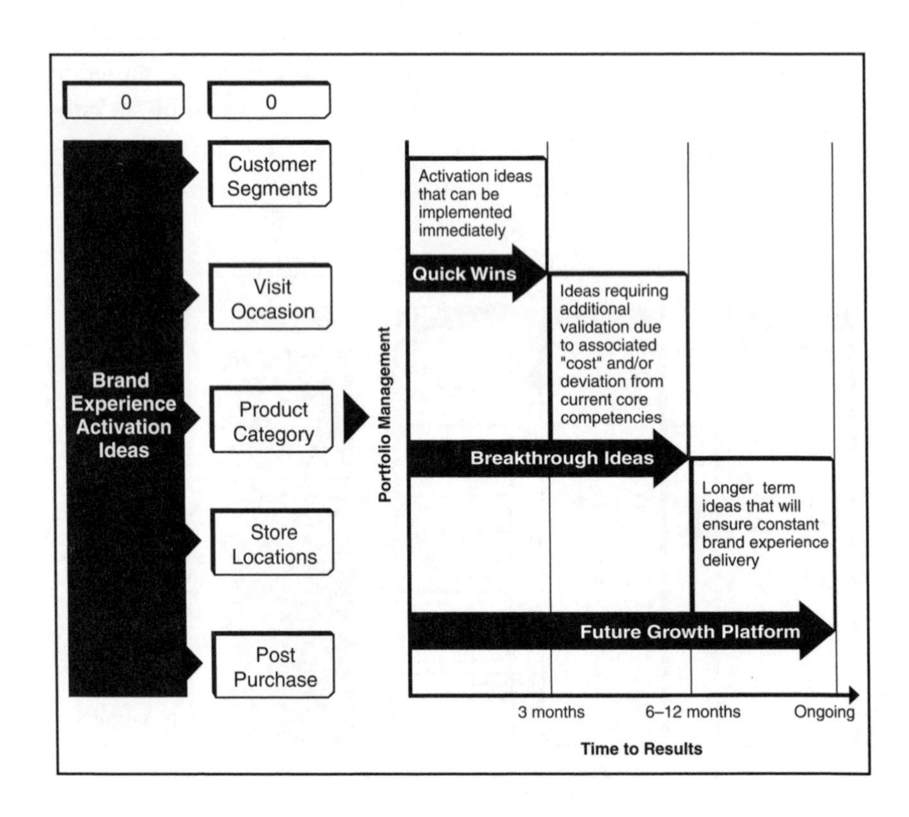

The Missing Piece: Postpurchase Brand Experience

Back in Chapter 7 (Brand Positioning), I talked a little about *virtual consumption,* which is when consumers love you and buy your value proposition but don't buy your product. Clearly, the goal of all your marketing-related efforts is to drive *real* consumption. But watch out: There are times when even that isn't enough.

The postpurchase experience is especially important when consumers buy products that should produce a change (such as the Crest Tartar Control example I gave above). If your product doesn't deliver, even if it's the customer's fault, you'll be blamed. For example, people don't buy Slim-Fast shakes for the taste; they buy them to lose weight. So if they watch those commercials featuring healthy, smiling people who lost a ton on Slim-Fast and they don't do as well, they're going to blame it on the product, even if they ate a double bacon cheeseburger every day for lunch.

The postpurchase experience people have with your brand may be as important as the original consumption. For example, part of the HBO experience is the discussions people have the day after they've seen a *Sopranos* episode. It's up to HBO to keep that experience compelling enough so that you'll keep tuning in—and keep paying extra for that premium cable package.

With very few exceptions, what you need in order to succeed in business is repeat sales. Getting everyone in your target market to buy *one* of your products will earn you a lot of money in a hurry. But then what? If you're interested in staying in business for longer than a few months, you're going to have to get at least some of those customers to buy another one. And another. And another. If they don't, you're gone. That probably explains why there's no market for pet rocks anymore—one was plenty for most people. And it explains why credit card companies keep advertising: If you don't take *their* card out of your wallet instead of one of the three or four others you probably carry around, they aren't going to make any money.

In a national study conducted by Brian Wansink, director of the Brand Lab at the University of Illinois, 63 percent of households had Tabasco sauce in the house—an absolutely amazing market penetration for one brand, until you hear the rest of the story. In more than half of those homes, the Tabasco had been on the shelf for so long that it had turned from red to brown. A third of the households had vitamins that they hadn't opened in the previous twelve months. And another study found that more than 40 percent of companies have "shelfware"—software that they've paid for but haven't gotten around to installing.

Tabasco and those shelfware companies created an experience that fulfilled enough customer needs to generate a sale. But then the system broke down. Because the companies didn't pay any attention to the postpurchase brand experience, consumers never got around to actually *using* the products that they'd bought.

Properly managed, the postpurchase experience will help you strengthen the relationships you have with your customers. But in order for that to happen, you need to be aware of how those experiences are created.

- It's the thought that counts. Consumers are naturally inclined toward second-guessing themselves, particularly when it comes to high-value purchases. This is such a common phenomenon that in many states, the law gives consumers a three-day grace period within which they can reconsider and call off the deal. What consumers are looking for is confirmation that the purchase they made was the right one. If buying Miller beer really does result in an improved sex life, or if the consumer's friends say "Cool car!" or "Cute skirt," the decision will be considered a good one. Purchase reinforcement can also come from you—in the form of price guarantees (find a lower price on the same item within thirty days and we'll refund the difference), some other kind of postpurchase support and contact, or even those commercials some car companies run that seem aimed at telling buyers they've made the right decision. A call from the manager of the Ritz-Carlton asking whether there's anything he can do for you is an attempt to make you feel good about spending $500 a night for a place to sleep.
- The actual experience. Although it may seem pretty obvious, you'd be amazed at how many companies don't get the connection between the expectations they create in consumers' minds before

they buy and the postpurchase reality. Ideally, the object is to leave as little difference between the two as possible. Taking an expensive vacation to a picture-postcard destination creates expectations of sapphire seas, drinks with little paper umbrellas, and massages under the palm trees. And paying for a premium cable TV package creates expectations of selection, quality, and availability. But if the beach is covered with broken bottles and there are bugs in your bed, or if the consumer realizes he now has 250 channels with nothing on instead of only 25, those prepurchase expectations have ruined the postpurchase experience. This is why I always suggest to my clients that they underpromise and overdeliver. It's safer that way.

- The future. This part's pretty simple. If you're happy with your decision to buy the product and your pre- and postpurchase experiences go together nicely, there's a good chance you'll become a loyal, repeat customer. But if you don't feel good about your decision, you could end up with a negative or neutral experience. If it's negative, you'll either return the product or become a dissatisfied customer and end your relationship with the company. If it's neutral, the product will end up sitting on a shelf somewhere gathering dust. People who donate unopened packages of software to Goodwill, or who pour nearly full bottles of Tabasco down the drain because it's been around so long that it went bad, won't buy software or Tabasco again any time soon.

Providing a good postpurchase customer experience, then, has two related goals: Encourage product usage and encourage repurchase. And it's up to *you* to keep giving purchasers good reasons to use and to buy your product. That could be any number of things, including loyalty programs, customer service surveys, a regular newsletter with tips and tricks and ideas for how to use the product, printing recipes that call for the product on the outside of the box or putting a leaflet inside, or effectively using marketing and advertising to remind customers of the needs and wants that the product satisfies and how using the product will improve their lives. There's no question that some companies do exactly these things—but most don't, and they suffer accordingly.

It's also especially important that you get straight in your own mind whom you're selling to. If you're selling directly to end users, those are the people whose experiences you need to worry about. But if you're a wholesaler or there are a few layers between you and the end user, you've got a little more to worry about: getting retailers to buy your product *plus* getting consumers to buy it from the retailer. In the wholesaler case, some of the responsibility for getting products into consumers' hands is clearly up to the retailer. But how confident are you that they're going to have your best interests in mind or that they're going to do a good job marketing your product? Frankly, I wouldn't trust them.

So it's up to you to help them out. For Kraft or Coca-Cola or any number of other consumer products companies, that means coming into the store and making sure the product displays are well stocked and look neat. It also means offering coupons, promotions, merchandise tie-ins, and advertising that reminds consumers of why they should buy your product and encourages them to do so as often as possible.

From the customer's point of view, buying your product at a retailer involves two completely separate experiences: one at the store where the purchase was made, the other delivered by the product itself. Sometimes, of course, the two experiences are related. A study at Washington State University found that—no big surprise here—price and color affect the decision to purchase an apple, while texture and flavor affect the postpurchase experience and determine whether the customer will make another such purchase. If the retailer prices your apples too high or doesn't display them in an attractive way and remove the rotten ones, consumers' experience of your product will suffer—and so might their experience of the retailer.

However, if a customer buys your cereal, gets it home, and finds a dead mouse in the package, his experience will probably guarantee that he won't be buying your cereal again. But it probably won't do much to change his relationship with the store where he bought it. Unless the store refuses to give him a refund or accuses him of killing the mouse himself, he'll continue to shop there. The bottom line here is that just like your customers' prepurchase experience, the quality of their postpurchase experience is up to you.

9

Forced Renovation—When Things Go Really, Really Wrong

As we've talked about throughout this book, any number of factors can make renovation a matter of life and death for your business. Ragú was involuntarily repositioned as watery by Prego; Singer Sewing Machines didn't renovate its destination and woke up one morning headed straight for a brick wall; the big television networks keep thinking they're competing with each other, but they're losing their market share to cable companies and DVD rentals; and the Democratic Party suddenly found itself irrelevant in the minds of its strongest base.

Failing to renovate one element of a business is enough to give most companies a brush with death—but the majority recover. They make the necessary changes and get back on their feet, or they manage to avoid stumbling in the first place.

But what happens when two or three or more factors need to be renovated at the same time? More to the point, what happens when those two or three or more factors get ignored? In most cases, the result can be summed up in two words: Chapter 11. No, it's not a chapter in this book—we've got only ten. It's a chapter in a company's history that, hopefully, you won't have to write.

In some ways, Chapter 11 can be a wonderful thing. It resets the clock, giving you a chance to do all the things you should have been doing all along. Got contract problems with your unions? Nothing to worry about; you can start from scratch in Chapter 11. Too much production capacity and too many employees? Chapter 11 lets you downsize in peace. Too much debt? That's okay, you can restructure it under Chapter 11.

I suppose I could argue that there's a healthy dose of willful ignorance here, that any company that lets things get so out of hand that it has to file for bankruptcy deserves what it gets. But over the years, I've found that things aren't that simple. Yes, bankrupt companies should have been on the ball and seen problems developing. And yes, they should have taken steps to correct those problems instead of letting deferred maintenance rot out their whole structure.

But it's a rare company that actually does those things. Instead, too many look at Chapter 11 as a business strategy. There's even such a thing as a "prepackaged Chapter 11," which allows companies to submit a reorganization plan at the same time as they file. That's completely nuts—kind of like meeting with a divorce lawyer before you get married.

Chapter 11 is *not* a quick and easy fix for what ails you. It's a huge branding event—usually the biggest in the company's history. It tells everyone who's got access to a newspaper or a television that the company is broken, that its value proposition no longer resonates with consumers. Chapter 11 is such a negative branding event that, in most cases, companies who file never recover.

So here's what I propose: Instead of filing for Chapter 11, why not do a prepackaged *renovation* instead? The end result will be the same—a completely renovated company with a newly focused destination and a solid plan to leverage the three elements of value that I talked about back in Chapter 1: core competency, assets and infrastructure, and core essence. The only differences are that it all happens without the negative publicity, and the company remains solidly in control of the dialogue with customers.

The Life Story of a Brand

Have you ever read a book that was so good you were sorry to see your bookmark move steadily toward the end? Unfortunately, most things (except the *Matrix* movies) have a beginning, a middle, and an end. Businesses go through the same kind of life cycle too. Most companies launch a business, spend some time relaxing in the middle stage, and then quietly slip into the final stage and out of business.

But for brands as well as businesses, life doesn't have to end this way. And the fountain of youth—you knew I was going to say this, didn't you?—is renovation.

In the beginning stage, every company starts off as the insurgent, whether it's going into an established market or creating a brand-new one. They invest a lot of money developing and executing a strategy, advertising, promoting, sampling, and doing everything else they can to stimulate desire and attract customers. After getting a foot in the door, the focus is on building the brand and defining what your company stands for. Whether you're running a shoe repair shop, a chain of pizza parlors, or United Airlines, it's all about building customer loyalty, increasing usage, and stimulating repeat purchases. Customer satisfaction is a key goal, and the company actively tries to identify underserved markets and segments that it can expand into.

Then they get into the middle, or mature, stage. And this is where the problems develop. Companies in this stage have three basic options:

1. Look the other way. This involves putting the company on autopilot and assuming that things will take care of themselves. The focus is on maintaining current positioning and profitability.
2. Circle the wagons. Although the goal is to keep from losing ground, adopting a purely defensive position like this has the opposite effect. The company just keeps on doing what it's been doing, exactly the way it's been doing it. At the same time, though, it incurs all sorts of additional expenses in an attempt to fend off insurgents. Sometimes companies slip into this mode without even realizing it. The way to tell is to crack open your books. Have some of your variable expenses become virtual fixed expenses? (A "virtual fixed expense" is one that gets booked as a variable expense but that's been on the books so long that it's as fixed as your rent and electricity bills. These include line items such as customer discounts, incentives, and multiyear sponsor-

ship agreements.) That's a sure sign of stagnation. Incremental increases in spending should generate incremental increases in sales. In other words, you should be spending to grow, not to maintain.

3. Renovate. This involves taking the offensive, having one eye watching your back while the other looks forward. The business, large or small, is continually improved to fill customers' needs and preempt the competition. New uses and new occasions are developed. Positioning, competitive space, advertising, and promotion are frequently adjusted to ensure continued relevance to consumers. Salespeople are retrained, customer plans are developed and refined, and the entire approach to bringing the company's product or service to market is reevaluated. The focus is on organically growing the business.

Obviously, if you go with option one or two, you'll move very quickly into the end stage, which is a place that's very hard to come back from. But if you go with option three, you can stay in the maturity stage for as long as you want to.

▪ ▪ ▪

Let me finish this chapter with a few examples of some companies (and industries) that are all in the middle stage of the brand life cycle and are all being forced to renovate by a variety of circumstances.

▪ ▪ ▪

Sun Microsystems is being forced to renovate by Intel-based PCs and by the economy. Spending on information technology is increasing worldwide, but Sun's business is way off. After all, who needs a Unix-based machine when a computer running Windows can do pretty much the same thing, and for a fraction of the price? Price and functionality are positioning Sun as outdated and inefficient and is making the company irrelevant. Customers are jumping ship and competitors have moved on to new and different things, leaving Sun as the dominant player in a shrinking market, selling products that fewer and fewer people want.

▪ ▪ ▪

Fixed-line phone telecom companies are being forced to renovate by wireless technology. Unencumbered by poles and cables and the labor it takes to maintain them, wireless companies have been able to make huge market penetrations. As with Sun, it's largely a question of price and functionality. Why even have a land line if your cell phone offers you free long distance calls, people can reach you on the same number wherever you go, and you can check your e-mail and even send and receive pictures? Of course the wireless companies still have to sort out coverage problems, but I can't imagine it'll be too long before they do. Some fixed-line companies are offering new services, such as unlimited local and long-distance calls for a flat fee. But they've still got a long way to go.

▪ ▪ ▪

Boeing is being forced to renovate by Airbus, and the whole commercial aircraft industry is being repositioned by low-cost carriers, terrorism, the Internet, recession, and other forces. Boeing used to be the largest commercial aircraft manufacturer in the world. Airbus was a very distant second, selling only half as many jets as Boeing as recently as a decade ago. But while Boeing was bogged down by its World War II-era factories and designs, Airbus designed cockpits that could be used in more than one aircraft. That made Airbus aircraft cheaper to operate because pilots could fly any size aircraft with no additional training. It's still a two-company market, but, driven by what its CEO calls the "mentality of a challenger," Airbus edged Boeing out of first place in 2003. They spend twice as much as Boeing on R&D (8 percent of sales versus 3 percent, respectively), and since 1988 they have introduced four new planes to Boeing's two.

Both companies are still financially strong. But you can't say the same about a lot of their customers. With budget carriers and cheap Internet tickets putting pressure on prices, margins are down and costs are still high. Fear of terrorism and SARS has also made people more reluctant to travel. It's still very much a buyer's market, and both Boeing and Airbus routinely discount their prices as much as 40 percent to get the business. Plus, more and more customers are leasing aircraft instead of buying them. All this translates into a far less predictable and stable income stream for both manufacturers.

Looking forward, both companies have made heavy wagers on very different futures. Airbus is betting on a resurgence of international travel and a growing demand for larger, more efficient aircraft. They peg demand at more than a thousand planes per year by 2020. Trying to position themselves as the leader in that sector, they're launching the A380, the largest and most economical airliner in history (it can hold as many as 550 passengers and has the lowest seat/mile cost of any plane).

Boeing is going in the opposite direction, estimating annual market demand for superjumbos at just over three hundred by 2020. Instead, Boeing is betting that low-cost carriers such as Ryanair, ATA, Southwest, and JetBlue will continue to expand; these airlines have four times the market share they did in 1990 and are ordering more planes all the time. (Unfortunately for Boeing, Airbus is writing a lot of those orders.) Boeing's new 7E7 is constructed from lightweight carbon fiber, uses 20 percent less fuel, and costs one tenth as much to operate than their current fleets. But that may be too little too late.

▪ ▪ ▪

Kodak is being forced to renovate by a shift to digital technology and plummeting interest in traditional film-based cameras. Since 1997, Kodak has cut its workforce 30 percent. In 2003 alone, net income dropped over 60 percent and share price dropped 30 percent. Sales of digital cameras are growing at 25 percent per year while traditional cameras have been steadily losing share since 1996. Kodak's competitors have jumped headlong into the digital space and Fuji is slashing prices on its traditional film. As a result, the brand that is almost synonymous with photography is on the brink of irrelevancy, with bankruptcy only a few steps behind.

▪ ▪ ▪

The pharmaceutical industry is being forced to renovate by generics, foreign competition, smart consumers, the media, and politics. Today, 1 percent of all spending in this country goes toward prescription drugs. And with our aging population, that number is only going up. People love stories of greed and the media are glad to oblige, running stories about high prices and huge profits generated by pharmaceutical companies. What the media don't report as often, though, is how those big pharmaceutical companies spend billions to research and develop drugs only to see them picked up for free by others the second the patent expires. Suspicious and dissatisfied, a lot of consumers are doing their own research. They're finding that they can get the same drugs in Canada and other countries—in person or by mail—for a lot less than from their local pharmacy. And 89 percent of doctors say that they've been influenced by their patients' health-care research.

▪ ▪ ▪

The low-carb mania sparked by the Atkins and South Beach diets is forcing bread and pasta manufacturers, potato growers, and all sorts of other carb merchants to renovate their positioning and brand destinations. The bread industry has seen sales decline by 2 percent over the past three years and has a lot of work to do to repair the damage. But Subway has avoided losing sales by renovating its approach and coming out with "Atkins Friendly" sandwichs and salads instead of continuing to push new bread recipes at carb-phobic consumers.

▪ ▪ ▪

As I suggested earlier, if these companies have the guts to do what needs to be done, you may read in *The Wall Street Journal* all about the fantastic turnaround job they did. But if they stick to the path they're on now, you'll find them in the *Journal*'s obituary pages instead.

10

Tying It All Together

Okay, for the past several chapters I've been telling you all about why you should stop innovating and start renovating. I've given you a close-up look at each of the six elements of my renovation plan and I've given you tons of real-life cases that illustrate what happens when companies do what I'm suggesting and what happens when they don't.

In this chapter I'm going to move back a step so I can give you a bigger-picture look at renovation. Instead of looking at individual facets of renovation, I want to show you how all six of these principles work together. To do that I'm going to take you through five case studies.

I'll start with two companies that failed to renovate when they should have. I'll tell you exactly what they did wrong and what they should have done instead. Then, because we're close to the end of the book and I don't want you to go away depressed, I'll finish up with a discussion of three companies that do it right.

These five companies represent a number of different industries. I deliberately selected them because, taken together, they offer enough variety that I know you'll find a situation that's similar to something you've faced or are facing now. Regardless of the industry you're in or the size of your organization, you'll be able to learn—from both the successes and the failures—and apply those lessons to your own company.

Let's get started.

What Not to Do

I'm sure that as you read the earlier chapters of this book you occasionally thought about companies you know of or do business with that could use some renovation. Most firms need to renovate more than one aspect of their business, but it's fairly rare to find a firm that has failed in all six areas that make up my renovation program. Still, it does happen, and when it does, the results are usually so severe that the company simply can't recover. In this first section I'm going to talk about two companies that have, indeed, failed on all six counts. But they're still breathing. And if their management teams are willing to do some major work the patients could be saved.

Diners Club

Got a charge card in your wallet? Well, you've got Diners Club to thank for it, because back in 1950 they came out with the first ever credit card and created a whole new industry. Aimed exclusively at business travelers, the card was a hit from the beginning and was so popular that it turned up in a Hollywood movie, *The Man from Diners Club*. But today, just about the only people who have a Diners Club card are longtime customers (there aren't very many of those around anymore) or those who use it for business. So let me tell you the sad story of how Diners Club was almost driven out of the industry it created because they steadfastly refused to renovate their business.

Failing to Develop a Renovation Mentality

Early in its history, Diners Club acted like the insurgent all the time. Not content with having created a whole new industry, they came back to the market with a number of renovations and refinements that addressed customers' needs and made the card even more attractive. They were among the first to offer primary car insurance and to create a credit card users' loyalty program (Club Rewards). For a while, Diners Club set a standard that most of their competitors couldn't come close to. But that didn't last too long. Sadly, Diners Club eventually became a textbook example of an incumbent company getting a little too cocky.

Insurgent companies broadened acceptance of their card by charging merchants lower fees. And they broadened usage by establishing consumer lines of credit so that individuals could rack up a lot of high-interest debt which would take years to pay off. As banks competed with each other for these lucrative individual cardholders, annual membership fees dropped to zero and sign-on benefits soared.

The credit card industry was now all about acceptance and lines of credit with flexible payment terms. But Diners Club didn't see the writing on the wall. Hell, they didn't even see the wall.

They held firm to their core essence of "the highest quality travel and entertainment card" when people were using their cards to charge a lot more than travel and entertainment. They were slow to pursue wider retail acceptance and even slower to offer payment terms other than "pay off your entire balance." They took their position in the industry for granted and slowly went from leader to follower, where they've been ever since.

In this chapter I've give you a few examples of exceptions to my "don't-lower-your-pricing" rule. Here's another. Ordinarily, brand loyalty allows the brand to charge a premium for its products. And that's exactly what Diners Club was doing with its $80 annual membership fee. The company was losing members by the thousands, and part of the reason was that fee—most other cards were free or a lot cheaper. (Loyal customers are often willing to pay a premium for your product, but there's always a limit.) But in what must have been a corporate suicide attempt, DC raised its annual fee to $95.

To be successful, a brand or product has to possess what I call the three *A*'s: availability, acceptability, and affordability. The Diners Club card didn't have even one. Few merchants would take the card (low availability), customers had more flexible options (low acceptability), and it cost too much (low affordability).

It's possible—though unlikely—that Diners Club will be able to make a comeback. Citigroup now owns the U.S. franchise and they know they've got a big job ahead of them. The first thing they need to do is give their few remaining consumers some significant reasons to stick with Diners Club. Then they can move on to giving *prospective* customers a reason either to add Diners Club or to use it instead of one of their other credit cards. A lot of damage has been done to the brand, and resurrecting it isn't going to be easy. But if anyone has the resources to do it, it's Citigroup—here's a good opportunity for them to leverage their financial services and credit card competencies, assets and infrastructure, and core essence to renovate their own business by acting like an insurgent. They're starting to make an impact. Citigroup announced that MasterCard and Diners Club have formed an alliance in the United States and Canada so that the Diners Club card will carry a MasterCard logo and be accepted at the right locations. It's a great step forward, but it's probably too late to really help.

Failing to Renovate Diners Club's Business Destination

Diners Club's initial destination was to be "the premier travel and entertainment charge card," and they've stuck with that destination ever since even though it's practically killed them. On the most fundamental level, DC has failed to expand their business destination to keep pace with a changing industry and underlying consumer dynamics. In the face of increasing consumer credit card usage and a shrinking travel and entertainment sector (especially after September 11, 2001), DC failed to identify new growth areas.

They needed to expand aggressively beyond travel and entertainment and into total consumer spending. A far better destination would have been (and possibly still could be) to capture a greater share of consumers' total disposable income.

Failing to Renovate Diners Club's Competitive Frame

Not understanding who their competitors are has hurt Diners Club in a big way. They claim, for example, that their biggest competitor is American Express, a similar charge card that also appeals to frequent travelers. But I can guarantee you that Diners Club doesn't keep many American Express employees up at night. That's because AmEx expanded its own competitive frame to include Visa and MasterCard, and all three left Diners Club off their radar screens.

Diners Club definitely should have expanded its competitive frame to include Visa and MasterCard and then kept right on going, expanding their occasions beyond travel and entertainment and into consumer spending. They also could have broadened their competitive frame to payment by cash and check, and aggressively tried to capture a greater share of all spending. MasterCard and Visa have been using this approach for the past several years. AmEx has too, entering into exclusive deals with retailers. Costco members, for example, can apply for a no-fee card.

Besides squandering opportunities to capture more consumer spending, Diners Club also failed to expand its competitive frame to capture greater merchant acceptance. Given the choice, why on earth would a local dry cleaner accept Diners Club and pay about two percent for the privilege when Visa or MasterCard would handle the transaction for half that? If DC wanted to keep charging merchants premium fees, they needed to come up with some pretty good reasons. But Diners Club just kept on keeping on, slowly strangling itself.

Failing to Renovate Diners Club's Customer Segmentation

For the last fifty years Diners Club has insisted on segmenting consumers into only two groups: frequent business travelers, and everyone else. And they've elected to go after only the business travelers. There's really no excuse for that. AmEx, which for a while was competing in the same niche, managed to keep their business travelers happy *and* introduce consumer cards with revolving balances.

There's no question that DC has a huge amount of data on their current (and past) customers—information on income, spending patterns, occasions, preferred types of products, and so on—and they should be able to segment them a little more accurately than two groups.

Actually, in recent years DC has made some stumbling attempts to do some segmenting of their frequent travelers, and they even tried to introduce a few new offerings in response to newly discovered customer needs. But for Diners Club suddenly to introduce new products is like Singer coming out with a top-of-the-line sewing machine or Smith Corona introducing a self-correcting typewriter. Too little too late.

Diners Club recently relaunched its premium Carte Blanche card, with a $300 annual fee. Carte Blanche was supposed to compete against AmEx's equally exclusive, invitation-only Centurion card. But who did they really think they were going after? With AmEx far more accepted (by merchants and card users) than Diners Club, it was hardly a fair fight. Plus, if they couldn't get people to pay $95 per year, how many could they conceivably expect to pay $300?

A year after the Carte Blanche launch, DC introduced another new product, the Montage Card. It's a design-your-own-card kind of thing, where you pick a number of fee-based travel benefits. So it's back to DC's unsuccessful high-fee, low acceptance formula. Montage has been a flop for several reasons. First, it launched in 2001, just a few months after the terrorist attacks, when people weren't interested in traveling at all, let alone in paying for travel benefits. Second, Montage doesn't seem to know what it wants to be when it grows up. The company says it will make an annual donation to three charities based on cardmembers' votes. But while it's a nice thought, people who are paying a few hundred a year for a credit card are more interested in their own tax deductions.

Failing to Renovate Diners Club's Brand Positioning

With at least three separate promotional campaigns, Diners Club seems a little confused about how it wants to position itself. Their "Travel in Good Company" campaign in 2002 didn't resonate with many people, partly because it kept hammering on the travel and entertainment aspects of the card, which consumers can get cheaper elsewhere. One of their billboards actually featured a picture of Dennis Hopper from *Easy Rider,* looking like a rebel, sitting on a motorcycle that anyone who's seen the movie knows has cocaine in the gas tank. What could that possibly have in common with Diners Club's core essence? Weird.

Then, in 2002, *Adweek* reported that Diners Club was cutting its advertising budget. With a declining customer base and a product that's fast becoming irrelevant, this was hardly the time to cut advertising. They should have *increased* it instead, but only after coming up with some clear and compelling points of difference supported by credible, relevant benefits.

Failing to Renovate Diners Club's Brand Experience

Years ago, Diners Club had the brand experience mastered. Their Club Rewards program offered hundreds of options and even allowed customers to use accumulated miles to buy airline tickets without having to worry about those annoying blackout dates. Diners Club cardholders also had up to two months to pay off their bill, longer than other pay-it-off-at-once cards. And while most other card companies automated their telephone customer support systems to save money, Diners Club made sure a human voice answered your call.

But the whole thing eventually fell apart because DC forgot that the complete experience is what counts. That includes not only direct contact with friendly DC employees (call that pre- or postsales support) but also customers' actual experience using the product. When their expensive Diners Club cards aren't accepted at very many places, and when the Diners Club card no longer carries any prestige, customers forget about the lovely chat they had with the customer service person and cut up their card instead.

On the various levels of the experience, Diners Club fails on almost all counts.

- Intrinsics. The plastic is the only physical part, and that's fine.
- Intention. You want to purchase goods and services.
- Interactions. The customer service is great, but it's frustrating not to be able to use the card with most local vendors.
- Impact. You may or may not be able to use your Diners Club card, so you better carry a backup card (or stop carrying the Diners Club card).
- Impressions. It's almost certainly not worth the $95.

Ford Motor Company

All of the Big Three U.S. automakers are in much the same situation, largely because they failed to renovate when foreign competition, rising fuel prices, and crushing pension obligations completely changed their industry. But while all three are guilty, I think Ford's story is the saddest because, like Diners Club, Ford launched—and once defined—its industry. And like Diners Club, Ford has stood by as other companies have whittled away at its market share. The big difference between the two, though, is that Ford's prospects are a lot brighter than Diners Club's.

In 2002, Ford posted losses of $980 million, which, if you can believe it, is a big improvement over 2001, when the company lost $5.45 *billion*. Frankly, it's hard for me to grasp how anyone can lose money when they have sales of $162 billion.

To its credit, Ford is making a valiant attempt to pull out of its current situation. The company plans to generate $7 billion in pretax profit by 2005, using a multiyear turnaround strategy (read "renovation") that is going to be very difficult to implement. Hopefully they'll read this book so they'll know what the plan should include.

Failing to Develop a Renovation Mentality

For too long, Ford and the other big U.S. automakers acted like incumbents, refusing to acknowledge the threat coming from overseas and laughing at the idea that the Japanese could possibly make a car that Americans would ever want to buy. But the situation isn't so funny anymore.

Toyota now sells more cars in the U.S. than Chrysler, which used to rank third in the Big Three. As number two, Ford knows it has a bull's-eye on its back and is running scared. They're already dangerously close to bankruptcy, and if the company doesn't change its attitude and start thinking like an insurgent pretty soon, the whole company will go the way of the Edsel.

On the pricing front, Ford let itself get suckered into matching General Motors' zero percent financing, a move that boosted unit sales but that almost eliminated any hope of profitability. (The company's financing unit was once its most profitable, but it's hard to imagine how they're going to make any money now.) It's also a move that's going to be hard to recover from, as consumers demand more and more concessions, incentives, and discounts.

Failing to Renovate Ford's Business Destination

Okay, here's a quick one-question quiz: Is Ford primarily a truck manufacturer or an auto manufacturer? Ideally, the answer should be "both."

But Ford seems to flip-flop between the two, focusing on one side at the expense of the other and then abruptly switching.

In 1984, Ford showed the world that it's possible for a behemoth of a company to act like an insurgent. The Taurus, a car that was designed based on extensive customer input, became the best-selling car in the United States and stayed that way for at least five years. But then Ford went back to its old ways, enjoying its profits and not worrying about the advancing competition. In the mid-nineties they completely redesigned the Taurus, but completely missed the mark with consumers. That would have been a financial disaster, but truck sales were booming and Ford was able to use its truck profits to offset it automotive losses.

But today, the situation is looking pretty grim. Ford took its truck sales for granted and didn't renovate its design much over the years. At the same time, imports started making bigger and bigger dents in Ford's truck sales. And in the fourth quarter of 2002, Chevrolet sold more trucks than Ford and moved into the number one spot. That's going to hurt Ford in a big way, in particular because while they were enjoying their status as the top truck company, they forgot all about cars, assuming that consumers would keep on buying whatever they produced. That approach worked for a while, but consumers want variety and they want car designs to change as their tastes and needs change. But it still takes Ford a lot longer than the Japanese to bring a car to market. So now both divisions are in trouble.

Failing to Renovate Ford's Competitive Frame

Of all Ford's problems, this one—their failure to acknowledge and respond to overseas competitors, particularly from Japan—has hurt the company the most. It's also highlighted the urgent need to renovate in a number of other areas, including destination, positioning, and segmentation.

In 1980, the Big Three had a 75 percent share of the U.S. auto market. The gas crisis didn't faze them at all, and they kept on making big cars and even bigger trucks. But while they were fiddling, Rome (or in this case, consumer passion) was sizzling. The Japanese gave people what they wanted, and by 2002, the Big Three weren't the Big Three anymore and their share had dropped to less than 63 percent.

Eventually, Ford caught on to the threat from overseas, but their epiphany may have come too late. Toyota and Honda had gained market share by satisfying U.S. consumers. They produced high-quality, low-maintenance cars, backed them up with long warranties, gave consumers a lot of different models and options to choose from, and did it all for a reasonable price.

Instead of responding by understanding their customers and trying to satisfy their needs, or (gasp) by producing better-quality vehicles, Ford (and the others) effectively turned cars into a commodity by offering insane discounts and promotional incentives. No question about it, short-term demand jumped. But at what cost? In 2002, incentives and discounts averaged $4,000 per vehicle—up 62 percent from 2001.

To make matters worse, Ford was suffering from some unforeseen effects of operational decisions they had made back in the days when they thought their market share was safe forever. For example, they're still operating a number of unprofitable and outdated plants across the country. Closing those plants, consolidating operations, and taking other steps would probably help Ford. And so could getting a handle on its health care and pension expenses. But that can't happen because Ford made too many concessions to the unions, thinking that consumer demand would never run dry.

Failing to Renovate Ford's Customer Segmentation

Years ago, Henry Ford's way of segmenting customers was pretty simple: There are people who can afford cars and people who can't. And his way of satisfying car buyers' needs was to give them a choice of any color they wanted—as long as it was black. With that kind of attitude, it didn't take long for Ford to fall into the number two spot behind General Motors, which is where they've been ever since.

This isn't to say that Ford never bothered to segment their customers. Of course they did. And it was through excellent segmentation and a commitment to satisfying customers' needs that Ford recognized consumers' increasing interest in trucks and SUVs, together with their decreasing interest in minivans and luxury cars. They responded quickly, and in the late eighties and nineties they were producing margins that were the envy of the industry and they became the leading truck manufacturer.

Unfortunately, as has happened so often in Ford's history, a moment of brilliance was followed by a long stretch of laziness. If you're at all aware of what's going on in the auto industry, you know that most of the Big Three's profits come from truck sales. But Ford doesn't seem to be doing much lately to protect its leadership position.

As bad as all this sounds, it's still a little premature to read Ford's eulogy. Despite teetering on the edge of bankruptcy, the company is still number two in the United States and sold almost seven million cars worldwide in 2002. Clearly, they're still doing a few things right. But if they spend too much time patting themselves on the back, they could end up being knocked out of their cushy number two spot by Toyota and their financial situation will get worse.

In recent years, the automotive industry has become much more like the consumer packaged goods industry in the way that consumers are continually demanding customization, options, and choice. And they want it *now,* dammit. Unfortunately, Ford suffers from incumbentitis and has a tough time responding quickly. For a long time, Ford took more than six years to get a model from the drawing board into the showroom. Foreign competitors were doing it in less than two years. Ford's design cycle is a little shorter now, but still too long.

Ultimately it all gets back to listening to what consumers are saying, segmenting them, and giving them products and services that meet or exceed their needs. Ford has had better luck doing this outside the United States, where they've developed models that meet local demands for smaller sizes and fuel efficiency. The Focus C-MAX, a small hatchback that seats five, is the product of good listening skills and good segmentation and will undoubtedly generate a lot of additional sales in the U.K. I can't figure out why they can't be as responsive to American customers.

Here, they're still trying to segment based on price and demographics, and the results have been pretty dismal. Ford's Premier Automotive Group, which includes Volvo, Land Rover, and Aston Martin, is losing money. The British-based Jaguar unit alone lost over half a *billion* dollars in 2002. Again, Ford's competitors—notably the Japanese—are producing cars that consumers actually want, and they're reaping the rewards.

If Ford is going to succeed over the long term, they'll have to understand consumers' purchase behaviors and attitudes. What are they buying and why? How often do they drive? To do what? Are they driving a carpool twice a day or schlepping Sheetrock? Are they looking for something sporty and practical, or will sporty alone be enough? The questions that need to be asked are nearly endless, and the more of them Ford asks, the more cars and trucks they'll sell.

Failing to Renovate Ford's Brand Positioning

Not so long ago, Ford had such reliability problems that many mechanics joked that the letters F-O-R-D stood for "fix or repair daily"—not the way any manufacturer wants to be positioned. Ford's response, "Quality is job one," was extremely successful and helped reposition the company back where it wanted to be. But since then I'm not sure Ford really knows where it wants to position itself.

One of the problems it's had is finding ways to differentiate itself from its competitors (which now include imports) in an industry where a lot of the differences are cosmetic. This problem is aggravated by the need to position and target each of Ford's brands so that each one is relevant enough to consumers that they'll buy it—with or without ridiculous financial incentives. That could involve discontinuing brands that have lost their relevance entirely, as General Motors did with its Oldsmobile line.

Frankly, I'm not sure that Ford will be able to do this. Between 2002 and 2007 they're planning to introduce sixty-five new models in North America alone. Forty-five new models will be introduced in Europe during the same period, and the Premier group is launching thirty-five. Pretty soon auto dealerships are going to be as overcrowded as the toothpaste aisle at the grocery store. And I think that with so many new models, Ford is going to have trouble positioning any of them in any kind of unique way.

One thing Ford has done right with regard to positioning is spending $100 million on a patriotic stars-and-stripes campaign introducing the new F-150 design. That has certainly helped solidify the F-150 as a sturdy, all-American truck. Early reviews suggest that the F-150 will continue to have the highest U.S. sales of any American-made vehicle.

Failing to Renovate Ford's Brand Experience

The experience of a car involves much more than comfort and fuel economy, and it starts long before the buyer walks into the showroom. In some cases, it actually starts years before the prospective buyer can even drive. Did his or her father or mother or older sibling have an earlier model? Was it fun to ride in as a kid? When the top was down, did the wind feel good? How did the interior smell? Once the buyer is old enough, the experience gets somewhat more tangible: How easy was it to find information about the car on the Internet? How did *Consumer Reports* rate it? How did it do at NASCAR? Are they getting sued for anything? All this is what brings the customer into the dealership . . . which is where the whole Ford experience could grind to a halt.

Too many people who come in ready to buy a Ford walk out without one. Why? Because they aren't getting what they want. These days Ford's cars are probably as well made as anyone else's, so quality isn't the issue. And since Ford is usually offering some absurdly low interest rate or equally absurdly high rebate, price isn't the issue either. What consumers want today is some control over their experience. They want to customize their car in the same way as Dell lets them "build" their own computer, selecting the exact processor, speed, RAM, graphics and audio cards, and other options that they want. But on many Ford models, customers have too few options to make them happy, so the Ford experience fizzles before it really has a chance to get started.

To renovate its brand experience, Ford is going to have to give customers more choices, in terms of both options and selection (although, as I mentioned above, introducing sixty-five models over five years is going make it even harder for Ford to differentiate itself from their foreign and domestic competitors).

The Ford experience includes all the traditional elements, and leaves many opportunities for mistakes:

- Intrinsics. The cars are good, but not the all-around best in quality or customer preference; some competitors satisfy customer needs better.
- Intention. You want a reliable, safe purchase for a good value.

- Interactions. Ford needs to interact with consumers at more places than just the dealership or when your car needs repair.
- Impact. Does the car last a long time at the same level of quality?
- Impressions. You want a good buy for your money and a car that does what you need it to do.

The Way to Go

The three companies that follow have, quite simply, done it right. They're all leaders in their industry, but they've got the renovation mentality down perfectly. They know their customers and do everything they can to satisfy their needs. They aren't afraid to take some chances and they aren't afraid to grow. But they make sure that the chances they take are grounded in their core essence and that their growth is organic, not simply acquired.

United Parcel Service of America, Inc. (UPS)

UPS started off in 1907 as a bike messenger service and has grown steadily ever since. Today, it's a massive global delivery business with a market capitalization of $72 billion and annual revenues of $31 billion. In May 2003, UPS received the American Business Award for "Most Innovative Company," but they really should have been recognized for *renovating* the company, which is what they've done continually—and very successfully—since their first days in business.

Developing a Renovation Mentality
UPS is the leading publicly held shipping company and the second most recognized corporate brand in the world (behind Coca-Cola). Its profits are four times higher than those of FedEx, which is widely considered to be UPS's closest competitor. A lot of companies in UPS's position would (and do) kick back and enjoy their status as incumbents. But UPS is always hungry. Or, as their chairman Michael Eskew recently said, "UPS has always been constructively dissatisfied. We're al-

ways looking for ways to do it better." It would be hard to come up with a better example of thinking like an insurgent, not like an incumbent.

There are very few companies out there that have internalized as well as UPS the message that *everything communicates*. Every new product or service they introduce, and everything they do on every level, is grounded in the company's core essence and consistent with its positioning and destination.

As one of the pioneers in package tracking, UPS is a master at letting customers know when their shipments will arrive and where they are every step of the way. The company applies that same kind of thinking to its own financials, tracking how well each new product or service performs as well as the effectiveness of individual marketing efforts. Collecting this kind of data makes it easy for UPS to track how well they're doing relative to their goals and to adjust their products and services to keep giving customers what they want.

UPS does a fantastic job of selling value instead of low prices. There are plenty of cheaper ways to get things from A to B, but UPS doesn't compete on price. Instead, they offer reliability, efficiency, safety, and speed, factors that are critical to a lot of shippers' businesses and that they're willing to pay a premium for. (I'm not talking about sending a birthday present to Aunt Millie. I'm talking about companies like Dell, which ships thousands of packages every day. Fast, efficient, damage-free delivery is part of "the Dell experience"—even if none of those factors are actually provided by Dell itself.) At the same time, UPS has an elaborate matrix of prices and services that gives customers an element of control over how much they pay and the kind of service they get.

Renovating UPS's Business Destination

Not satisfied to remain a simple package delivery business, UPS has recently redefined its business destination as "Enabling Global Commerce." The "enabling commerce" part of UPS's elegantly simple destination gives the company the mission to move anything—goods, services, and even money—use any mode of transportation, and offer any service a customer wants, many of which don't even involve shipping. These include international trade management, customs brokerage, consulting, and, as I'll discuss below, supply chain management.

The "global" part of the destination has made it possible for UPS to establish a significant international presence. Overseas operations grew 10 percent in 2002 and now generate 25 percent of the company's total profits. All this growth is coming from offering additional services to existing customers. For example, through its recently introduced Intra-Asia network, UPS is now the only company that delivers packages in Asia by 8:30 A.M. Intra-Asia is growing at a rate of 13 percent per year.

Renovating UPS's Competitive Frame

The small package delivery sector is a $60 billion per year market, and it would have been easy for UPS to stay happy being the big fish in the pond, competing only with FedEx, Airborne, and a few others. But being "constructively dissatisfied" makes that impossible, and over the years UPS has redefined its competitive frame to include the U.S. Postal Service, e-mail providers, and financial institutions.

The company has no intention of getting out of small package delivery. In fact, thanks to the growth of Internet commerce and globalization, that sector of UPS's business is quite profitable. But it's now only one of the many reasons customers turn to UPS.

In 2002, UPS launched a new unit to help customers outsource supply logistics. This is a wonderful example of a company intelligently growing by leveraging its assets and infrastructure (750 distribution centers), competencies (tracking and transportation), and core essence. The proof is right where it ought to be: on the bottom line. In it's very first year, UPS Supply Chain Solutions captured 20 percent of the entire market of outsourced logistics.

Renovating UPS's Customer Segmentation

UPS's customer segmentation goes far beyond typical demographics such as package origin and destination. The company segments its customers by their actual behavior and needs, such as urgency, in-house services, delivery and shipping patterns, budget, company size, services used, shopping patterns, package volume and size, and estimated future demands. This has enabled UPS to tailor its marketing and customize its fees and services so customers can choose the exact service they need and get it at the right time and price.

For example, after analyzing the services their corporate and individual clients value most, UPS recently launched online customer service, ordering, and package tracking to ensure customers that they'll always have efficient access to their information. They also added a money-back guarantee for residential shipments within the continental United States, a full range of Saturday services, and even same-day delivery in some markets.

And UPS's close relationship with eBay has led to numerous improvements in sales and customer services; eBay shippers and buyers can now easily compare shipping times and prices, track them, and even print labels.

Renovating UPS's Brand Positioning

UPS has continually renovated its brand positioning to highlight its core attributes and the benefits it provides. Just take a look at the way the company's ad slogan has changed to reflect its ever-evolving positioning, from "The Package Delivery Company More Customers Count On" (we're a simple, reliable package delivery company) to "The Tightest Ship in the Shipping Business" (we're reliable and ship more than just packages) to "Moving at the Speed of Business" (we move anything and everything quickly). The most recent slogan is "Synchronizing the World of Commerce" (we ship anything and everything, quickly and globally).

As huge as UPS is, and as many areas as they operate in, it would be easy for them to lose control of the dialogue they have with their customers. But they haven't. They've positioned themselves as international and timely and have ensured that every employee in every division in every country supports that positioning. As a result, UPS owns that space and no one can even come close. Unfortunately, space ownership is often thought of by companies as a license to get fat and lazy. UPS's challenge is to avoid making that mistake. They've avoided it for a hundred years and I see no indication that they're going to stop now.

Renovating UPS's Brand Experience

If you've ever sent or received an important package, you know that your experience with the shipper depends on a lot more than whether the package got picked up and delivered on time. You're also taking into consideration questions like Was it easy to ship? Was it damaged? Was I able to track it? Was the tracking information accurate? If there was a problem, was it resolved in a way that made me feel good? Did I see the person who delivered it? Was that person friendly? The answers to all those questions will contribute to your next shipping decision. As economics, technology, and prevailing trends change, so will customers' needs. UPS clearly understands that and continually renovates the experience it offers so that customers will have an excellent one on every possible level:

- Intrinsics. Shippers have access to a highly sophisticated set of transportation and customer service logistics to deliver packages and services.
- Intention. Packages are delivered on time and without being damaged.
- Interactions. UPS systems are electronically tracked, and customers can access a variety of information online or over the phone.
- Impact. The overall UPS experience makes you feel that you were charged a fair price and that you got nothing less (and maybe more) than you expected.
- Impressions. You're glad you shipped with UPS.

Walgreens

Like UPS, Walgreens has been around for a hundred years. And like UPS, Walgreens is continually renovating its business, always in a way that's grounded in its core essence: convenient health-care and basic needs retailing. The results have been remarkable: Just staying in business for a century is a pretty big accomplishment, but Walgreens has also posted twenty-eight consecutive years of growth—a record few companies can even come close to.

Developing a Renovation Mentality

With a 12 percent market share, Walgreens is the country's biggest drug retailer. It would be easy for them to act like an incumbent, contentedly running their existing stores and watching the money roll in—for a few more years, anyway. But Walgreens is about as far from being an incumbent as you can be.

Over the years, the company has very deliberately chosen *not* to be just another drugstore. Oh, there's no question that their pharmacies provide a huge chunk of their income. But again, instead of resting on their laurels, they leveraged their pharmacy profits and their core essence as a brand consumers trust to become an insurgent in the larger retail business, filling other needs for customers who are already in the store waiting for their prescriptions. All those incremental sales add up: Between August 2002 and August 2003, overall sales went up over 13 percent. To put it differently, compare Walgreens' average sales of $654 per square foot to the average for drug superstores (just under $200 per square foot) and drug stores in general (just over $200 per square foot).

This isn't to say that Walgreens hasn't made its share of mistakes. Not long ago, they slipped into the biggest incumbent trap of them all: Thinking that they could coast on their brand awareness, they lowered spending for promotional advertising. The drop in front-end sales was immediate. When they stopped constantly reminding customers why they should shop at Walgreens, customers went somewhere else.

Fortunately, it didn't take Walgreens too long to recover their senses and get back to thinking like an insurgent. They're launching new national and local advertising and promoting the hell out of their new digital photo and photo restoration services. The ads are straightforward—no chance they'll win any awards for cleverness or creativity. But that's okay with Walgreens because they've figured out what advertising is all about: to sell stuff. They're also putting up displays and advertisements *inside* their stores, with one simple goal: to give existing customers—people who are already in the store—a reason to buy more.

Walgreens does have low prices, but for the most part they've managed to keep themselves out of the downward spiral of pricing concessions. Sure, there are some specials and loss leaders designed to get people in the door, but their prices on a lot of other products and services are often slightly higher than the competition. They can get away with it because they offer—and deliver—a wider range of products than other drugstores, along with convenience, which is something people are willing to pay a premium for.

Renovating Walgreens' Business Destination

Walgreens is a company with a clear destination: Increase market share and become the local neighborhood store to as many Americans as possible. As I mentioned, their share right now is around 12 percent, which makes them the biggest drugstore chain in the United States. And they're growing at an incredible clip, opening stores at a rate of more than one per day. By 2010 they expect to have seven thousand stores in the United States, almost twice what they have now. One third of their stores have been open less than three years, and half have been open less than five years.

The most impressive thing about all this growth is that it's not cannibalizing sales from existing stores. Even in this tough economy, same-store sales went up more than 10 percent from 2001 to 2002.

Renovating Walgreens' Competitive Frame

You might think that Walgreens would see the other big drug chains—Eckerd, CVS, Duane Reade, Rite Aid—as their major competitors. That was probably true at one point, but Walgreens successfully renovated its competitive frame, expanding into a much larger competitive space, one that's currently occupied by retailers such as Wal-Mart and even local supermarkets.

Anyone who decides to compete with Wal-Mart had better have his eyes wide open. And Walgreens certainly does. They recognize that going toe-to-toe with Wal-Mart on price is a losing battle (Kmart's attempt to do so contributed to their eventual bankruptcy). But just being in the same competitive space as Wal-Mart has forced Walgreens to identify and eliminate operational inefficiencies, monitor consumer tastes more closely, and find ways to keep those customers emotionally connected to the Walgreens brand.

At the same time, the company hasn't forgotten its roots. They've broadened their competitive frame in the overall drug market, expanding from in-store pharmacies to include mail order. That natural extension is perfectly grounded in Walgreens' core essence and leverages their existing core competencies in a convenient new channel. The mail-order side of the business now brings in over $1 billion a year.

Renovating Walgreens' Customer Segmentation

Because Walgreens serves such a wide range of customers, continually renovating its segmentation has played a big role in its longevity. Of course they use the usual demographics such as age, income, and ethnicity. But they cross-reference them with local trends and with psychographics such as what people's specific needs are and what drives their purchase decisions. They then use this segmentation data to match each store's product and service selections to the needs of the local market. In some cases, they actually develop new products to satisfy those needs. For example, Walgreens came out with two ethnic makeup lines and in-store marketing targeted at specific segments. They also now offer prescription label data in eight different languages.

The result of this simple commitment to finding out what people want and giving it to them (instead of trying to shove down their throats a bunch of stuff they don't want) has enabled Walgreens to make each store profitable. As mentioned above, Walgreens' same-store sales from 2001 to 2002 went up more than 10 percent. At the same time, the other players in the drugstore space were reporting *declining* same-store sales.

Walgreens has even leveraged its understanding of customers' wants and needs to figure out where to build stores. As of this writing, about 40 percent of the U.S. population lives within two miles of a Walgreens. Almost 60 percent are less than five miles away. And although stores are customized to local markets, they're still similar enough that consumers can feel at home in any Walgreens store anywhere.

Renovating Walgreens' Brand Positioning

A company's positioning needs to establish consumers' expectations while remaining relevant. Walgreens' slogan does a pretty good job on both fronts. "You're always welcome at Walgreens" is about convenience and dependability and says, in a folksy kind of way, "Come on in, it's your store. We've got what you need and we'll always treat you nicely."

Walgreens has developed a brand consumers can trust. Even so, positioning can sometimes be a precarious thing. To keep from being involuntarily repositioned by its competitors, Walgreens must firmly control the dialogue it has with its consumers. It does that by making sure that its product and service selections, marketing, promotion, real estate choices, and even employee training *all* reinforce the company's core essence of convenient health-care and basic needs retailing.

Renovating Walgreens' Brand Experience

As I've discussed throughout this book, customers' experience with a company rarely begins and ends with the product itself. The same is true at Walgreens.

Product performance is certainly important, but customer service, employees' product recommendations (especially in the health and supplements areas), store layout and displays, lighting, availability of other products or services, and much more all shape customers' experience and keep them coming back.

Recent renovations, such as the mail-order business I mentioned above and twenty-four-hour pharmacies, give customers a lot of control over how and when they use the store. (Walgreens actually runs nine hundred twenty-four-hour pharmacies—55 percent of the nation's twenty-four-hour stores.) Walgreens' photography service prints 4.4 million photographs every day and gives customers a choice of one-hour or twenty-four-hour developing. Customers can also bring in old, damaged, aged, or faded photos for restoration.

A robust Web site lets consumers check specific store information online. Food aisles provide products when consumers are in between trips to their local supermarket. And back in the pharmacies, Walgreens offers money-saving generics, personalized consultations to explain how to take the drugs, and a huge database that flags potential interactions between drugs.

Looking at the whole Walgreens experience, you can see they've addressed each important issue:

- Intrinsics. Convenient locations and wide range of products.
- Intention. Consumers get the health and everyday items they need, at a decent price.

- Interactions. Employees are trained to communicate effectively with customers in the store, on the phone, and through the mail. All of the marketing supports the brand.
- Impact. Consumers get a user-friendly, comfortable shopping experience.
- Impressions. Consumers feel they got a good deal on the products they needed.

Washington Mutual

Yet another company with a long legacy, Washington Mutual (WaMu) first opened up shop in 1889 in Seattle, lending people money to rebuild their homes after a devastating fire. From the very beginning, WaMu's core essence has been relaxed, warm, customer-oriented financial services. They've leveraged that core essence, along with their core competencies and assets and infrastructure, to build a financial services empire that in 2002 had $283 billion in assets and chalked up $3.9 billion in net income. Pretty big numbers, especially when you consider that just ten years earlier the company had only $34 billion in assets. Still not impressed? How about this: Washington Mutual has increased its per-share dividend for more than thirty consecutive quarters.

Developing a Renovation Mentality

It's not always easy for a $283-billion-dollar company to act like an insurgent, but that's exactly what WaMu does—and has done for decades. While a lot of financial services incumbents retrench or grit their teeth when things get dicey, Washington Mutual sees tough times as a challenge. During World War I they grew by 68 percent. During the Great Depression they bought up a lot of their competitors. And it's looking as if they'll do the same thing in the post-dot-com recession.

While their competitors have been hoarding their pennies and delaying investing in their own growth, WaMu has continued to expand, moving into New York, Denver, and Chicago in just the past couple of years, successfully challenging regional incumbents like Chase Manhattan and Bank One on their own turf. (Over the course of just one year, WaMu went from being an unknown to being the second most recognized bank in New York). In 2002, they opened 266 new retail branches; 2003, about 250 more (49 in August 2003 alone!). People need loans in these tough economic times, and Washington Mutual isn't afraid to make them. They're also building customer relationships that will become extremely profitable as the country recovers.

WaMu understands that every aspect of their marketing must help generate sales while supporting and reinforcing the brand image. All of their advertising does exactly that, presenting a brand that is warm, good-humored, and likable. It's advertising that's aimed at winning customers, not awards. And it's very successful.

WaMu handles transactions every day for more than 12.5 million households and 7.3 million checking accounts. That's an amazing amount of information, which the company uses to improve its understanding of its customers, to measure the effectiveness of its marketing efforts, and to track branch and corporate performance.

Back in Chapter 3 I warned you not to get caught up in the downward spiral of pricing concessions, that it's better to compete on value instead of price. Given that, you'd think that I'd be all over WaMu because of their free checking—after all, how much lower can they price something than zero? And how can they possibly make any money if they don't have any income? In this case, though, I've got to admit that it's not a bad strategy—but *only* because WaMu is so good at cross-selling revenue-generating products to free-checking customers.

Renovating Washington Mutual's Business Destination

When Washington Mutual was lending money to fire victims in Seattle, their business destination was probably to be "Seattle's leading mortgage lender." Over the years, as the company grew, they renovated their destination at the same time. "The Northwest's leading mortgage lender" was renovated into "The Northwest's leading retailer of consumer financial services" and finally into WaMu's current destination: "to be the nation's leading retailer of consumer financial services."

That last one is part of a five-year renovation plan started in 1999 to broaden the bank's business destination and improve its internal processes. Even spread out over five years, striving to be "the nation's leading retailer of consumer financial services" is a pretty gutsy destination, given how overcrowded the financial services market is. But WaMu gets closer every day.

Renovating Washington Mutual's Competitive Frame

The bank's competitive frame has expanded right along with its destination. When they went from just mortgage lending to "consumer financial services," they were suddenly competing with investment banks, stock and insurance brokers, and financial planners. When their destination went national, so did their competitive frame. And that struck fear into the hearts of local, regional, and national financial services companies everywhere. If you're in the financial services business, you're either competing with Washington Mutual already or you're thanking your lucky stars that they haven't hit your market yet.

If Washington Mutual decides to move into your market, watch out. They start by introducing mortgage banking services. That leverages their competencies in mortgage lending, their substantial financial resources, and their core essence of relaxed, warm, customer-oriented financial services. Once they've established a foothold in the market and consumers are familiar with them, they open retail banking offices in the community, offering additional services to existing customers.

It's an extremely successful approach. They're doing commercial lending in all of the top fifty metropolitan areas in the country, and they've got retail branches in twenty-eight of them. In twelve of those cities they have a 30 percent share of the market.

Renovating Washington Mutual's Customer Segmentation

WaMu really understands what their consumers are looking for in their financial services. Yes, they frequently rely on demographics, particularly socioeconomic groupings, to target new services and loans. But within those groups, WaMu digs deeper, targeting consumers based on their shopping behaviors, communication needs, desired financial services, potential future value, attitude and approach to banking, and much more.

This kind of segmentation has enabled WaMu to respond quickly to the specific needs of a variety of groups of customers. They put computers to work to help improve their customer service; they introduced the first telephone banking and shared ATMs; and they've expanded to include brokerage services, mortgage lending, annuities, insurance products, and select commercial lending. And it's all been done while staying true to their core essence of relaxed, warm, customer-oriented financial services.

In another example of WaMu acting like an insurgent, the company is aggressively targeting groups—particularly low-income customers—who have largely been neglected by other banks. Because WaMu is willing to take the time to understand these customers, they've been able to create or modify services that meet their needs. The results have been extremely profitable.

Renovating Washington Mutual's Brand Positioning

In an industry where there's not a lot to differentiate one player from another, Washington Mutual has positioned itself as a whole different way of banking: friendly, funky, and with a good sense of humor. Kind of like Southwest Airlines without the planes. They offer a unique level of personalized service, plus no-fee ATMs and free checking. All of that, of course, positions their competitors as unfriendly, stodgy, strait-laced bankers who are out to squeeze every last nickel in fees out of their customers.

In a way, WaMu uses its competitors' own bank statements against them. When a non-WaMu customer opens up his statement and sees that his bank charged him two dollars for using a WaMu ATM, he's also going to get a reminder that WaMu didn't charge him anything. Eventually, that non-WaMu customer may move his accounts. Getting competitors to negatively reposition themselves is brilliant, and it leaves them with a simple choice: Renovate from the ground up, or watch more and more of their customers walk across the street to a WaMu branch.

Washington Mutual does a great job of thinking globally while acting locally. They contribute billions of dollars to local communities, and WaMu employees perform more than two hundred thousand hours of volunteer work every year. A big part of that community involvement is driven by a genuine desire to do good and to help local organizations and charitable causes. But another part is driven by the bottom line. Community involvement helps the bank establish relationships with local customers. In addition, WaMu understands that people feel safe investing their money in a bank that gives back to the community, and that doing so may be the factor that persuades some customers to choose WaMu over the competition.

Renovating Washington Mutual's Brand Experience

A lot of companies don't think much about their customers' experience with the brand. But WaMu does. In fact, they actually have a goal: "Create a consistently inviting experience whenever and wherever customers come in contact with Washington Mutual." That experience is consistent with WaMu's core essence as a warm, friendly bank. And all fifty thousand WaMu employees are trained to make that experience a reality.

Famously free checking and no-fee ATMs are certainly part of the WaMu experience by reminding customers that they're getting a good deal and being treated fairly. Eventually, WaMu's competitors will match this deal, which will make it little more than a price-of-entry attribute.

But it's the rest of the experience that has played a major role in WaMu's success and truly set it apart from the competition. By encouraging customers to meet with friendly, live bankers, the company establishes a personal relationship with people and makes them feel comfortable. Employees' casual-yet-professional clothes and a clean, lighthearted decor further reinforce the experience.

- Intrinsics. Comfortable retail locations and helpful telephone and Web site services.
- Intention. A competitive interest rate on investments and loans.
- Interactions. Consumers communicate with the bank through several channels, so employee training is very important.
- Impact. Consumers deposit money with or take out loans from WaMu.
- Impressions. Consumers can trust WaMu as a friendly, convenient, and competent bank.

Where Do You Go from Here?

I have a reputation in the business world for being something of a contrarian, criticizing everything in sight. In my first book, *The End of Marketing as We Know It,* I explained why marketing as it's being done today simply doesn't work anymore, and I gave marketers the tools they needed to refocus their efforts on the bottom line. In the follow-up book, *The End of Advertising as We Know It,* I went far deeper and showed how companies are being snowed by fast-talking ad execs who convince them that success is measured by brand awareness and winning awards for clever television ads. And I gave them the tools to eliminate wasteful and counterproductive advertising expenditures and, again, to refocus on the bottom line. Are you noticing a theme here?

For me, it's all about the bottom line. Whether you want to admit it or not, the reason you're in business is to make money. The simple truth is that while I may be a little abrasive at times, I'm not really anti anything. I'm just looking for ways to drive organic, profitable growth, and when I see companies missing opportunities, I feel I need to say something. Hey, someone's got to do it.

Hopefully, between the specific steps I gave you in earlier chapters and the more detailed examples in this one, you've learned enough to honestly evaluate what your own company needs to renovate so it can stay relevant and profitable. Better still, you now know exactly how to do it.

- You know why it's better to start with what you can sell and see whether you can make it, than to start with what you can make and then see whether you can sell it.
- You know how important it is to think like an aggressor, not like a leader, and how to keep from getting suckered into price wars.
- You know how to identify a destination and articulate a plan for getting there.
- You know how to figure out who your competitors are and how you can expand into areas that are logical extensions of your brand.
- You know how to figure out who your customers are and how to get them to buy more of your product more often.

- You know how to position yourself in the market, how to position your competitors as irrelevant, and how to avoid being repositioned yourself.
- You know that none of that is worth anything if your customers' *experience* doesn't live up to—or exceed—their expectations.
- And you know that whether the story of your company ends with Chapter 11 or Chapter 10 depends on how well you renovate.

But no matter how much you've learned, there's always more. I could probably give you another thousand examples and not even come close to identifying all the different ways that companies fail to renovate. So every time you turn on the television, read *The Wall Street Journal,* go out to eat, buy a book, ride a bus, take your clothes to the cleaner, or buy groceries, pay attention. Companies that are renovating—and even more that *should* be—are everywhere. Keep an open mind and you can learn a lot from them.

Whether you're a hot dog vendor on a street corner or the CEO of a Fortune 100 company, renovation is a process that never ends—or at least never should. And once you've put your renovation program into action, don't let yourself get too comfortable. Stay connected to your customers and their needs, and develop strategies that leverage your assets and infrastructure, core competencies, and, most important, your core essence. Doing this will help you stay ahead of your competition and capitalize on opportunities to grow your business intelligently and organically. And through it all, you'll be able to sell more stuff to more people, more often, for more money, more efficiently.

Conclusion

I own quite a few cookbooks—hey, I like to eat!—and I've tried out a lot of the recipes. But that doesn't make me a chef. In a lot of ways, the same applies to this book. Over the course of any given year I spend a lot of time talking with corporate execs and CEOs. Whenever I bring up renovation and the ideas you've just finished reading about, they get all excited, and many of them invite me to do presentations to their managers and other employees.

But thinking about renovating their business and bringing me in to fire up the staff (or, in your case, reading this book), although they are great first steps, are not enough. In order to truly renovate a company, every single employee from top to bottom has to take some cooking lessons. And there has to be one chef who has a deep, almost religious belief in the importance of business renewal and renaissance. He or she will have to visualize, lead, and create an environment where people *implement* these ideas and make them a part of everything they do, from hiring and training employees to allocating spending and tracking results. Everything.

One of the big stumbling blocks that keep companies from renovating is a little condition I call *but-we've-always-done-it-this-way-itis*. "We know what we're doing," people say. Or "We've been successful until now, and what got us this far will take us the rest of the way." Or "You don't understand. Our situation is different." What a load of crap.

When I worked for The Coca-Cola Company, the things that dragged us down the most were the behaviors that we repeated over and over for no other reason than that we always had. We did various sponsorships and always ran promotions at Christmas, New Year's, and Labor Day, or Ramadan, or whatever the holiday was in whatever country we were operating in. And we never bothered to ask ourselves (or our customers) whether we were doing the right thing.

▪ ▪ ▪

According to publishing tradition, authors aren't supposed to introduce new ideas in the conclusion of a book. But since I'm not a big believer in blindly following tradition, I want to take a moment to have you consider an idea I raised early in the book, but from a slightly different angle: the idea that renovation requires flexibility. Most execs make the mistake of vastly overestimating their current flexibility and what I call their *aptitude for flexibility*—their ability to change direction in the future.

In the early stages of a company's existence, being flexible is easy. There are no long-term commitments, no regular expenses, and hardly even any employees except for the guys who started the business. In short, almost everything the company does and every expense it incurs is flexible. As time passes, though, the business's behaviors and spending patterns become more and more predictable and fixed. When you hire a bunch of employees, their salaries become essentially fixed because you're going to be paying them for a long time. When you start offering discounts to your customers or sign a long-term lease, those expenses become fixed too. But rather than move those expenses from the *variable* line of the income statement to the *fixed* line, where they belong, most companies leave them where they are.

The problem with keeping expenses that have become fixed in the variable category is that it deludes you into thinking you're more flexible than you actually are. When too many expenses (and attitudes) are set in stone, you can't possibly think like the challenger, and you'll never be able to adapt your business to your customers' changing needs and desires.

The bottom line is that if you're not flexible, you're dead. Many times when we do business planning we forget that previous results don't guarantee future ones. You may have sold a hundred cartons of your product last year and you may have increased sales 5 to 10 percent per year for the past ten years, but can you really and truly bank on that to continue this year? Are you absolutely sure that your customers' needs and requirements will grow at the rate you've plugged in? And even if they do, can you really be sure that none of your expenses—salaries, overhead, marketing, customer discounts, and so on—will change?

Too many companies that overestimate their own flexibility also underestimate their customers' flexibility. They assume that brand loyalty is fixed, that usage frequency won't ever change, and that people's needs and wants are slow to change. The truth is just the opposite. The tremendous variety of options and the freedom of choice that most consumers have actually *encourage* variable behavior.

▪ ▪ ▪

I've devoted a lot of space in this book to discussing core essence and core competence. But because they're such critical ideas, I'm going to contribute a few more paragraphs here.

Let's start with core competence, because it's critical to have a firm grasp of what it is that you do best and how that can be leveraged to create a distinct advantage. Unfortunately, that's easier said than done. Many times when I do destination planning sessions with clients, I ask them this fairly simple question: "If I were to go out and build a company to do what you do, what would I have to do?" Amazingly, a lot of companies can't come up with a clear, concise answer. They start by saying that they're good at manufacturing product X, or great at sourcing raw material Y. But the more I dig, the less confident they become, the more they hem and haw, and the more obvious is it that they need to rethink their core competence.

Besides knowing what they do best, companies also need to know what their core essence is and what the core essence of their brands is. As I discussed earlier in the book, Pepsi's core essence is about being the challenger, Coke's is about continuity and stability, and Microsoft's is that no product is ever fully developed and finished. Brands—no matter how big or how established—need to figure out what their core essence is, and the best way to do that is to look back at their origin. The core essence of a brand usually arises at about the same time as the brand itself. Companies often add benefits and give customers more reasons to buy or use their products or services, but almost never abandon their core essence.

At the end of the day, renovation is a holistic process. And as is true for any process, there are routines and dependencies, rhythm and sequence, pace and pause, and an ability to continually regenerate and renew. Overall, it brings together your core essence, core competence, and assets and infrastructure. Throughout my career, I've been involved in transforming or renovating a number of companies. Let me give you just three examples. Two you've heard of and one you'll probably hear of soon.

When Bruce Rohde took over as CEO of ConAgra, it was a mishmash of brands, products, and companies that had been acquired over the course of a number of years. One of the first things Bruce did was to figure out what ConAgra's core essence and core competencies were. Once he did that, he went out and spent $3 billion to acquire companies that supported ConAgra's core essence and competence and sold off $3 billion worth of products, brands, and companies that didn't. In short, Bruce created a completely different model for how to grow the company. It involved precise communication, new tools and frameworks, relentless follow-up, and an unwavering belief that ConAgra can be America's favorite food company. It wasn't easy, but Bruce is well on his way.

Similarly, Alcoa's CEO, Alain Belda, completely retooled what the company does and stands for. For decades, the company—a major producer and fabricator of metals—had focused on running its plants at near capacity. That approach worked well for a while, until a number of their big customers began switching to other suppliers. By understanding what Alcoa's customers needed, Alain was able to come up with products that people wanted instead of continuing to produce a lot of stuff their customers didn't need or want.

Finally, there's Alejandro Santo Domingo, the twenty-six-year-old CEO of Bavaria, a company that owns a large number of breweries and other businesses throughout Latin America. Alejandro and his father completely transformed Bavaria, dumping assets that didn't support the brand's core essence or competencies. He also created a management model that allowed for centralized corporate strategy but decentralized execution. People often talk about how they need to centralize and decentralize stuff, but Alejandro actually did it. Perhaps most importantly, though, he established rules, metrics, and processes to measure success and to ensure that his brand not only survived but thrived.

The reason I'm bringing up these three CEOs is simply to drive home the point that some people truly *get* how important renovation is. They see it as almost a religion. It's hard work and it means performing at a level that's always ahead of the market. It means remembering that growth and thinking are variable behaviors. It means changing the old saw "There is no finish line" from a cliché to a reality. And it means having the courage to continually reinvent and disinvent components of what makes the company great *now* in order to create the components that will make the company great in the *future*.

▪ ▪ ▪

To a great extent, my company, the Zyman Group, came about as a direct result of the lessons about renovation that I learned during my years at Coke. After my first book, *The End of Marketing As We Know It*, came out, a lot of companies called to say things like "Wow, now we understand what marketing is" and "I got to get me some of that." So I started the Zyman Group to consult with companies that needed to renovate their business. I didn't put it in those exact terms, though. In fact, I didn't even use the word "renovation" at all when I first started out, even though that's exactly what I was telling my clients to do.

Renovation was what Roberto Goizueta, Don Keough, and I did at Coca-Cola when we finally figured out that the core competencies of the company weren't clear and we sold off our shrimp farming and plastic cutlery businesses. Renovation meant coming to the harsh realization that the entire bottling system needed to be restructured and retooled and then doing both. Ten years later, renovation was completely overhauling the way the company went to market. And renovation was what we had to do after New Coke was introduced. (At every speech I give, people still ask me about New Coke. Roberto and I often discussed writing a book about it, but he died before we could get started—a great loss for humanity and for the business community. I've been bugging Don Keough to collaborate with me on a book. Maybe he'll do it one day.)

Today, at the Zyman Group, renovation—the word and the concept—is front and center. It's the foundation for all our beliefs and it drives the way we serve our clients. It's a part of everything we do and everything we say. Hopefully, the ten chapters that make up this book will help you embrace the "religion" of renovation as much as we have. If you do, you'll be on your way toward achieving the goal we set for all our clients: to sell more stuff to more people, more often, for more money, more efficiently.

Renovating the Coca-Cola Company

From 1990 to 1993, Coca-Cola's earnings per share grew 16 to 18 percent per year. Arguably the bluest of the blue chips, Coke became a must-have stock for every portfolio, and its successful forays into China, Vietnam, East Germany, Russia, and other new markets cemented the company's status as the most global of global institutions. As my boss, then-Chairman and CEO Roberto Goizueta, put it, "Coke was global before global became cool."

But in 1993, in the midst of one of the most successful periods in its hundred-plus-year history, Coke began a process of top-to-bottom renovation.

Why try to fix something that clearly wasn't broken? I guess it was a strong sense of déjà vu. Back in the 1980s, Coke went through a period of intense focus on growth. Theoretically, that isn't a bad thing. But in the process the company lost track of its own identity and what it stood for, and it strayed far, far away from its core business. The results were obvious: stagnating or declining market share and profitability.

In trying to figure out what went wrong, Coke analyzed every aspect of its go-to-market strategy, from pricing and distribution to advertising and promotion, and came to the unpleasant (but honest) conclusion that it would have to overhaul the whole thing. It dumped its strategy of growth by acquisition and focused instead on growing organically.

So in the mid-nineties, when Coke's management team saw the enormous wave of mergers and acquisitions that dominated business, its reaction was "Been there, done that, didn't like what happened, and we'd better do something now to keep it from happening again."

That's where I came in. Goizueta, Coke's chairman, and Don Keough, the president, invited me to rejoin the company to kick-start the renovation process before the situation got out of hand. I jumped at the chance.

At the core of my strategy was one simple idea: *It's all about the consumer.* If we could get more people to buy more of our products more often, we would continue to grow the business profitably. This was the mantra that the company began to chant. More important, this was the mantra that Coke began to live by and that became the focus of everything it did. From 1994 to 1998, the company grew twice as fast as it had from 1990 to 1993, which, as I mentioned, had been a wildly successful time.

Take a look at the step change that this renovation created:

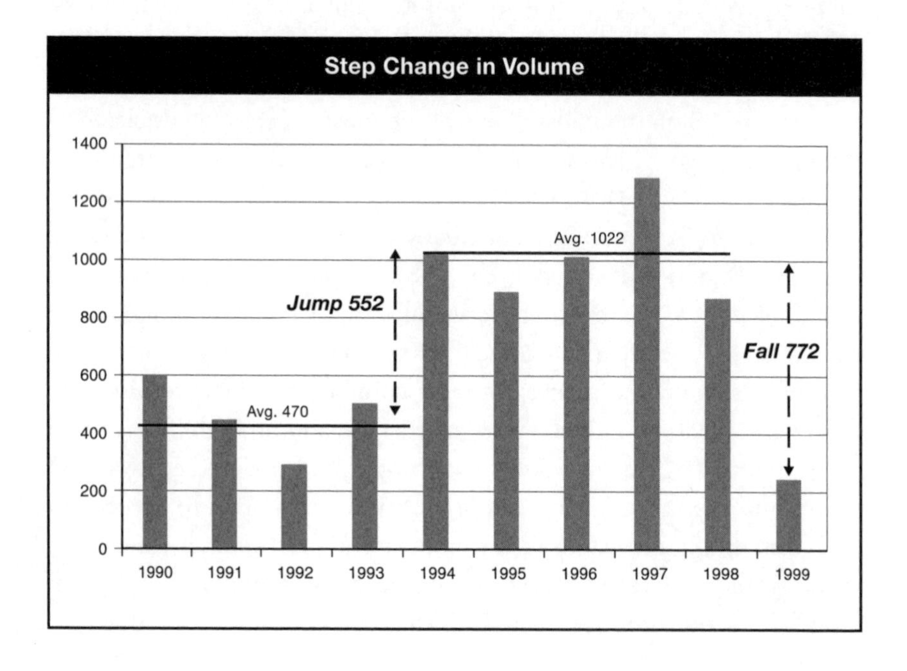

and how that impacted the financial performance of the Company:

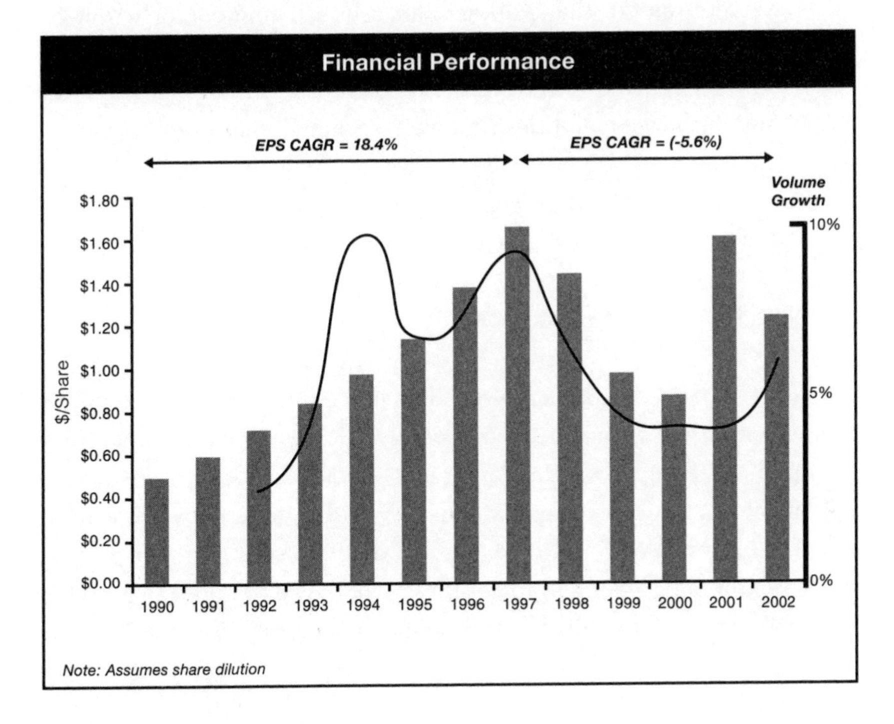

In the years since I left Coke and started my own consulting firm, I've had a chance to look back at what, specifically, we did to renovate the company. I believe there were five facets that were especially instrumental:

- Staying true to our core essence. We believed in the carbonated soft drink business and in the growth potential of our core brands, and this helped us strategically pursue organic growth opportunities.
- A clear purpose and destination. We articulated this through several guiding principles, which I called Conviction, Mandate, and Indicated Actions.
- A new set of tools, frameworks, and theories to implement these guiding principles and make them tangible and usable. These were developed through the application of scientific method and refined with experience and insight.

- Changes in the structure, processes, and measurement systems. We determined what work got done, how it got done, where it got done, and how success was measured.
- New blood. We introduced into the business new people who brought new capabilities that were germane to our renovation.

Let me take you a little deeper.

Staying True to Core Essence

With its lucrative fundamentals and enviable long-term growth potential, Coca-Cola was uniquely positioned to deliver superior value. Most compelling, though, was the company's unwavering belief in its brands and its ability to achieve sustainable success by continually reinventing itself. Coke's leadership firmly believed that what got them where they were would not be enough to get them where they wanted to go. They had the guts to consciously "disinvent" components of Coke's *current* greatness in order to create components of *future* greatness. Here's what I mean:

- **From** . . . building the distribution infrastructure with bottlers . . . **to** . . . building brands with consumers. Coke had achieved its objective of being within "arm's reach of desire," meaning that the product was so widely available that customers would have one whenever and wherever they wanted. Now the issue was to build desire for Coke over the other choices, as soft drinks suffered from sameness at the point of sale.
- **From** . . . capturing all the growth . . . **to** . . . capturing all the potential. That was seen to be the quintessential quality of leadership—neither accepting any natural limits to growth nor assuming there were any insurmountable obstacles.
- **From** . . . share of soft drinks . . . **to** . . . share of daily liquid requirements. That one simple change completely refocused the way we looked at opportunities for growth.

- **From** . . . aspirational goals . . . **to** . . . aspirational plans. Aspirational *goals* were seen as merely the desire to get to a better place. Aspirational *plans,* on the other hand, were blueprints for making those goals a reality, embodying the belief that neither growth nor change was optional.

Purpose and Destination

Roberto Goizueta and I established a five-year plan to turn Coke, a growth company with the world's most valuable brand, into the premier marketing organization in the world. My strategy was to differentiate and cultivate distinctiveness and relevance for our company, which would give us a sustainable competitive advantage.

Step one was to develop three guiding principles and communicate them to everyone in the organization, from top to bottom. These principles were as much about the business as they were about the people responsible for it.

- Convictions. I believe that that consumers ultimately determine the success or failure of a business. That means that great marketing starts and ends with the consumer. Should have been pretty obvious, right? Unfortunately, it wasn't. Companies say all sorts of things about how important their customers are, but words aren't worth much unless the actions are there to back them up. So we deliberately set out to understand fully, and at the most fundamental level, the people who voted with their dollars, pesos, pounds, and rupees every day, several times a day. Who were they? Where did they live? Where did they buy? How did they shop? What did they perceive Coca-Cola's core essence to be? Why did they choose what they chose? What was important to them and what motivated them to buy?

  The answers to these questions became the foundation of our renovation process. They forced us to reexamine what we knew and what we thought we knew but didn't. And they made us recalibrate our measures of success.

- Instead of focusing on how many bottles we sold, we shifted our thinking to figuring out how many daily drinkers we had created and retained, how many weekly drinkers, and how many monthly drinkers.
  - Instead of worrying about whether people liked our advertising and getting excited when we won awards, we focused on results: How many people bought our products after seeing those advertisements, and over what time period?
  - Instead of marketing one way to everyone, we changed the ways we approached daily, weekly, and monthly drinkers.
  - Instead of focusing on availability, acceptability, and affordability, we shifted to pervasive presence, preference, and price-value.
  - Instead of concentrating on the properties and sponsorships we should own, we looked deeper, determining how to use those properties and sponsorships to sell more Coke.

Let me illustrate this last point with an example. Coca-Cola has been a sponsor of the Olympics since 1928 and since then had approached the Games every four years as a sponsorship event. Until 1996. As I'm sure you know, Coke's corporate offices are in Atlanta, which is where the 1996 Olympic Games were held. We realized that with the world's attention on Atlanta, we had a lot to gain—not only financially, but also in terms of the potential impact on the Coca-Cola Company's reputation. We knew we had a great opportunity to renovate the way we conceived of and activated our sponsorships.

Our approach to the 1996 Games is best summed up in a line we used when we first started rethinking the true purpose of our sponsorship: "To sponsor is to believe." That seemed just fine and dandy—until we started asking questions such as What does Coke's sponsorship of the Games mean for consumers? Will our sponsorship change the way they think and feel about our brands and our company? Will they buy more or fewer Coke products if we do the sponsorship?

What we found was that in consumers' minds, a corporate sponsorship meant that the sponsor had deep pockets. They saw no integral role for the brand in the sponsorship, and they expected large organizations to sponsor big events simply because they could afford to. None of this translated into either higher preference or purchase intent.

So we went back to square one and did some serious soul searching, starting with a thorough reexamination of Coke's core essence, the core essence of the Olympic Games, and the core essence of our long-term partnership. We realized that ultimately it was all about "common ground" and "shared ideas" between Coke and the underlying spirit of the Olympics, which culminated in a major event every four years. We also concluded that Coca-Cola was unique in the sense that it represented more than a refreshing and delicious beverage that people enjoyed. It was an idea, a concept, that was motivating and inspiring, and it provided a unique connection between fans and athletes.

Putting all these insights together, we came up with a new idea that we felt captured our new understanding: "Coca-Cola is for the fans." This connected Coke's core essence (unique and delicious refreshment) with the core essence of the Olympics (the purity of people striving to do their best) and the role that fans played by being there (cheering and supporting to make the dreams of young men and women from around the world come true).

Then we went a step further, using the "Coca-Cola is for the fans" idea as a way to bring the Olympics to all Americans and get them to participate in the spirit of the Olympics by giving them a chance to carry the Olympic flame in their own city. For the first time, the Coca-Cola Company sponsored the torch relay, and it became a grassroots movement.

Our experience with the Olympics led us to change the way we looked at our other sponsorships: football, cricket, baseball, and all the rest. We created new benchmarks for those initiatives, ones that took into consideration Coke's core essence as well as the core essence of the sport. The integrated idea then became a part of every element of the marketing mix, from packaging to mass advertising and everything in between.

- Mandate. I felt that our business mandate was clear and simple: to achieve profitable volume growth for the four core global brands, Coca-Cola, Diet Coke, Sprite, and Fanta. The problem was that the overall Coke brand had become so big that most marketers either didn't fully understand its core essence or couldn't tell what drove purchase and consumption. Brand ubiquity—being everywhere all the time—was seen as an end in itself, which is why we sponsored everything from sports to concerts to flower shows.

So we took all four brands apart and put them back together based on a deep understanding of their core essence and how we could use it to fuel new value and new growth.

Each of the brands accelerated its growth trajectory over the five-year plan, with the most dramatic results coming from the largest brand: Coca-Cola. To put this into perspective, here was a brand that had a more than 50 percent share of worldwide carbonated soft drink consumption and was growing at approximately 4 percent annually. During the period from 1994 to 1997, we boosted the compound annual growth rate to 8 percent. Contrary to popular belief, most of that growth didn't come from horizontal expansion and new markets like China, India, and Russia. Instead, it came from existing markets with a long history with Coca-Cola, like the United States, Mexico, Brazil, and Germany.

- Indicated action. In a very deliberate and systematic fashion we set about uncovering and activating the core essence of Coca-Cola, which, as I've said, was all about unique, delicious taste, physical and emotional refreshment, and authenticity. The brand was multifaceted and multidimensional and therefore relevant to multiple consumer segments, and it had a rich folklore and mythology (which we called "Coke Lore").

  Our most recognized and trusted icon was the uniquely shaped "contour" glass bottle. But in several markets around the world, including the United States, we had abandoned the contour bottle in favor of a straight one. In doing so, we had inadvertently diluted Coke's core essence.

  We recreated the contour bottle and relaunched it all over the world. In a way, the bottle became the stimulus for communicating not just what surrounded the brand, but the great taste and refreshment that was contained in that bottle. It also enabled us to create a wide variety of packaging and pricing options, which we segmented by channel and how consumers shopped in those channels.

In addition to the contour bottle, we reinforced Coke's iconography through the use of the color red, especially for celebrations like the Chinese New Year where red had meaning and significance both for the celebration and for Coke as a part of that celebration.

While all this was going on at the front end (the part that was visible to everybody), we were also completely renovating the back end, collecting information about our consumers and building the databases and analytics to determine consumer segments, drivers, and differentiators, and doing marketing-mix analysis to chart the relative importance of individual marketing activities such as advertising, promotions, pricing, and distribution. From the worldwide Christmas campaign to the activation of Coca-Cola at the Atlanta zoo, we evaluated what worked, what didn't, and why.

These databases served as the foundation for the tools and frameworks we created and utilized to grow the business.

Tools, Frameworks, and Theories

If you want people to think differently you have two choices: Teach them how to think, or give them different tools which, when used, will require new ways of thinking. As you might guess, we opted for option two. Let me give you an example of just one of these new tools.

We determined that 70 percent of Coca-Cola's volume came from people who were daily drinkers. Clearly, understanding these consumers was critical to the success of the brand and the business. But we needed a methodology that would give us this information on a real-time basis across the world. So my marketing leadership team and I came up with eleven imperatives, defined them, and created the supporting tools to make it possible to deliver on them:

1. Daily consumers are the key to growth. We will act upon the differences among daily, weekly, and monthly consumers relative to their attitudes and behavior. Based on that knowledge we will prioritize our marketing efforts and key messages to maximize the number of daily drinkers for each of our brands.
2. Consumers will elect us every day of the year. We will create ways to sell every case we can produce every day regardless of the season. We know that continuous communication works best.
3. Marketing is a business and we firmly believe that it works. Every brand is a business in itself. Tracking P&L by brand ensures that we get value for what we spend. We will only invest resources that drive profitable volume growth and brand equity, but just to the point of diminishing returns.
4. We will differentiate each brand in the marketplace. Consumers need a unique reason to buy our brands. We will interpret, not define, the brand for the consumer. Our brands will be worth more than they cost.
5. We will manage all our messages. We are aware that everything we say or don't say, and do or don't do, communicates something about our brands, our company, and ourselves. All communications will be actively managed around the world. Every vendor, every uniform, every truck back will communicate a key message to drive volume consistent with the company's positioning.
6. We will drive purchase and consumption. Our job is to ensure that our marketing plans close the gap between purchase intent and daily consumption.
7. We will plan and measure our business results weekly and monthly.
8. We will secure and develop the marketing talent we need to optimize our brands in the marketplace. Leaders love talent and know where to find it. People should be viewed as valuable assets that create value for our brands and business. We will continually invest in developing our talent.
9. We will be a continually learning company. It is the responsibility of every member of the marketing team to be relentlessly curious, to leverage their knowledge of the entire marketing system,

to share learning with the total system, and to seek learning from the total system.

10. Management will be involved in the details of the business. Managers will be knowledgeable about the key drivers of profitable volume growth.
11. We will systematically evaluate every property or event in the context of its ability to drive profitable volume growth and brand equity. To own is not enough; we will activate and utilize properties we buy and match the relationship the consumer has with the property or event with the company's values.

These imperatives ultimately led to the creation of a performance management system called INforM (information for management) which housed a fifty-country database of information on sales, consumers, and customers. With INforM as a foundation, we could scientifically analyze everything we did, from positioning research to forecasting the underlying momentum of the business to isolating base volume from the incremental volume generated through marketing activity.

INforM was the final move from gut-based to fact-based decisions. It created an undisputed fact base so that numbers were not a matter of debate. Instead, numbers became a matter of dialogue and discussion. That helped people come up with even more new ways of thinking about the brands, advertising, media, sponsorships, pricing, the business as a whole, and how to grow it.

Changes in Structure, Processes, and Measurement Systems

We believed that global brands would benefit from global positioning, architectures, and strategic frameworks that were centrally developed, and adopted or adapted to meet the specific needs of local markets.

To make that happen, we created the Coca-Cola Marketing Division in Atlanta and gave it global responsibility for strategy on brands, advertising, media, sponsorships, and research. Our emphasis was on taking the global architecture and localizing it appropriately, so we set up a parallel structure in each country.

Conversations at the annual planning sessions moved from plants, trucks, and promotions to daily and weekly drinkers, marketing variance analyses, and debriefing success and failure. But whether in Atlanta or Timbuktu, we measured success the same way: It was about getting more people to buy more of our products more often.

New People, New Competencies

We believed that global brands need global leadership and that we needed specialists rather than generalists to raise the level and quality of our work outputs. As I've always said, once you've identified the gaps and voids in skills, you can train the gaps, but you have to fill the voids. And we had plenty of voids. So we made it our mission to attract and retain the best marketing talent in the world. We hired several recruiters around the world to help us search out the best talent—the best advertising people to develop advertising, the best consumer strategists to develop brand strategies, the best media people to work on media strategy, and so on.

What set Coke's hiring strategy apart from most other companies' was that *not* having prior beverage experience was an advantage! What we were looking for were individuals who had demonstrated their consumer marketing chops in a variety of industries and markets and who would bring that competency to Coke.

We knew that with the exponential growth of a business came exponential demands on the competencies of people, and that meant hiring people who had:

- The values that would allow them to make decisions based on a shared framework of priorities and judgments, coupled with
- The skills that would make them effective agents for making the company perform to new, higher standards;
- The knowledge that comes from having meaningful and actionable information at the right time;

- The creativity to discover, develop, plan, and execute the ideas that would create new value; and
- The accountability that clearly defines roles and expectations and rewards performance.

From 1993 to 1995, Coke hired more than three hundred consumer marketers around the world and charged them with giving more people more reasons—both rational and emotional—to buy and enjoy our products.

▪ ▪ ▪

The renovation of the Coca-Cola Company was successful because the foundations were anchored in both the theoretical and the practical, the tangible and the intangible. The tools and frameworks we created, for example, made new ways of thinking easy to understand and act on. At the same time, we built a completely new corporate culture. Throughout the process, though, we knew that the only way to win in the marketplace was to win with the consumer. And the only way we could sustain the momentum that was there before we started renovating was to constantly come up with new ideas, but to keep them true to the core essence of both the brand and the company.

Index